The Professional Photographer's

Digital Wedding Album Design Guide

The Professional Photographer's
Digital Wedding Album Design Guide
by Kathy Woodford

This book may be purchased at www.carilloncreek.com.
Or contact sales@carilloncreek.com.

Print history
October 2005: First edition

ISBN: 0-9766646-0-7
Library of Congress Control Number: 2005902350

Technical Editors:	Richard Lee and Russ Madeira
Content Editor:	Todd Manza
Proofreaders:	Rosemary Lee and Carol Nickols
Indexer:	Melody Englund

This book was typeset using Adobe InDesign CS and the Adobe Garamond Pro and Adobe Myriad Pro typefaces.

9 8 7 6 5 4 3 2 1
Printed in China

To my husband Dale,

whose technical wizardry and unfailing support
make everything possible

The Professional Photographer's

Digital Wedding Album Design Guide

Kathy Woodford

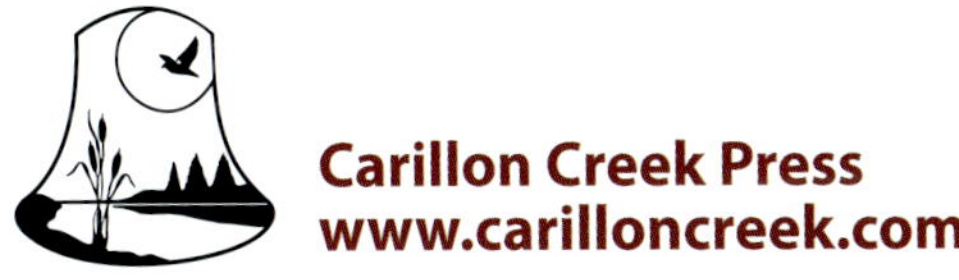

Carillon Creek Press
www.carilloncreek.com

Contents

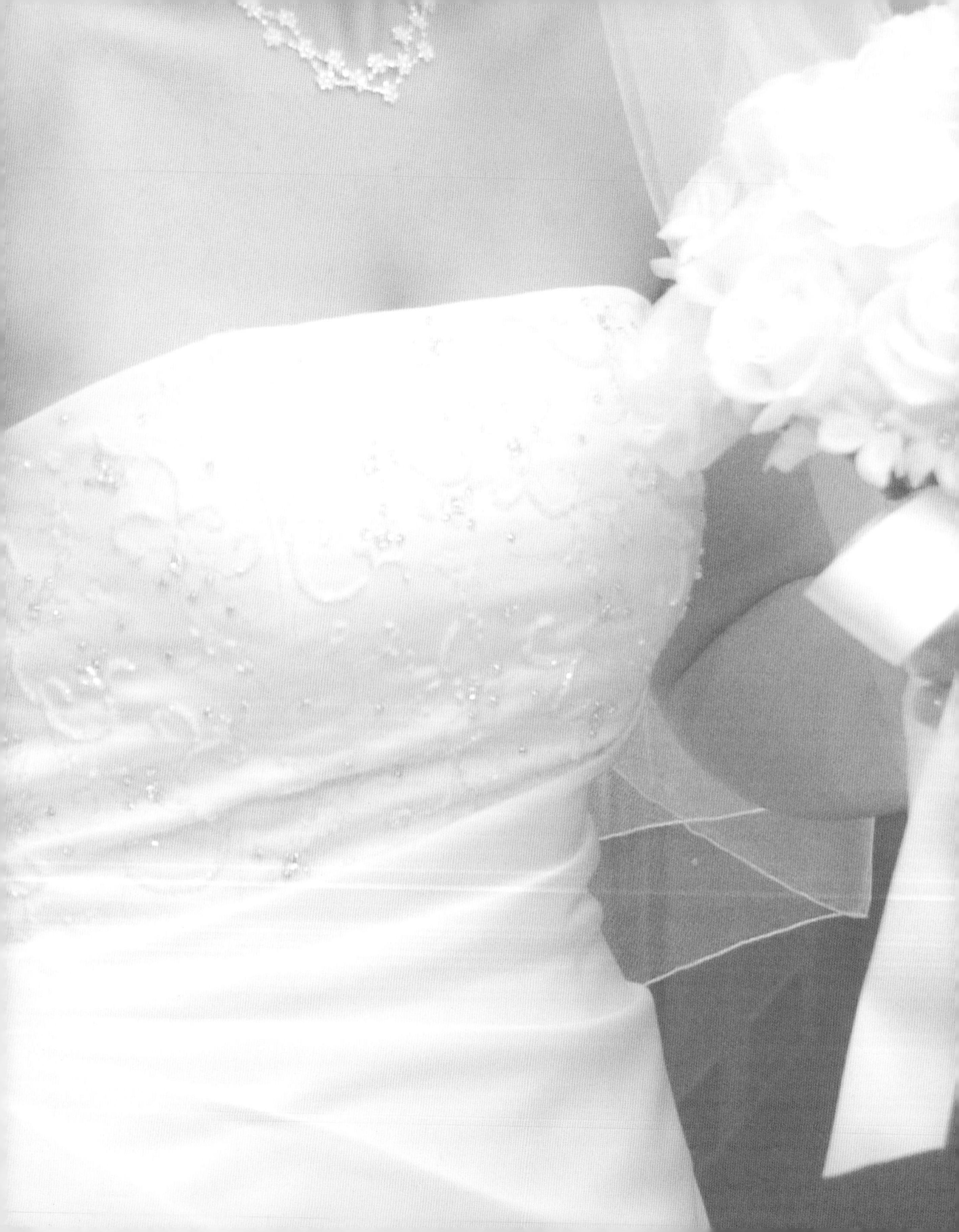

Preface

When I began designing digital "magazine-style" albums, there wasn't a single book or website to be found that explained anything about that process. And even today it's difficult to find answers to questions like these:

- What images should I capture for the most creative layouts?
- What's an effective digital workflow?
- What questions should I ask an album company when I'm looking for a good flush-mounted album?
- What unique characteristics of digital album production do I need to know about when I'm setting package prices?
- What's a good software program for presenting proofs and selecting album images?
- How can I use the Photoshop Browser (and now Adobe Bridge in CS2) to do all the sorting, selecting, and batch-processing needed for an efficient digital workflow?
- Which Photoshop features are needed to produce digital albums?
- Where can I find step-by-step procedures for creating professional-looking designs?
- How can I reduce the number of requested changes after clients have looked at the album proofs?

This book answers these questions, and focuses on everything you need to know to produce beautiful digital albums quickly and efficiently. Think of it: all the Photoshop features used to design digital albums distilled here into two chapters, covering *only the features you need to know.* And in addition to learning the Photoshop features, you'll also learn the creative techniques used to produce all the sample album pages shown.

How the book is organized

For the sake of grouping information generally in chronological order, I've placed most of the pre-wedding information in Chapter 1. This includes the decisions you'll need to make regarding images to shoot, pricing, and what to say during the consultation. Chapter 2 discusses an effective digital workflow after the wedding and how to run an in-studio session with clients to select album images. Chapter 3 covers information about designing pages, including techniques for working quickly, helpful graphic design principles to keep in mind, and a method for experimenting with design ideas. You'll also find out how to prepare digital album pages for the lab. And finally, in Chapter 4, you'll find step-by-step instructions for producing all the designs shown in the sample album page spreads.

The album examples

The album pages shown came from our studio, Calypsis Designer Wedding Images (www.calypsis.com), and I designed all but a few, which were the work of my talented assistant, LeAnn Raschke. The album shown in Design 23 (p. 124) was the first one I produced, and it won the Judges' Choice award in a Seattle print competition. The example shown in Design 2 (p. 80) is from an album judged Best Wedding Album of the Year in a 2005 print competition held by the Seattle Professional Photographers Association.

Software and hardware requirements

All the album pages in Chapter 4 were created using Adobe Photoshop CS and then the techniques were tested again in CS2. You may be able to do many of the designs using Photoshop 7, but the techniques were only tested in CS and CS2. Where features have changed for Photoshop CS2, those changes are noted. For the purposes of this book, CS2 changes are mostly found in the new Adobe Bridge (which now replaces the File Browser) and in the way linking works in the Layers palette.

Keep in mind that the most expensive element in the design process is your time. Photoshop is a "resource hungry" application, and it performs best with fast processors, fast disk drives, and plenty of memory. In designing digital albums, you'll be working with large, high-resolution images. If you find that Photoshop doesn't perform quickly on your computer, you may need to upgrade your hardware.

Memory is getting less expensive every day, and there's no reason to put up with a slow computer when you don't have to. Adding random access memory is the least expensive, easiest, and most useful improvement you can make. If you don't already have a gigabyte of RAM, you'll want to upgrade.

If you're in the market for a new computer, look at the top systems recommended by reputable dealers. You'll pay a premium for the fastest processor speed, and this isn't necessary. It's more cost-effective to choose a system a step or two below that, and you'll still be happy with Photoshop's performance.

Acknowledgements

I owe thanks to many people for making this book possible. First I want to thank my husband, Dale, with all my heart. Dale not only created our studio website, but he writes every software program we need to run the studio efficiently. Whenever I need a new software tool, he says, "Write a spec and tell me when you need it." In addition to administering our domain and our e-mail accounts, he found the time to design and create a beautiful digital marketing piece that was a finalist in the PPA AN-NE competition for 2004. And after designing software at his "day job" all week, Dale accompanies me to every wedding, where he sets up equipment, takes creative images, and generally enables me to focus on capturing the special moments of the day. I'm so fortunate to be sharing life with him.

My mentors, Randy and Michele Santee, have been more than generous with their knowledge and their time. Without their help and guidance years ago, I would probably not be photographing weddings today. I learned many of the design techniques from the gorgeous albums they produce in their studio in Rocklin, California.

Thank you to my peer reviewers, especially Bob Gassen and Chris Sollart, who provided valuable feedback about content. Thank you to Richard Lee and Russ Madeira, whose careful technical reviews ensured the accuracy of the procedures. My editor, Todd Manza, lent his content editing expertise to help turn a rough draft into a finished work. Melody Englund produced a great index to make finding information easy.

And thank you to my sweet girls, Alaina and Claire, for their patience with a mother who loves her work.

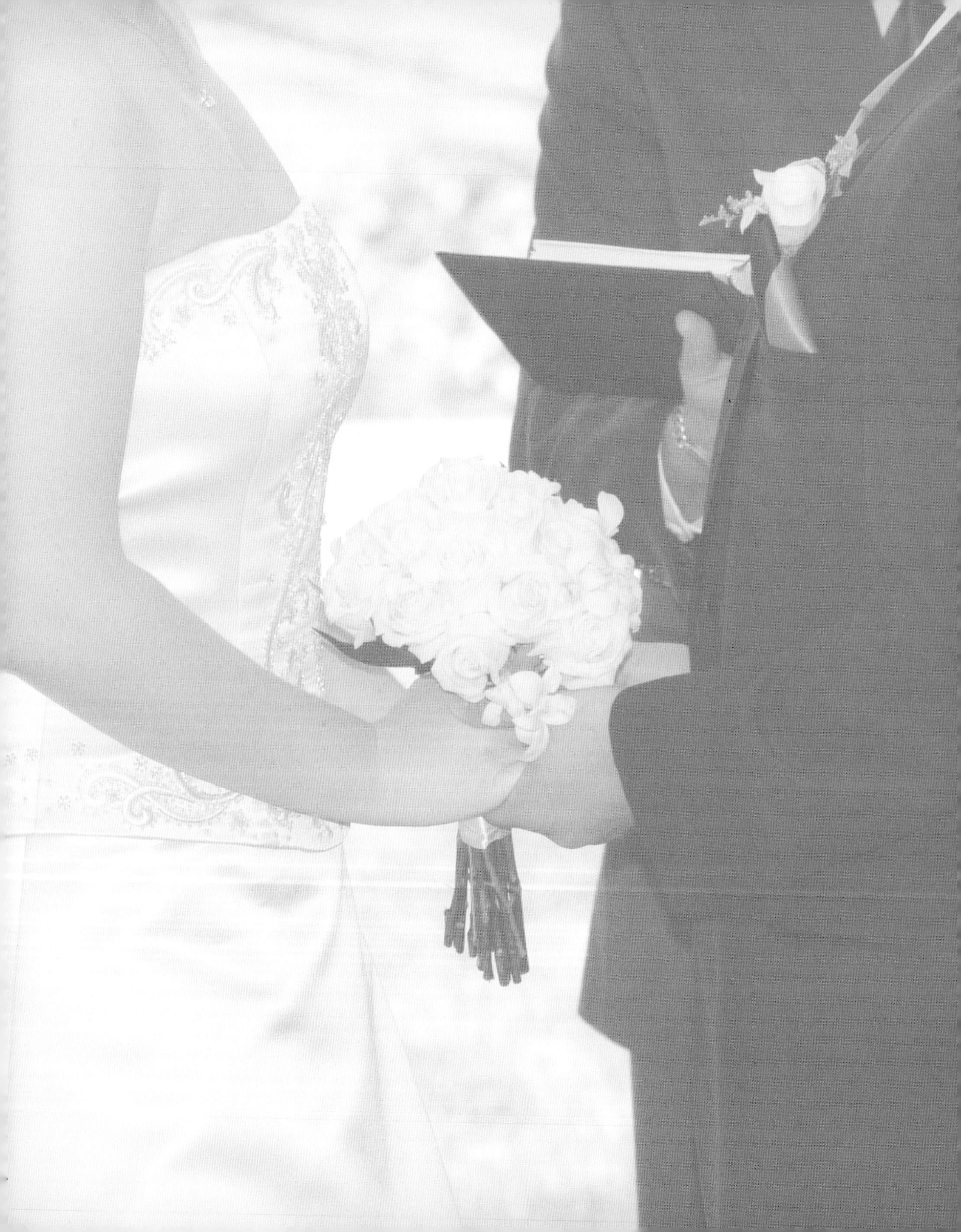

Business issues

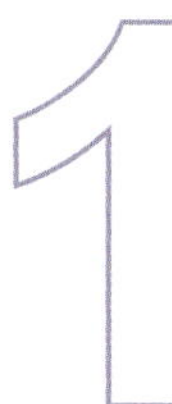

Introduction

The only kind of wedding album available to brides and grooms used to be the matted album. But now, with today's professional-quality digital cameras producing images indistinguishable from film, the market for digital magazine-style albums has exploded.

Many brides and grooms would like to see their wedding story in a digital album. You may want to offer these albums, but you've probably heard (or found) that the design process can be difficult and can take a great deal of time. You may be unsure how to go about designing an album or which software to buy. You may have bought several thick books about Photoshop but have been unable to find the time to get through all those tutorials or to figure out which features and tools are needed to design albums.

Photoshop can be intimidating if you're not familiar with it. It's rich with features, each with a unique set of controls. However, you need to know only a small subset of these features to produce beautiful digital albums, and you'll learn every one of these features here.

Learn a small subset of Photoshop features here, and you'll know everything you need to know to create beautiful digital albums.

As you read the instructions for the design techniques illustrated in Chapter 4, you'll learn many additional Photoshop tips and techniques. If you want more information about any of the Photoshop features, I recommend the book *Real World Adobe Photoshop CS* by David Blatner and Bruce Fraser.

How long will the album designing actually take? With the techniques you'll learn in this book, laying out the pages can take as little as twenty minutes for each double-page spread. That's just six hours for a thirty-four–page album.

What is a digital magazine-style album?

In the classic matted album, each image chosen by the couple is printed individually, and these prints are attached behind a mat on each page. A mat might have one large cutout for a single 8 x 10 print, for instance, or four smaller cutouts to hold 4 x 5s. The mats offered by the album company determine your layout options.

With the new digital albums, however, the layout options are limitless. Once a couple has chosen their album images, you can design pages with a new freedom that allows incredible creativity. After you build all the two-page spreads for the album in Photoshop, you'll flatten the composite images and order them as large prints from your lab. When these come back, you'll trim them if necessary and then send them to the album company for mounting and binding.

The most common form for a digital album is one in which the prints are flush-mounted on each art board page and the book is bound with a leather cover. There are two common types of flush-mounted albums: those with split pages, and those with fully panoramic images on each page spread.

Split-page album

Split-page albums use a separate print for each page, with either a taped or hingeless binding showing between pages.

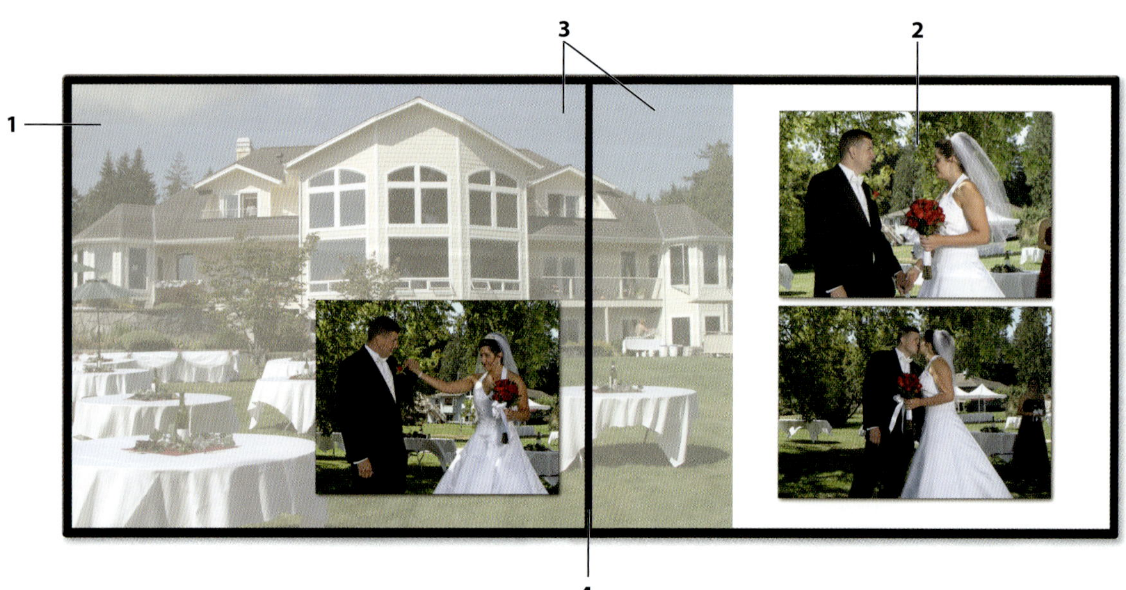

1. Background image
These are made partially transparent, adding a subtle design element without taking attention away from the images placed over them.

2. Image
Images are combined in one Photoshop window and then modified with layer styles and other enhancement techniques.

3. Flush-mounted prints making up a two-page spread
After you finish designing the pages in Photoshop, you'll send the files to your lab. When the prints come back, you'll package them to send to the album company, where they'll be mounted and bound.

4. Core
This shows between the pages in a split-page album. Some albums are made with white cores, and some with black. (I prefer the black core, as it matches the usually black album cover that "frames" each two-page spread.)

Panoramic album

Panoramic albums use prints that are two pages wide, without a split down the middle.

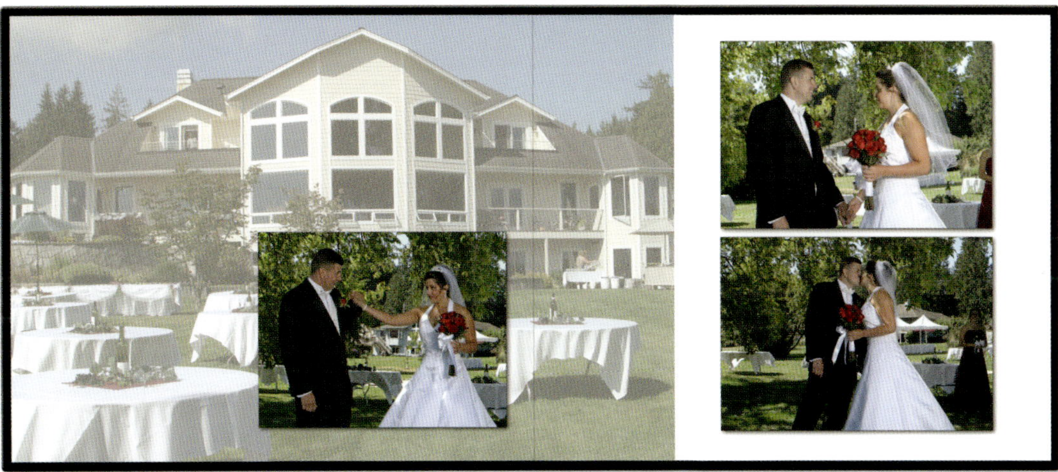

Why not pay an album company to design your digital albums?

Many album companies are offering design services now. Besides the obvious fact that those services are expensive, here are some factors to consider:

- You have no control over the style, and the results could be different each time depending upon the designer.
- Design styles vary considerably among different album companies.

If you maintain control of the design, you can be more confident that clients will be happy with their album.

- Once the design is complete, the album company will charge for revisions. (What if clients ask for quite a few?)
- The album company works with its own lab to print the final images, and you won't be able to check the prints before they're mounted and bound into the album.
- Once you've created your own sample album, clients will want an album just like that, and you will need to be able to promise them the same look.

For these reasons, it's much better to maintain control over the design. This way, too, you can use the professional lab you know and trust to provide high-quality prints, which you will then send to an album company for mounting and binding.

What about template and design programs?

Should you buy a program with templates for designing? Template packages are pre-designed album pages that enable you to drop images into digital "mats." It seems that every lab and album company either has an album design program now or is planning to announce one soon.

Here are some factors to consider:

- Some of the software packages are expensive. If you have Photoshop, you don't need to buy an additional software package to achieve the same results.
- These packages might have limited options for enhancement effects such as layer styles. You can add a shadow, for example, but it might be the one the program designer determined looked best. You'll want to be able to customize layer styles for the most creative designs.
- You'll have many, many templates to choose from (sometimes thousands), but it takes time to look through these and select the right one for the specific set of images on every page.
- After you find a template that's close to what you're looking for, you'll need to modify the images to fit the template, or to modify the template to fit the images. And you'll need to know Photoshop to do that well.
- And finally, some of these programs create proprietary files, so you're locked into using albums from only one company.

Even if you use a template program, knowing the features used in Photoshop will allow you to creatively enhance the template designs.

Even if you're already using a template package or design program, you can use the sample pages in this book for design ideas. Some template programs produce layered files in Photoshop, which you can then modify. But in order to modify them, you need to understand what Photoshop features were used to build them in the first place. Learning how to create the sample designs presented here will give you the skills you need to customize the files created by this kind of template program.

What you'll find in this book

Here you'll find an inside look at how to handle all aspects of using Adobe Photoshop to create digital albums "from scratch." We'll walk through business issues to consider, creating an efficient digital workflow, selecting album images with clients, and necessary Photoshop features for designing pages. Finally, you'll learn step-by-step methods for creative page design.

You may already have your own strategies in place for some of these processes. The ideas presented here will help you streamline your workflow and produce better albums faster.

Getting started on your first digital album

The first thing you'll want to do is create a sample album (or some sample page spreads) and make the business decisions necessary to market this product. You'll need to decide:

- Which wedding images to use
- Which album company to use
- How much to charge
- What to say to clients during the consultation

Even if you haven't created a digital album before, you may not need to produce an entire sample album to sell the idea to the first client.

Before I designed my first digital album, I put together three sample magazine-style pages from a particularly nice wedding which I could show to potential clients.

I projected images of these sample pages during a consultation, and then offered one couple a low album price because I would be using their images to produce my first digital album. They were excited about the offer, and they couldn't wait to see what their album would look like.

I spent weeks designing that first album. I looked at many online albums for ideas, but I hadn't yet figured out the techniques for designing quickly and efficiently. The bride and groom loved the album, and the album company asked for permission to print its own samples to display at trade shows.

Images to use for the sample album

You might already have the digital images from a beautiful wedding you recently photographed. If you do, you can start designing an album right away. The disadvantage is that you may not have taken as many background or detail images as you need to produce the most creative designs. (You'll see ideas for these images later in this chapter.)

Ideally you'll plan to use the recommendations in this book when you are photographing an upcoming wedding that you know will be beautiful. Shoot plenty of background and detail images, and capture transitional moments that help tell the story. Then choose only the best images from this wedding and create a stunning sample album.

You might think that you can save time by designing just one album and getting two copies printed—one for the couple and one as a studio sample. However, I don't recommend this in most cases. For your studio sample, you'll want to include only the very best images, whereas the bride and groom may choose images that are not necessarily representative of your best work.

Your sample album doesn't need to be large. The album I designed that won Best Wedding Album had just twenty-four pages (twelve double-page spreads).

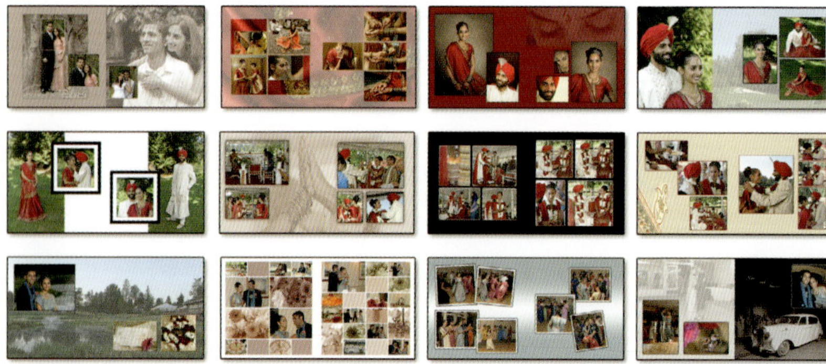

Resolution

If you shoot with film, you will be happiest with the resulting album if you have your negatives professionally scanned. For digital, you'll achieve the best results if you use a camera that produces files with at least 2,000 x 3,000 pixels (the typical size from a 6-megapixel camera).

You'll want files this large because most of the time, you won't want to scale up images on the page. When you scale up, Photoshop creates pixels to fill in and make the image larger. These made-up pixels are never as sharp as the pixels in the original image.

Look at this example. In this page spread, you see two versions of the same image.

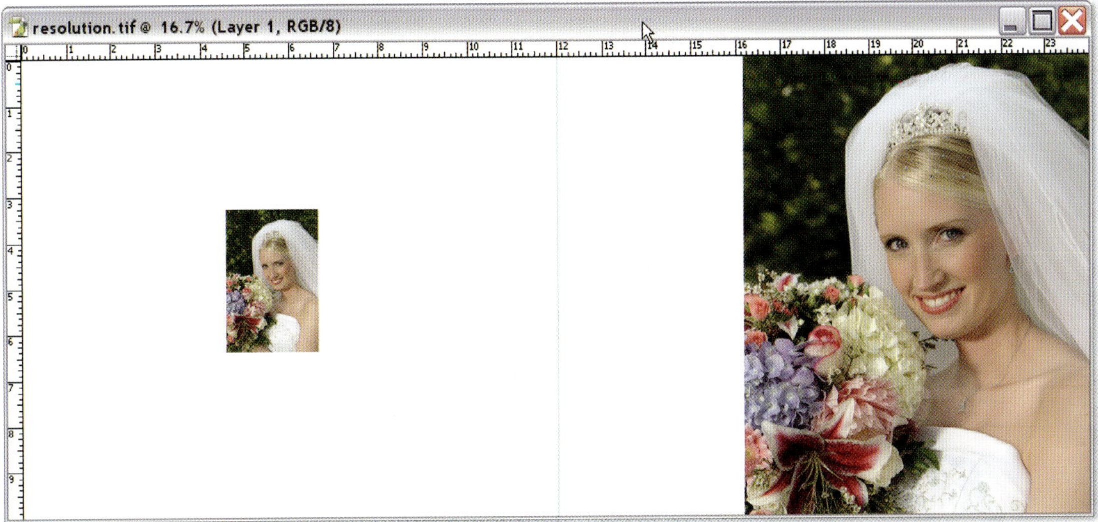

The large version contains all the original pixels captured with a 6.3-megapixel Canon 10D. When the large image was pasted into the page spread window, it filled the page without resizing. This is because the image itself is 3,000 pixels high, and the page spread window is about 2,500 pixels high. This is ideal, and provides a clear, sharp image when printed.

The small version was resampled in its own window to a maximum height of 800 pixels, and was then pasted into the page spread window. This demonstrates what can happen if you crop a larger image down to just a face, for example, and try to enlarge the cropped image in your page spread.

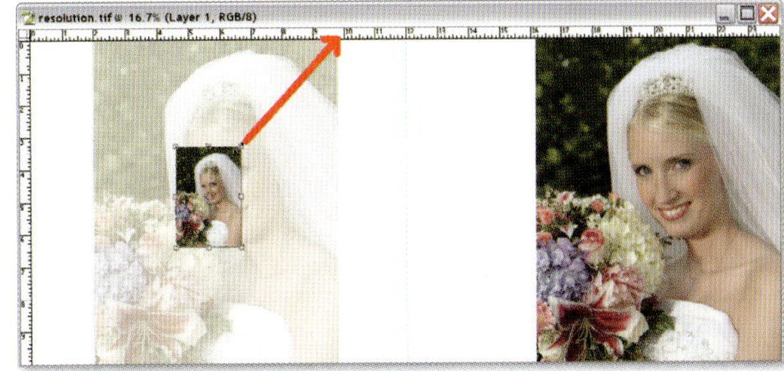

The small image will look fine in the album, *if* you leave it at that size on the page. But imagine if you cropped a face from a larger image, and then scaled it up on the page. Here the enlarged version on the left looks just about identical to the one that started out with a lot more pixels.

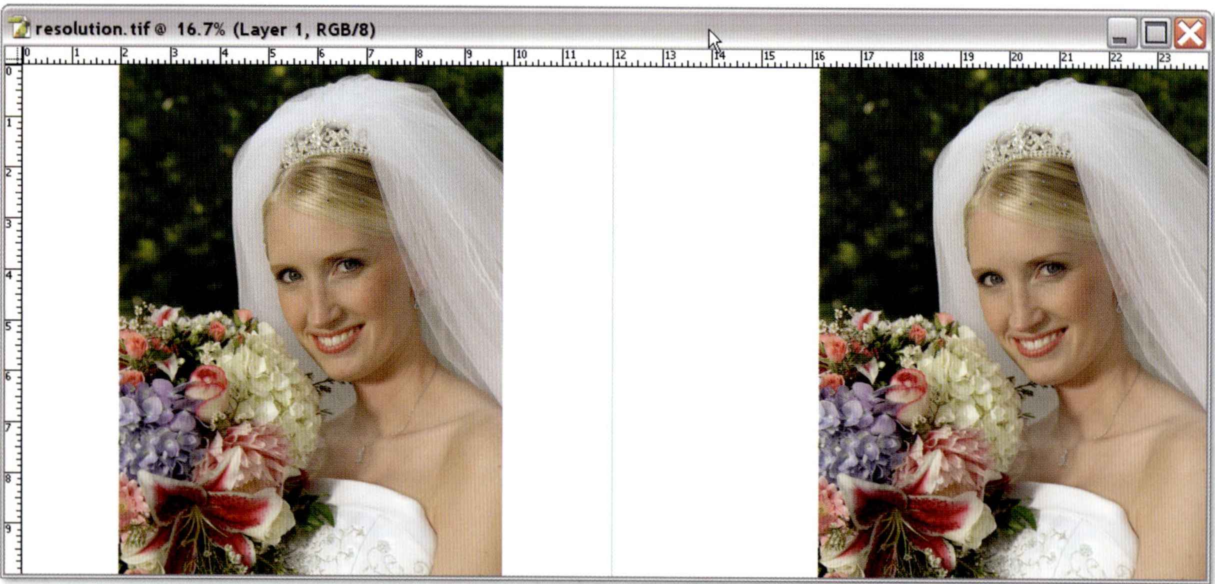

But look what happens when we zoom in. The image on the left with the pixels added as a result of enlarging has become unacceptably soft, and no amount of sharpening will restore the necessary clarity.

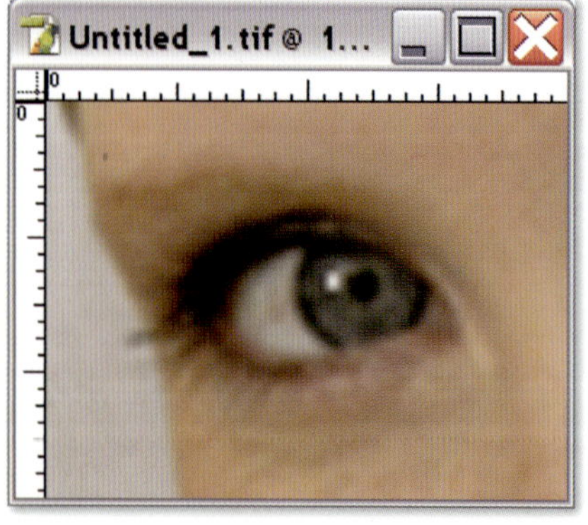

Close-up view of an image enlarged from 800 pixels to 2500.

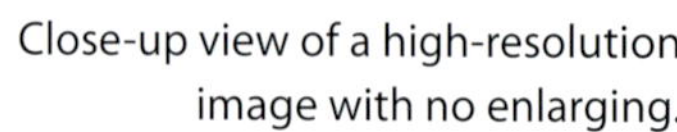

Close-up view of a high-resolution image with no enlarging.

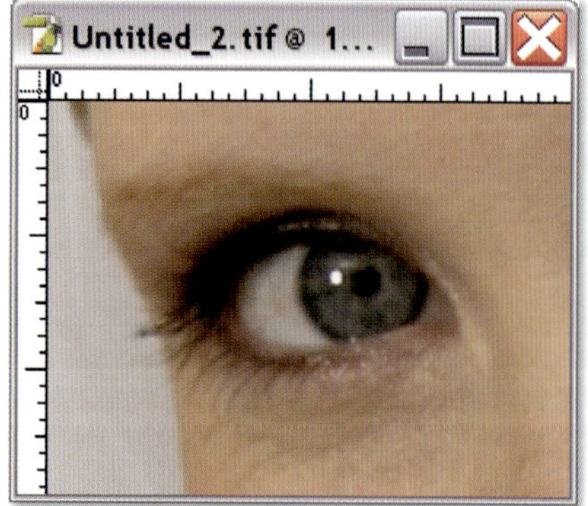

The more you enlarge an image on the page, the worse the blurring will become. This is why you want to start out with high-resolution images and avoid enlarging them whenever possible.

Images to capture

Let's talk a little bit about the pictures. Besides the usual images you shoot of people, it's also useful to have both background and detail shots to incorporate into creative designs. Make sure you capture many images that will be appropriate for backgrounds. Do some vertical and some horizontal shots of the same scene, in case one orientation works better for a particular layout. You'll use close-up detail shots for highlights as part of page spreads.

I tell prospective clients that we use only images taken on their wedding day. I think this is important to people. Most probably don't want to see someone else's idea of appropriate clip art in their timeless keepsake.

Images that make good backgrounds are often images without faces. These allow you the greatest freedom in positioning images over them. If a background image has faces in it, you will either need to cover a face completely with an image or to leave plenty of room around it.

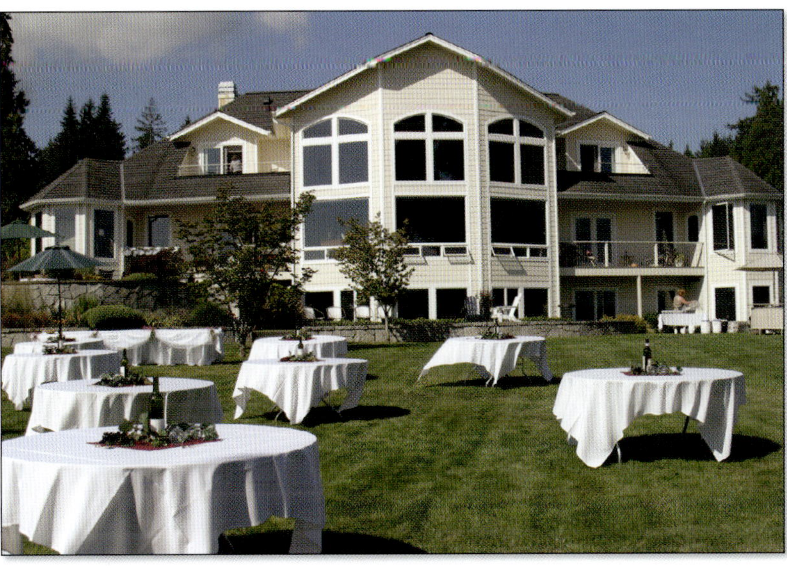

Suggested images

- Close-ups of flowers
- A close-up of the bouquet, with the bride blurred in the background
- The wedding dress
- Details of the dress
- Stained glass in the church
- Wide views of the church exterior

Be careful about using a scaled-up image of the bride's and groom's hands and rings for a background image. It may look fine in the small size you're viewing on your screen, but when large hands are printed on a 12 x 12 page, they can look claw-like and scary!

- Wide views of the church interior, both empty and during the ceremony
- Wide view looking up the aisle from the altar, with the church empty
- The sign for the church or reception venue
- Wide views of the reception hall before guests arrive
- Wide views of the reception hall full of people
- A place setting before anyone sits down, especially the bride's and groom's place settings
- The head table
- A centerpiece
- All the place cards in rows before they're set on tables
- Creative views of the cake and cake details
- The sky (if there are interesting clouds), the sunset, the moon
- A flower arrangement in the church, or candles on a stand
- The guest book
- Sheet music played at the ceremony or reception
- Hands and rings
- Rings on an invitation, with flowers or petals placed around
- Just the bride's and groom's hands, clasped, with a nice blurred background
- Bride's hands fastening her shoes
- Shoes with jewelry and bouquet or garter
- The couple's toasting glasses on the table with a candle and the bouquet
- Any details unique to the location

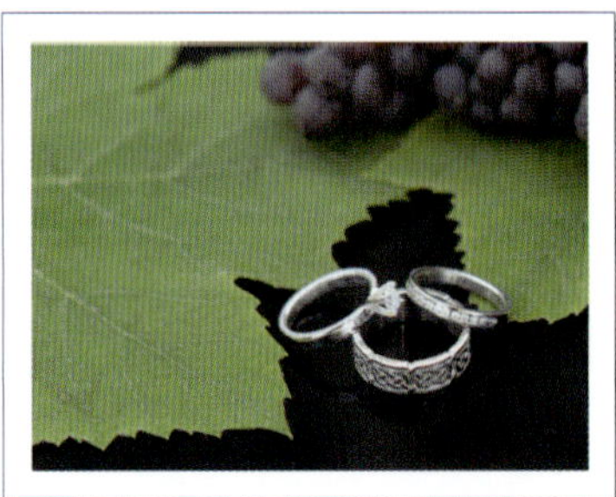

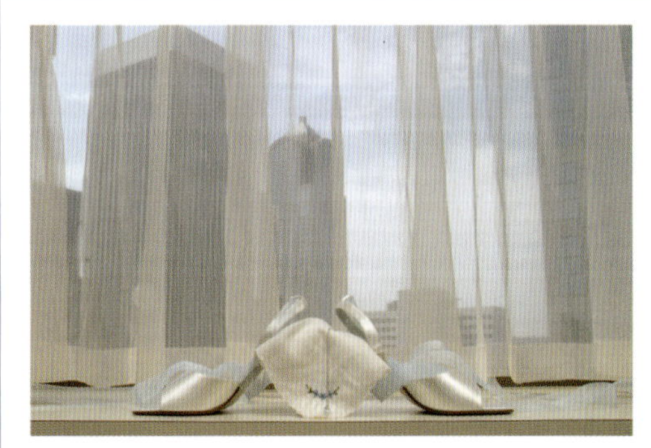

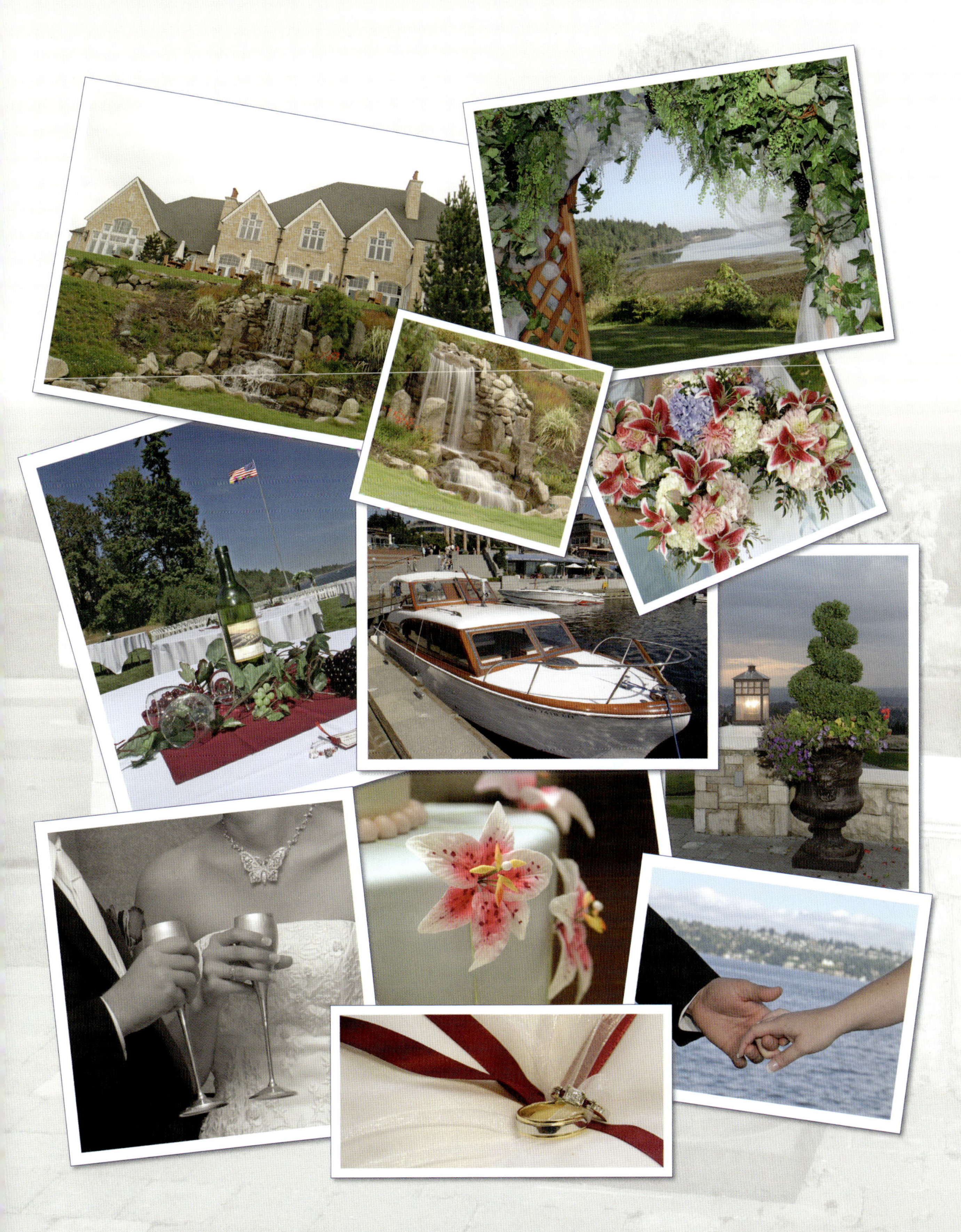

Using the invitation and vows

Ask the bride to send you an invitation so you'll be able to bring it to the wedding and take a shot of it in the context of the reception. We usually borrow a flower or two from a centerpiece or a bridesmaid's bouquet to use in the picture.

Also ask the bride to send a copy of the vows. Keep text in the album to a minimum for simplicity, but a line or two from the vows on a ceremony page spread works nicely. Because some people don't finish writing their vows until the last minute, you may have to get them via e-mail after the wedding.

Researching album companies

After you've decided which wedding images to use, your next step will be deciding which album company to work with. You need to know what sizes they offer for flush-mounted albums so you can choose a page size before you begin designing. Believe me, after you've designed even one page spread, you will not want to redesign it for a different album size.

Most of our clients like the 10 x 12 horizontal album that we order from Classic Album. I like the horizontal format because there's plenty of room on the page for a full-length image and for other images beside it.

Call several album companies and have them send you a price list for flush-mounted digital albums. Some of them may say they only work with people who use their proprietary design program or template package. If this happens, push a little and find out if they will allow you to submit finished prints, paying only for mounting and binding. They may allow this option, but simply not print it in their catalog.

Here are some things you'll want to ask about their albums:

- How much is the discount for a studio sample?
- What cover sizes are available?
- How much are the covers for various sizes?
- How much for mounting and binding in the various sizes?
- What are the options for cover finishes and styles?
- Do they offer a leather-like alternative? (Some of our clients prefer not to have a leather cover.)

- Do some of their albums allow full panoramic pages (pages that are not split in the middle)?
- What color is the core in their split-page albums?
- Will they send order forms and cover-material swatches?
- How much do they charge for the inscription?
- How much do they charge for a cover cameo?
- Do they charge extra for a protective coating on the pages?
- What is the typical turnaround time?

Here are some companies to contact:

- **Renaissance** www.thebookalbum.com
- **Classic Album** www.classicalbum.com
- **General Products** www.gpalbums.com
- **Capri** www.caprialbum.com
- **Leather Craftsmen** www.leathercraftsmen.com

These are companies that I've enjoyed working with or that my colleagues recommend.

Pricing issues to keep in mind

The process of producing digital albums is considerably different from the process of producing matted albums. Because of these differences, you'll need to decide what to charge for various new areas:

- The time you spend working with the digital images and designing
- Elements such as background images, digital enhancements, and miniature replica albums

Charging for your time

After you've designed and ordered your first album, you'll know the cost of the album itself and of the prints from your lab. You'll have a good idea how long the designing takes and what you'll need to charge to make it worth your time. Be sure to take into account the hours involved in all the tasks comprised in producing digital albums.

The table on the following page gives you an idea of the kind of time you can expect to spend on the whole process of photographing a wedding and using the digital images to create an album.

Task	Hours
Consultation	1
Phone calls and e-mails	1
Engagement session, including putting proofs online	4
Photographing the wedding	9
Copying flash memory cards, paring down images, and preparing proofs	3
Preparing for and hosting the album design session	4
Color-correcting images for print orders, submitting the orders, and shipping prints	2
Color-correcting selected album images and enhancing selected images	3
Designing pages	6
Making requested revisions	1
Preparing album images for the lab and placing the order	1
Trimming prints, packaging prints, and shipping to the album company	1
Total	**36**

Keep in mind that you don't want to provide designing time at no cost. Clients are commissioning you to produce a work of art from their wedding images. If you show them lovely samples of your work, those with discerning taste will be willing to pay more for quality designs.

You might consider offering a lower-priced package for an album of one size, and a higher-priced package that includes a larger album. In addition to this, many photographers charge a base price for a certain number of images. For instance, you can charge a price that includes eighty images and then set a price for each additional image. If you charge by the page, budget-minded clients might ask you to fit more images on fewer pages. You'll need to educate them about the fact that they would be disappointed by the number of small images if fewer pages are used.

Let clients know in advance how much you charge for change requests they might have after they preview the album.

You'll want to set a policy regarding requested changes. I've heard stories about clients who have strong opinions about the design and who ask for many specific changes after previewing the album. Changes can take a great deal of your time, so it's a good idea to have a written policy that specifies the number of changes included in the package, and how much you charge for additional changes.

Should you charge for background images?

Background images are the semitransparent images that fill the page behind the other images placed on the page. You'll need to decide whether the background images you choose will count toward the total number included in the clients' package. This is a little tricky because you won't know during the proof selection session just how many background images you'll actually use.

Once clients understand what a background image is, they usually have opinions about which images they'd like to see used. If clients expressly choose an image to be used as a background, that image becomes part of their total number of selected images. As we're selecting the images to include, I also make a list of the ones I've decided to keep as good possible backgrounds. I don't include these as part of the clients' total because I may not use them.

What will you charge for digital enhancements?

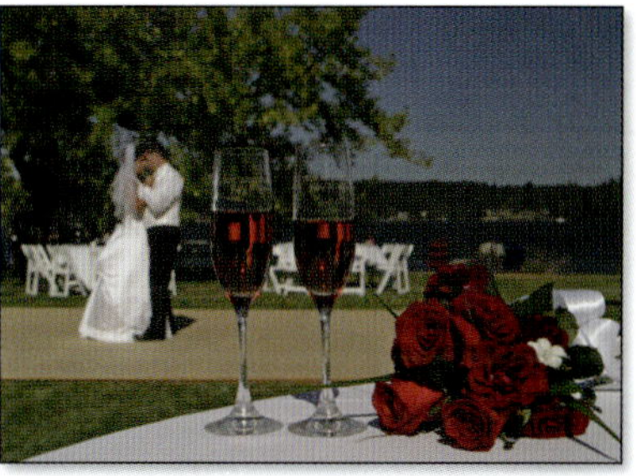

You can enhance digital images for clients in any number of ways: turn them to black and white or sepia, add or remove people, take out distracting background elements, or give a bride a smaller waist.

You will want to determine how much you charge for these kinds of enhancements. I recommend charging something per hour, or offering three free enhancements and then charging for others. If your clients think you'll do any number of enhancements free of charge, they will ask for a considerable number of changes; you'll find yourself spending many hours working on a handful of images.

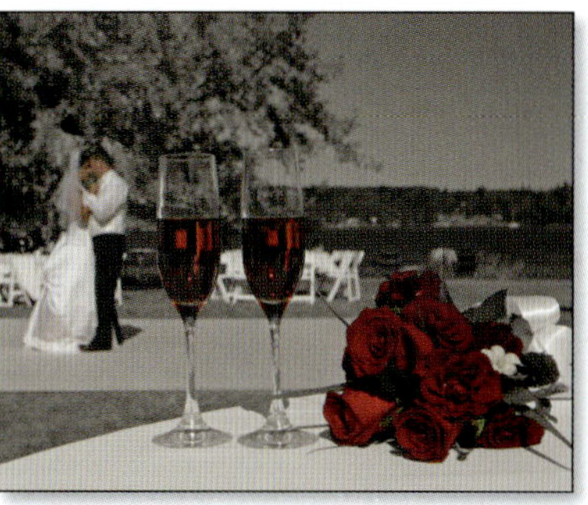

What about miniature replica albums?

A great add-on to offer couples is a miniature replica album. This is an exact copy of their album, only smaller. Once you have the design finished, it's easy to order another set of prints in a smaller size and an additional album from the album company. These are great for parents. In addition to the 10 x 12 album, we offer a 5 x 6 miniature replica album.

You'll also need to decide how much to charge for these. Most album companies offer them, and brides love them (and so do their mothers!). These albums require very little work from you because the design work is finished. But they're expensive. Make sure you know exactly how much a miniature replica album will cost, including the cost of the prints from your lab and shipping. And be aware that if parents decide to order one, they may be purchasing just the album instead of ordering many prints of their favorite images. By selling a replica album, you may be giving up a large print order.

You need to charge enough for a miniature replica album to make up for the potential loss in print sales.

Another thing to decide before talking with potential clients is how much to charge for changes to parent albums. I tell clients that the parent albums are miniature replica albums—a smaller version of the large album. But I've had a few parents ask if they can, for instance, add more grandparent portraits to the family portrait pages. What will you charge for switching one image with another? Will you charge one price per changed page, no matter how many changes? How much will you charge to add another complete page spread? It's a good idea to be prepared with answers to these questions. You might charge $20 per page spread changed, for instance, and $30 if changes require a new page spread.

The consultation

After you've read this book and created your first sample album, a bride and groom will be sitting in your studio, admiring the album. They'll know they want to see their wedding story in an album just like that.

When you show clients a sample album, handle it very carefully. Turn the pages slowly. This shows clients that you believe this work has great value.

At this point, most couples want to know that they'll be able to preview their album before it goes to print, so you need to have decided how you're going to provide that opportunity. You can put preview images on your own website, or on one of the many event-hosting websites, such as Collages.net, Pictage.com, or Eventpix.com. You can send clients a CD with low-resolution images. You can bring clients in and display the images using a projector or display them on a wide-screen television connected to your laptop computer.

If clients want to know how many pages the album will be, you'll need to give them a range. The number of pages will depend somewhat upon how many images the clients choose in each category. For instance, if they choose four cake images and four dance images, those eight images might make one page spread. But if they choose eight dance images, the cake images will need to go on an additional page. Our albums usually include about ninety images, and they range from thirty-two to thirty-eight pages for a 10 x 12 horizontal album.

I make it a point to mention to couples that when other clients have previewed their album, they're excited about the design, and they may request one or two small changes. This way, clients are more likely to believe that when they see the album proofs, the album is in its final form, except for one or two minor requests. Keep in mind that the more professional the design looks, the more likely clients are to see the album proofs as a finished product. You'll learn about how to produce a professional look in Chapters 3 and 4.

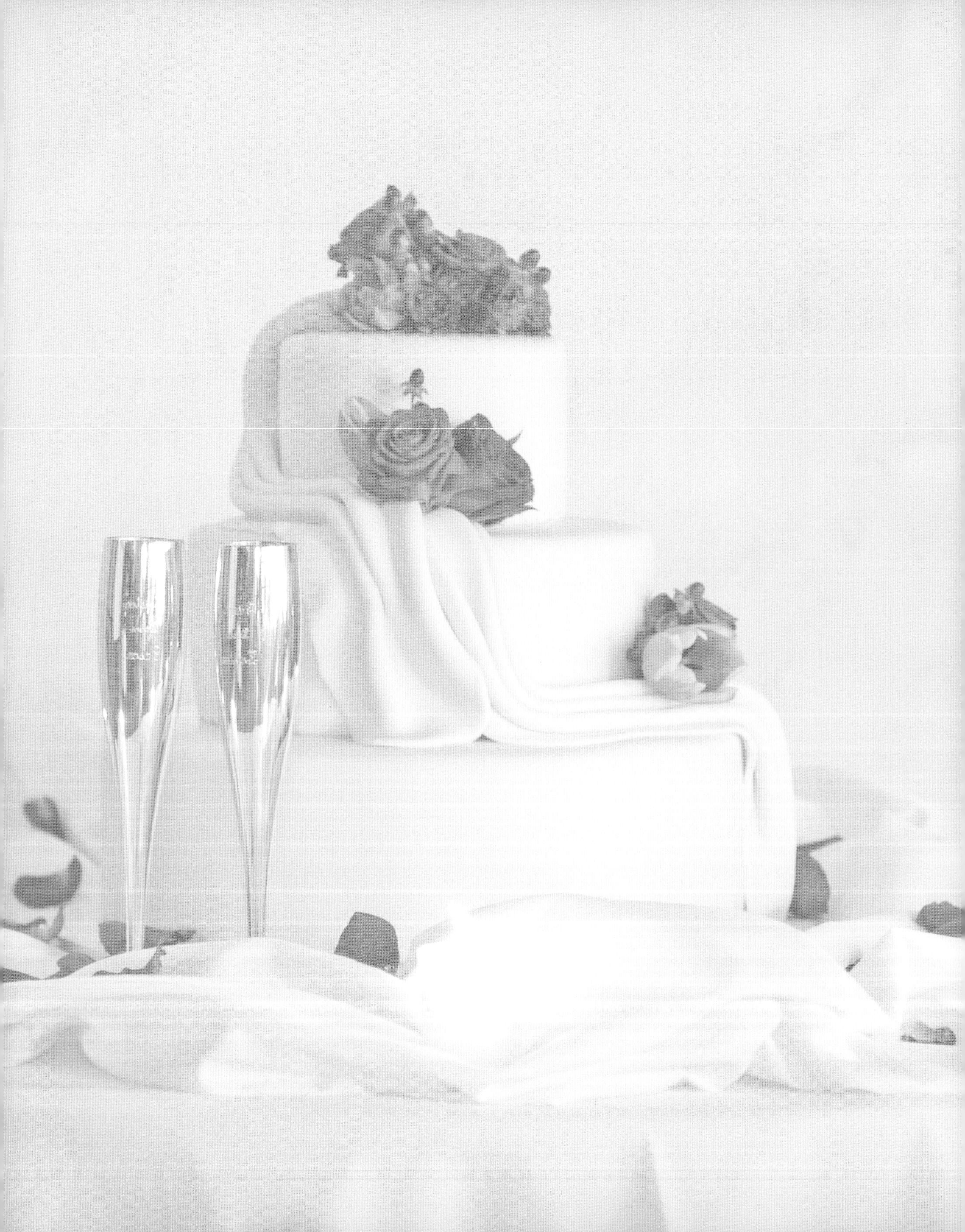

Getting from 900 proofs to 100 album images

2

Digital workflow

You may already have processes in place for exactly what happens with the images when you shoot a wedding. It's helpful, though, to take a look at another system to see if there's a particular step you might want to add or change. First we'll look at how to pare down the entire set of proofs to create the set we show to clients. And then we'll look at how to run a session with clients to select their album images.

Before the wedding

If you use multiple cameras, it's important to synchronize their times before the wedding. Later, you'll be putting the images from all the cameras into one folder and sorting them by date/time created, and you want all of these images to fall into the right order. If two cameras used during the ceremony are off by even a minute, you'll find "exchanging rings" images from one camera interspersed with "kiss" images from the other, for instance, and you'll have to manually move these into chronological order.

Synchronize the times on all cameras used to shoot the wedding.

When we show proofs to our clients, we do a Premier Show, putting proofs in an order that tells the story of their wedding, rather than in the order the images were shot. Synchronizing camera times is a big help in customizing the sort order to produce this show.

Also look at the numbering on all the cameras. If you use two of the same kind of camera and the numbers are close, reset the numbering on one of them. If two images are called "IMG_4622.jpg" you'll have to rename one set in order to copy all the images into one folder later.

After the wedding

Throughout the wedding day, we copy images from flash memory cards to a laptop, looking at a few in each section to make sure that no equipment malfunctions (or other unfortunate circumstances) have created the need to redo an image.

Here's an overview of how we get from 900 images to the approximately 350 proofs we show to clients:

- Flash memory cards are offloaded at the studio into a folder called ClientName\Wedding\Originals.
- All the original images are burned onto two DVDs. (One of those DVDs is stored off-site.)
- Another folder is created called ClientName\Wedding\Proofs.
- All the originals are copied to the Proofs folder.
- These images are moved into the appropriate order and are pared down for proofs using the Adobe Photoshop File Browser.
- Files are renamed to preserve the custom sort order.
- Another DVD, containing the proof images, is burned and stored in the client file.
- Proofs are copied to a Small Proofs folder and are set to a maximum height and width of 800 pixels.
- Any proofs needing cropping or brightening before being shown to clients are given quick enhancements.
- Proofs are uploaded to our website.

In addition to the DVD back-up, the entire hard drive with all the client images is backed up automatically onto an additional hard drive every night. Once a week, this back-up hard drive is swapped with another one stored off-site.

Using the Photoshop File Browser

Take a moment to look at the following illustration. As you do the techniques in this section, it'll be helpful to know the terminology.

If you shoot with RAW capture, you're no doubt already familiar with the File Browser as a useful tool for selecting images. If not, you'll find that the File Browser is a good tool for paring down images to the set of proofs you'll show to clients. Here you'll learn

In Photoshop CS2, the File Browser has been replaced by a stand-alone application called Adobe Bridge. Many of the features discussed in this chapter have nearly the same functionality in both programs.

what you need to know about the File Browser to prepare a set of proofs for presenting to clients.

File Browser window

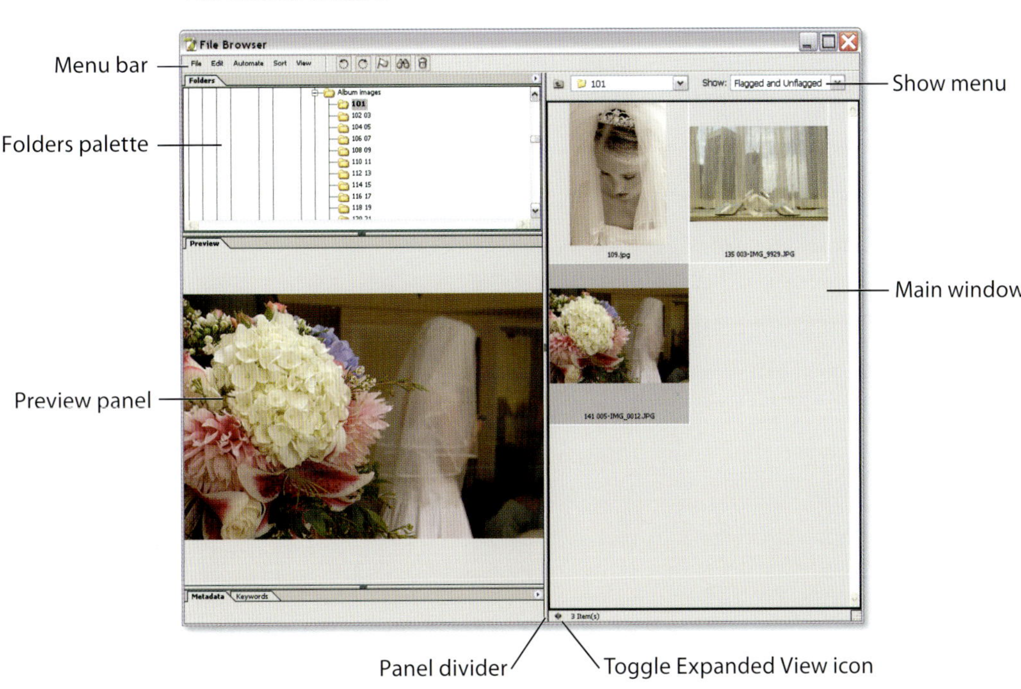

Customizing the File Browser

As you're paring down images for the set of proofs, you'll want to see each image large on the screen to check the quality. Here's how to modify the File Browser window to make this easy.

1. From the File menu in Photoshop, choose Browse to open the File Browser.
2. From the File Browser View menu, choose Large Thumbnails. (In CS2, drag the slider below the thumbnails for a custom thumbnail size.)
3. In the folder list, drag the horizontal panel divider up so that the Folders palette is small.
4. Double-click the Metadata tab to minimize that palette if it's not minimized already.
5. Drag the vertical panel divider to the right to increase the size of the Preview panel, leaving the main window only large enough to show a vertical strip of thumbnail images.

When working with the File Browser, it's helpful to press Tab to hide all the Photoshop palettes so they're not in the way. To show them again later, press Tab again.

In CS2, Adobe Bridge appears in front of the Photoshop palettes.

Customizing thumbnail size

If you'd like to see thumbnails larger than the Large Thumbnails view, you can specify a custom size.

1. From the File Browser Edit menu, choose Preferences.
2. Type a new number, such as 200, for Custom Thumbnail Size. Click OK.
3. From the File Browser View menu, choose Custom Thumbnail Size.

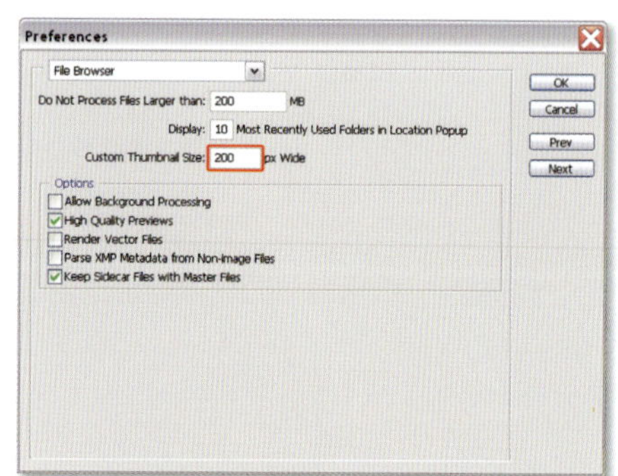

Saving File Browser configurations

Photoshop saves your custom File Browser configuration from one session to the next. However, if you find that you use more than one view of the File Browser, you can save the views you find useful so that you can simply select the different views from a menu later.

1. Arrange the palettes in the appropriate configuration.
2. From the Photoshop Window menu, choose Workspace, and then choose Save Workspace. (In CS2, this command is on the Bridge Window menu.)
3. Give this workspace a name.

To open a saved workspace in CS2, open the Bridge, and then choose the workspace name from Workspace on the Window menu.

The next time you want to use the File Browser with this configuration, you'll find the name listed on the Workspace submenu, and you can select it from there. You can even choose the name of your workspace to open the File Browser.

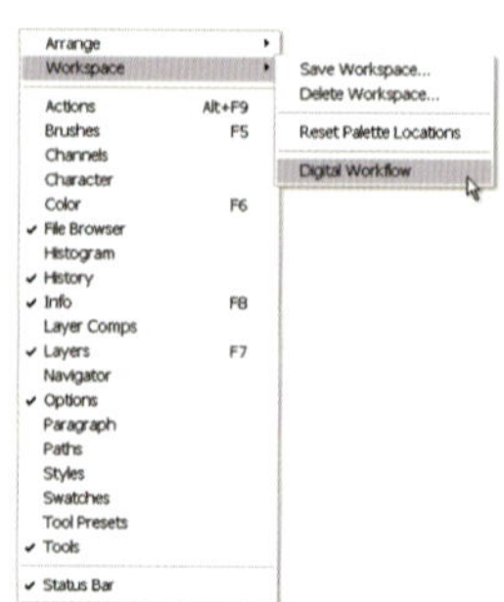

Renaming files

If you do end up with some wedding images having the same file names, you can copy the images from each card into a separate folder, and then rename them using the File Browser. This way you'll be able to move all the images into one folder for paring down.

1. From the File menu in Photoshop, choose Browse.
2. In the Folders palette, locate and open the folder containing the images to rename.
3. Select all the files in that folder by pressing Ctrl+A (⌘-A).
4. From the Automate menu in the File Browser, choose Batch Rename.

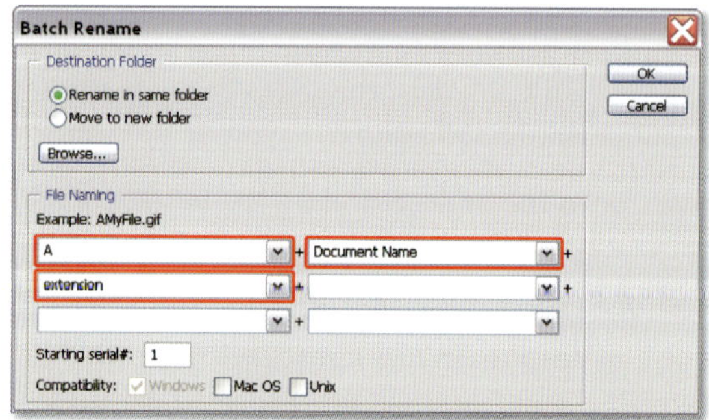

5. Add something to the name that will differentiate it from the other files.
   - In the first dropdown list box, type the letter A and a space.
   - In the list box to the right of the first one, select Document Name.
   - In the third list box, select "extension."

To rename images in CS2, select the images in the Bridge, right-click (Ctrl-click) an image, and choose Batch Rename.

This would rename IMG_1435.jpg to A IMG_1435.jpg. Once you've renamed the files, you'll be able to copy them all into the same folder.

Rotating images

Rotating images is easy using keyboard shortcuts.

1. In the File Browser, click the Toggle Expanded View icon to hide the palettes and make more room for thumbnail images.
2. Hold Ctrl (⌘) and click one by one all the images that need to be rotated clockwise.
3. Press Ctrl+] (⌘-]) to rotate the images clockwise.

To make more room for thumbnail images in CS2, drag the vertical panel divider to the left.

Photoshop displays a message telling you that only the thumbnail versions of the images are rotated. When you open the file in Photoshop, the rotation will be applied, and then you can choose whether to save the rotated version.

If you want to apply all the rotations without opening the files in Photoshop, select all the files (you can press Ctrl+A to select even those files that have not been rotated) and choose Apply Rotation from the Edit menu in the Browser. This overwrites the existing files with the rotated versions.

Creating a custom sort order

After you've created a set of proofs in one folder, you'll probably want to move images into a custom sort order. For instance, you may have found time to get pictures of the cake while you were waiting for the bride and groom to arrive at the reception, and then you captured the rest of the cake pictures later. You'll want to move earlier cake pictures next to the pictures of the bride and groom with the cake, to make their job of selecting album images easier.

If some images are out of order, use the File Browser to create a custom sort order.

1. In the File Browser, locate and select the Proofs folder.

   If you've just finished rotating images, you may need to click the Toggle Expanded View icon to show the Folders palette.

2. From the View menu, choose Large Thumbnails.
3. From the Sort menu, choose Date Created.
4. Drag the thumbnails into the correct order.

Click Toggle Expanded View to hide or show the panes on the left.

Now you're ready to select proofs.

Selecting proofs

We'll talk here about two ways to select proofs in the File Browser: by flagging the acceptable images, and by deleting the unacceptable images. The following information will help you decide which method to use:

In CS2, be sure to have Show Thumbnail Only unchecked on the Adobe Bridge View menu if you want to see the star rating for each thumbnail.

- If, as you go through the images, you want to see the entire proof set during the selection process, so it's easy to change your mind later about whether or not to keep an image, you'll want to use the flagging method.
- On the other hand, if you're a very decisive person, and you know that when you decide an image is unacceptable you won't change your mind later, you'll want to use the deleting method.

Selecting proofs by flagging images

The flagging feature is a handy way to specify which images you want to keep. First, flag all the "keepers," and then at the end, delete all the unflagged images. You can also choose to copy the flagged images to another directory.

1. Use the arrow keys to move through the images.
2. When viewing an image you want to keep, press Ctrl+' (⌘-') to flag it.

If you change your mind about keeping an image, press Ctrl+' (⌘-') again to remove the flag.

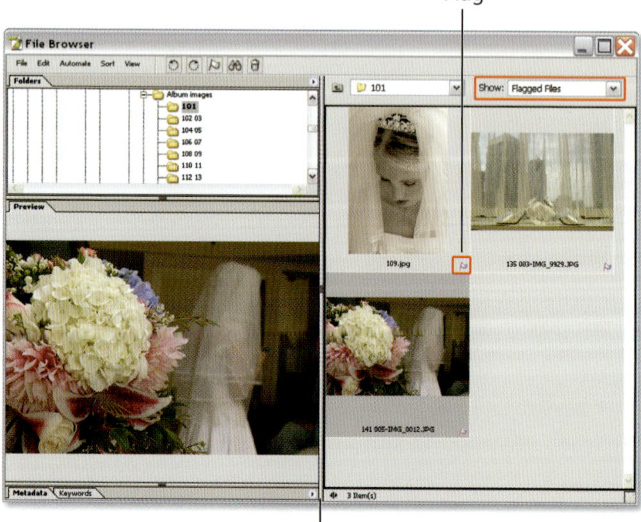

At any time you can see how many images you've flagged by choosing Flagged Files from the Show menu. If you can't see the Show menu, you might need to drag the vertical panel divider to the left so there's room for it at the top of the Main window.

To copy all the flagged images to another directory:

1. Choose Flagged Files from the Show menu to display only the flagged files.
2. Press Ctrl+A (⌘-A) to select all the flagged images.
3. Holding Ctrl (⌘), drag the images to an empty directory.

If you want to move the files instead of copying them, drag them to another directory without holding Ctrl (⌘).

Selecting proofs by deleting unwanted images

The advantage of this method is that you can see at all times which images remain and how many.

1. Select the first thumbnail image in the folder by clicking it.
2. As you press the right arrow on your keyboard to move through the images, press Delete (and then Enter) to remove those that won't be included in the proof set.

   You can check the Don't show again option in the delete confirmation dialog if you don't want to press Enter to confirm every time you press Delete.

Renaming files to maintain the custom sort order

After you've moved images in the File Browser into the order of the wedding story and deleted those that will not be shown to clients, you'll want the images to show up in this same sort order in your file browser and in whatever program you use to show the proofs to clients.

To retain the custom sort order, you'll need to rename the files. (I also rename them because our website upload tool uploads them in order of file name; you may find this is also the case with event-hosting websites.)

When you rename files to maintain the new sort order, it's important to retain the original file names and simply add a prefix. You'll probably make "quick and dirty" modifications to some of the files for the sake of showing them as proofs—for instance, cropping or brightening.

Adobe Bridge uses a system of stars to rate images. Press Ctrl+. (⌘-.) to increase the number of stars for each selected image. Press Ctrl+, (⌘-,) to decrease the number of stars.

After applying star ratings in CS2, use the Filter menu at the top of the thumbnails to specify which images to display.

When clients select the files they want in their album, you'll need to be able to trace the proof image back to its unretouched original so you can do a more careful job of cropping and color correction.

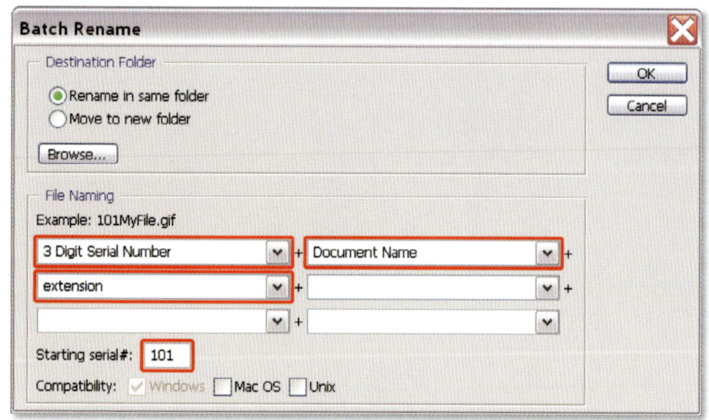

1. From the File menu in Photoshop, choose Browse.
2. Locate and open the folder containing the images to rename.
3. Select all the files in that folder by pressing Ctrl+A (⌘-A).
4. From the Automate menu, choose Batch Rename.
5. Click Rename in same folder.
6. Add a three-digit prefix to the file name.
   - In the first dropdown list box, select 3-Digit Serial Number.
   - In the second list box, select Document Name.
   - In the third list box, select extension.
   - For Starting Serial #, type the number you want to start with, such as 101.

To rename images in CS2, select the images, right-click (Ctrl-click) an image, and choose Batch Rename.

Batch resizing using droplets

After preparing the proof set, we create another directory called Small Proofs. The proofs in this set will be sized down to a maximum of 800 pixels because our proof presentation program runs more quickly with smaller images. You may also want to resize images for placement on your website or for burning onto a CD for clients.

A droplet can be used as a powerful automation feature that allows you to quickly batch-process image files. To quickly resize a set of images using Photoshop, first create an action that resizes one image. Then create a droplet that uses that action to process entire folders of images.

Creating an action

1. Open an image in Photoshop by double-clicking it in the File Browser.
2. In the Actions palette, choose New Action from the flyout menu.

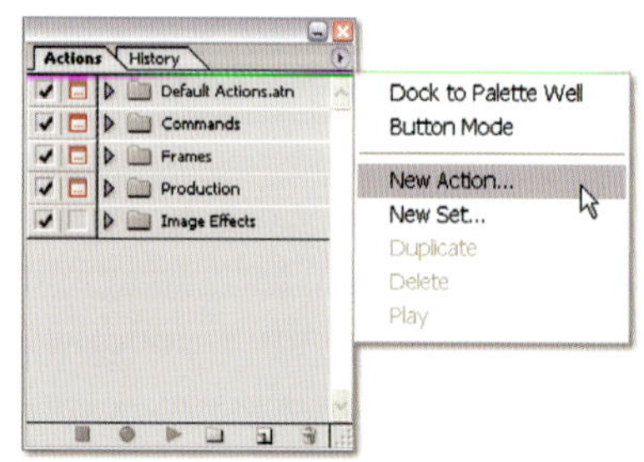

3. Type a name for the action, such as "800 max."
4. Click Record.
5. From the Photoshop File menu, choose Automate, and then choose Fit Image.
6. Select the existing dimension for Width, and type 800.
7. Select the existing dimension for Height, and type 800.
8. Click OK, and then click the Stop Recording icon in the Actions palette.

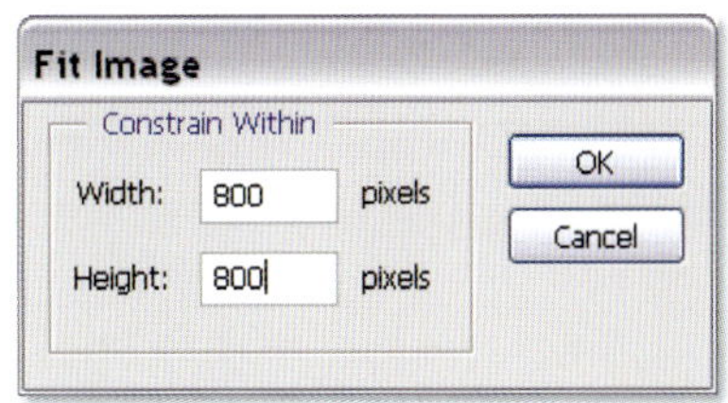

Now you've created the action to apply to all the files. Next you'll create the droplet that allows batch processing.

Creating a droplet

1. From the Photoshop File menu, choose Automate, and then choose Create Droplet.
2. Click the Choose button, and choose where you want to save the droplet.
3. For Set, choose the actions set containing the new action you created.

   If you didn't create a new action set, the new action was saved in the Default Actions set.
4. For Action, choose the new action. Leave the next four boxes unchecked.
5. For Destination, choose Folder.
6. Click the Choose button, and choose a folder where you want the copied, resized images to be placed, such as Small Proofs. Type a name for the droplet.
7. For File Name, choose Document Name in the first drop-down list box, and extension in the second one. Click OK.

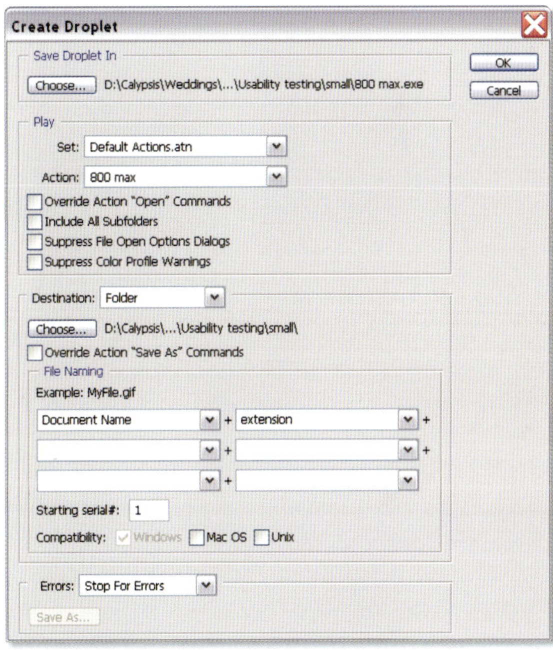

Now you're ready for batch processing. Find the droplet file you created, in the folder where you saved it, and drag it onto your desktop. To resize an entire folder of images, simply drag the folder over the droplet icon, and drop it there. All the images in the folder will be opened one by one in Photoshop, resized, and then saved in the destination folder you specified. You'll want to move the small files out of this folder before resizing another set of images.

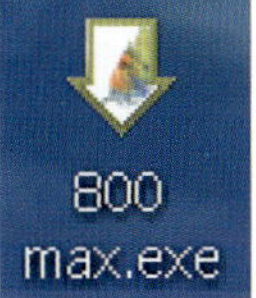

Whether to show proofs on a website

Whether to make proofs available online is a decision you'll need to make. Some photographers choose to show clients their proofs only once, during the album design session in the studio. Clients are likely to order more prints if they know they won't see the images again.

I've found that telling brides at bridal fairs that their wedding proofs will be available online in a matter of days is something they get excited about. More and more couples choose to stay in touch with the world, even on their honeymoon, so they take a laptop or find a digital café where they can get online and relive their favorite moments from the wedding day.

Once we have the set of proofs ready, we upload them to our website in a password-protected account. Our custom upload program automatically creates images with a watermark and a maximum dimension of 400 pixels.

We invite you to view
Scott and Lisa's
wedding online

- *Go to www.calypsis.com*
- *Click the Events link*
- *Click the event name*
- *Type the password: 4Seasons*

Images will be available on June 29th

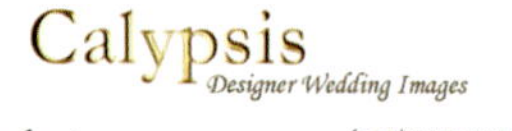

info@calypsis.com *(425) 957-0225*

At the reception, we will have handed out a quarter-page sheet to guests with instructions about how to view the proofs, and the date when those proofs will be available on the web-site.

Selecting album images with clients

After clients return from their honeymoon, we schedule an album design session. We prepare a light dinner, and the bride and groom come prepared to spend two to three hours, sometimes bringing both sets of parents. If you choose not to make proofs available on a website, and this is the first time the bride and groom have seen their proofs, the album design session will probably take longer.

During the album design session, we use a laptop connected to a wide-screen television, and custom proof selection software that we developed for the studio.

Proof selection software

When we first began showing proofs digitally, we looked for a program that had all the features we wanted for proof presentation and selection. None of the programs on the market offered everything we needed. We were looking for a program that enabled us to:

- Show thumbnails in a custom size
- Show images in a full-screen slide show
- Exclude an image with a keystroke during the slide show

- Instantly change an image to black and white or sepia
- Display two to four images on-screen in a Compare window with resizable panes
- Show either included or excluded images at any time
- Jump to a specific image by proof number, allowing clients to check print order forms
- Print a list of selected images with proof numbers mapped to original file names
- Automatically locate the originals of all selected images and copy them into a new directory
- Use dual monitor capability to show clients only the parts of the program they need to see

Because my husband is a software developer, we decided to create our own program, Calypsis Album Designer, which includes all the features needed for the proof presentation and selection process. In addition, it provides an easy way to design matted albums and to export designed album pages as .jpg images.

Calypsis Album Designer was written for the PC only.

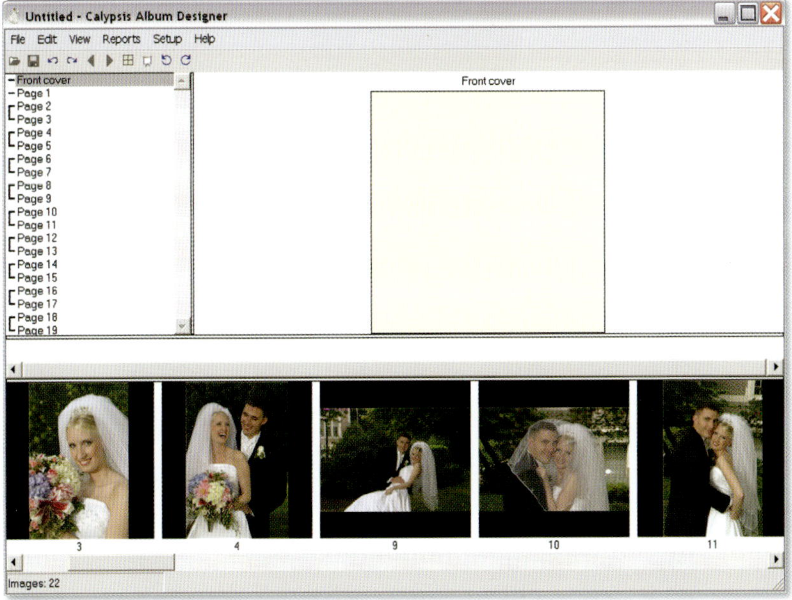

Calypsis Album Designer

If you'd like to try Calypsis Album Designer, you can download a free trial version at www.carilloncreek.com. You can learn how to use all the program's features in the online help.

To prepare for an album design session, we import proofs into Calypsis Album Designer. They appear in the thumbnail strip at the bottom of the screen.

Dual monitor mode

One handy feature of Calypsis Album Designer is its Dual Monitor mode. If the laptop or desktop computer used for running the software is equipped with two video cards, you can use this feature to show clients a different view from the one you see. Dual Monitor mode allows you to show on the viewing monitor or wide-screen television only the thumbnail strip, the page spreads, the slide show window, and the Compare window. On the monitor you're using, however, you'll be able to see everything you need to, including the invoice, all the menus, and the number of included images.

Running a slide show

When clients come to the studio for their album design session, double-click a thumbnail image to open the slide show. If clients have not seen them before, you can show all the images in an automatic slide show, setting the transition you'd like and the display interval for each image. You'll want to play appropriate music along with the slide show. Music will tremendously enhance the clients' enjoyment of the images, and will help them to remember the emotions of the day.

If the clients have already seen the images on a website, you can begin the selection process immediately.

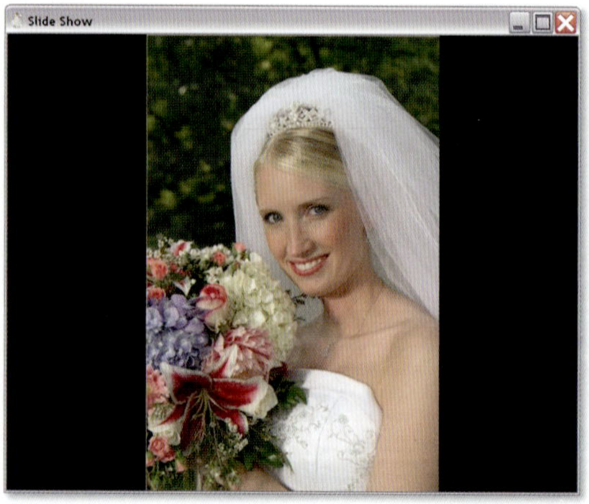

Slide Show

The slide show window

Excluding images

As we move through the slide show during the proof selection process, clients will say yes or no to indicate whether they want each image in their album. If they say yes, pressing the arrow key moves to the next image. If they say no, pressing E excludes that image from the thumbnail strip, leaving only the images they like.

At any time, you can show clients all the excluded images alone, so they can be sure those are the images they choose not to include in their album.

Modifying images

Clients may want to see what an image would look like in black and white or sepia, or what an image would look like cropped. These are easy changes to make by selecting the appropriate command on an image context menu.

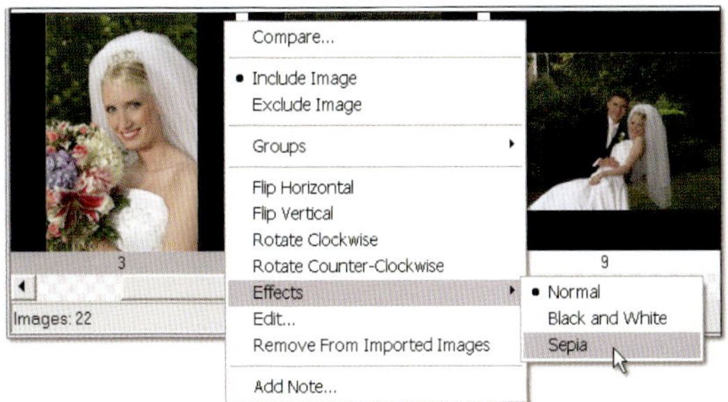

Instantly change an image to black and white or sepia.

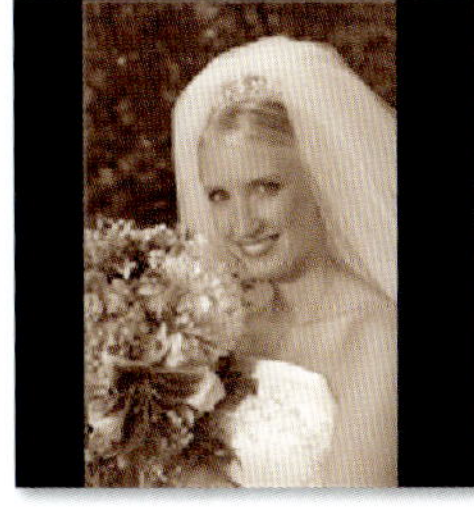

Comparing images

Another handy feature is the Compare window. You can open up to four images at a time to help clients decide between similar images. You can also drag the panes to resize the images, allowing clients to see a larger view of the ones that most interest them.

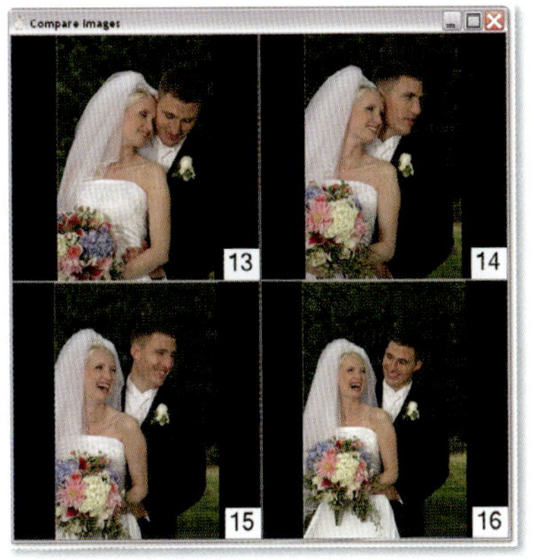

Display up to four images for easy comparison.

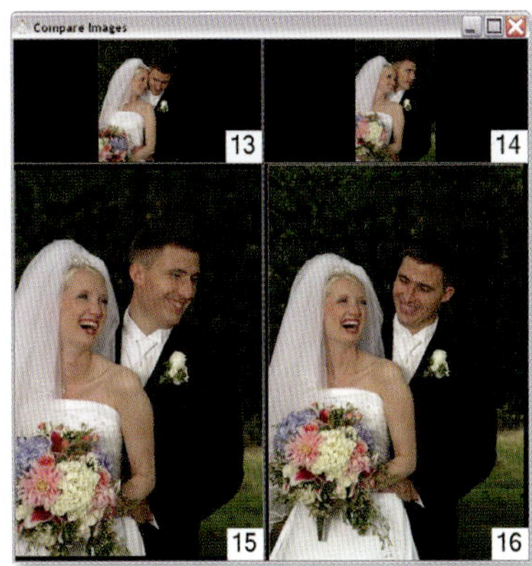

Drag the panel dividers to enlarge the view of specific images.

Jumping to a specific proof number

After the selection process for album images, clients and their family members often want to finalize their list of images to order as gift prints. At this point, you can enter proof numbers and jump to any image so they can make sure the number they wrote down on their order form is the image they wanted. The Go To Image command makes this easy.

Generating reports

The two types of reports generated by Calypsis Album Designer are invoices and album summaries. The invoice provides the option of adding any line item or payment. For digital albums, the album summary lists the client name and the proof numbers and original file names of all included images.

For matted albums, the album summary report also lists number of pages designed, the type and number of mats used, the file names of all images placed in mats, and the print sizes of images placed in mats.

The selection process

As we go through the images, couples say yes or no to each image. I demonstrate how this will work: "So you'll say, 'No, no, yes, no, no, no, yes.'" This shows them both that they can say no without causing offense, and that they'll need to say no a lot more often than yes.

During the album design session, it's important to give each couple a clipboard with an order form so they can write down the proof numbers of the images they'd like to order as loose prints. Let them know that it's a good idea to take notes as they see images they like, such as the proof number and who or what is in the image. And make sure this order form includes a place for their e-mail address and phone number, in case you have questions later about their order.

We offer a discount for any prints ordered at the album design session, encouraging everyone to get their orders in at the same time.

As clients are making their selections, I take notes regarding the images they like best (so I can make those larger on the page) and which images one person insists on but the other doesn't care for (so I can make those smaller).

Make sure you're clear about which grandparents go with which family so you can place those images on the correct family pages.

Clients choose about one hundred images, and we talk about what will work for backgrounds. I'm deliberately vague about which ones I'll use, saying I'll know later what will work in the album, depending upon which images end up on which pages.

After clients have excluded all the images they don't want in the album, Calypsis Album Designer generates a list of the included images.

Copying included images to a new folder

A feature you'll use at the end of the album design session is Copy Images. If you imported small proofs, it's handy to let Calypsis Album Designer locate and copy the large, original versions of the included images into a new folder called Album. You can specify the source (where the original images are) and the target (where you'd like them copied). This way, the high-resolution versions of all the included images are in one place, ready for you to begin color correcting and designing.

The commission agreement form

At the end of the album design session, you'll talk with clients about the details of their album. It's a good idea to prepare a form to fill out, so you can make sure you get all the information you need. It's also a good idea to have clients sign this form so they are clear about what they will be receiving.

The form includes:

- Size of the album they selected
- Price of the large album and any additional parent albums
- Price of any album images chosen beyond what was covered in the package
- Amount owed
- Album cover material and color
- Album liner material and color
- Number and size of parent albums
- Name and date text exactly as they will appear on the cover
- Color of cover inscription
- Which proof number they've selected for the cover cameo, if appropriate
- Date on which they agree to provide text from vows, if appropriate
- The approximate date on which they will be able to see their album proofs (maybe in one month)
- Your policy about how many changes to the album design they can request, and how much additional changes will cost
- Text emphasizing the fact that they are commissioning a work of art and that they understand that after the album is produced there is no way to change it
- A place for client signatures

Collecting payment

Before clients leave, you'll want to collect payment for any loose print orders and for albums, if they're not already paid for. Have a policy in place regarding payment for additional album images not covered by the original package—do you take full payment for extra images at this point, or do you allow the bride and groom to pay this when they pick up their album?

About preparing images for print

After the design session, print the list of included images and copy the corresponding original images to a new directory. It's a good idea to print this list and keep it in the clients' file, in case anything happens to the hard drive where your proof selection software resides.

The day after the design session, we compile the orders for loose prints and color correct all of those images, sending them to the lab right away.

Many of the images ordered for loose prints will be the same as images included in the album. In this case, copy the color corrected images into the Album folder, replacing the unretouched duplicates there.

Calibration

When you order thirty-six 10 x 13 prints and thirty-six 5 x 7 prints from your lab (for the bride and groom album and the parent album, for instance), you want to be confident that they will look great.

You'll need to adjust your monitor so that the results you get back from the lab match what's on your screen as closely as possible. To achieve this, you'll want to use a ColorVision Spyder or other calibration device. You can find information about the ColorVision Spyder at www.colorvision.com.

Your best bet is to work with a professional color lab. We use H&H Color Lab (www.hhcolorlab.com). If you want the best possible results from your prints, I highly recommend working with H&H. They will do everything they can to help you calibrate your system and to achieve beautiful results even from images that were not captured under ideal conditions. You can upload images to their website, and beautiful prints arrive at your doorstep just a few days later.

Color correcting

If there were a way to condense the information about color correcting digital images into a few pages, I would cover it here. However, color correction is a complex topic that is best learned from books written entirely on that subject. Two books I highly recommend are *Professional*

Photoshop: The Classic Guide to Color Correction by Dan Margulis, and *Real World Camera Raw with Adobe Photoshop CS* by Bruce Fraser.

For regular matted albums, you can submit images to your professional lab knowing that each image will be individually balanced so that every print looks as good as possible. However, once you've created a digital album page with several images flattened together as one image, the lab can no longer adjust the individual images.

If you're having a hard time matching the color of a particular image to other images on the page, change the problem image to either sepia or black and white.

Therefore, it's very important that you carefully color correct every image, paying particular attention to the sets that appear together on a page spread. For instance, you don't want the wedding dress to look a little blue when the bride and her father are about to walk down the aisle, and then on the opposite page, a little yellow in a photograph taken later in the ceremony.

When you're finished color correcting all the album images, you'll be ready to begin designing pages.

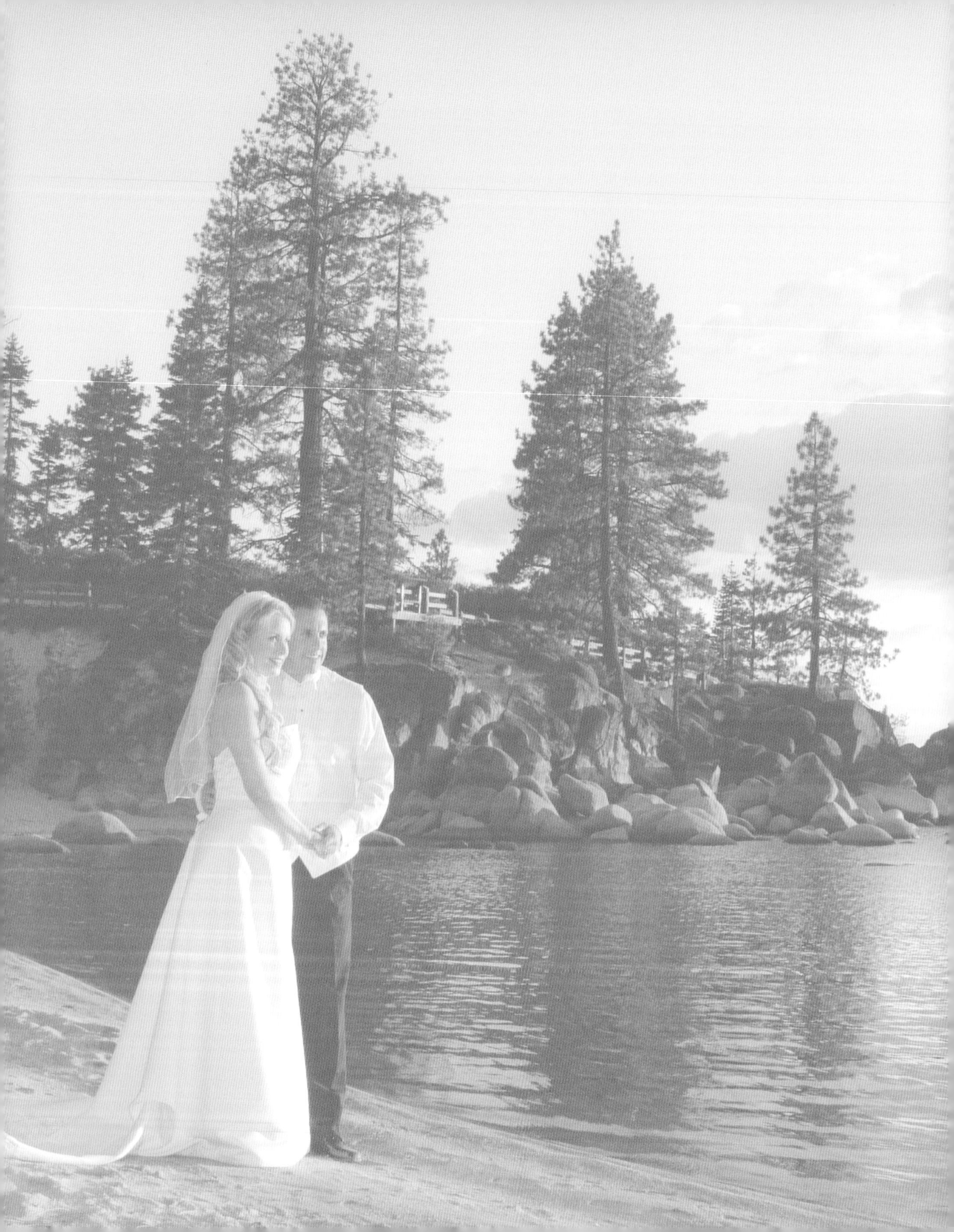

Designing pages

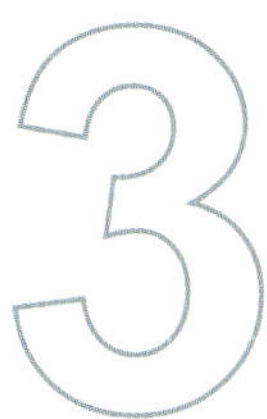

Working efficiently

Designing digital albums is a fun and creative process that can be rewarding simply for the sake of the art you produce. However, from a business perspective, the design process must be all about making it worth your time. You need to be able to design albums quickly enough that you won't have to charge more than your market can sustain.

Before you design your first page, here are some things to keep in mind. Because it's sometimes difficult to feel that a page is finished and to move on to the next, I recommend three strategies that will speed up your designing time tremendously:

- Setting goals
- Using a timer
- Looking at other albums

Setting goals

You will be able to produce page spreads much faster with each album that you design. For your first album, though, you'll probably find that you want to spend a very long time experimenting with various ideas and perfecting each page.

When would you like this album ready to show to prospective clients? An upcoming wedding expo is a good target date, for instance. Here is the kind of timeline you can expect when producing a digital album:

Day 1 Select album images and color-correct them

Days 2-3 Design the album

Day 4 Upload images to a professional lab

After you've designed an album or two of your own, you'll find that designing gets much faster.

Day 7 Receive prints from the lab; trim prints, pack them for shipping, and fill out the album company order form

Day 8 Ship prints to the album company

Day 48 Album arrives

You can probably count on about a two-month process—*if* you can dedicate enough time during designing days.

If you want the album finished and in your hands in two months, you need to set goals for how many page spreads you will complete in a day. If the album is going to be twenty-four pages long (eleven page spreads plus the first page and the last page) and you want to finish the designing in two days, you'll need to complete about six page spreads each day.

This sounds straightforward, but you may find that with your first album, you'll want to spend many hours on the first page. This is simply not practical. If you have six hours each of those two days to spend designing page spreads, you need to spend no more than one hour on each one. If you've spent half an hour moving images around on the page, you need to make decisions that will allow you to move on after the next thirty minutes.

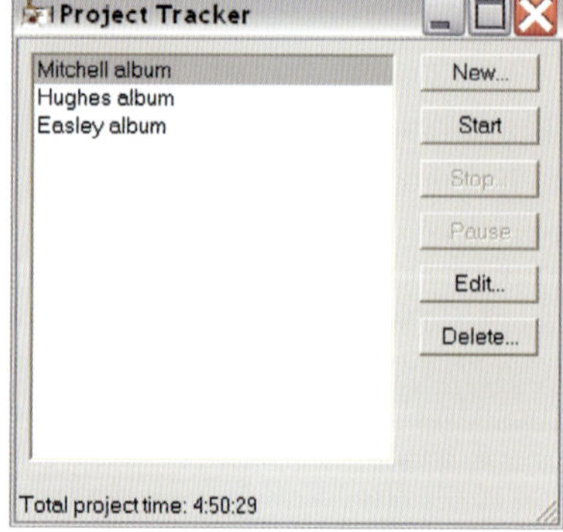

Calypsis Project Tracker was written for the PC only.

Using a timer

I highly recommend using a timer. Time every minute that it takes you to design each page spread. This encourages you not to spend too much time on one design and to always think about moving forward. In addition, this will tell you exactly how long it takes you to design an entire album, and you'll be better able to decide what you need to charge to make it worth your time.

If you don't have an online timer, you can find Calypsis Project Tracker, an inexpensive little utility, at www.carilloncreek.com.

Looking at other albums

I also highly recommend that you look at examples of other magazine-style albums online. Type "magazine style wedding album" into Google, and you'll get thousands of links.

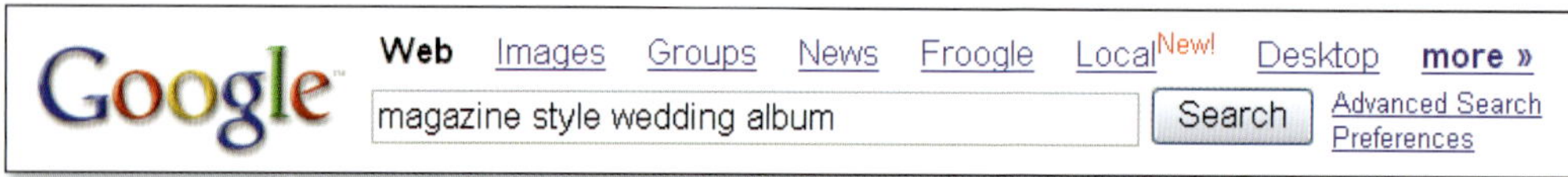

Using these design ideas for inspiration and adding your own creative touches will take *much* less time than starting with blank page spreads. Look at examples and find what appeals to you. Your best bet is to keep the style simple and elegant.

Creating a folder structure

The easiest way to plan what images will go on which pages is to create a folder structure that includes every page spread.

Create a folder for each page spread.

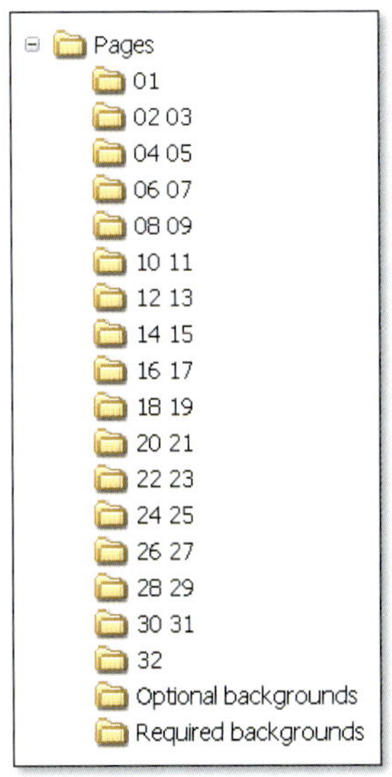

The images will naturally fall into various categories, such as getting ready, couple portraits, and ceremony. I usually put two to four images on each page, or four to eight per two-page spread.

Think about telling a complete short story on each page spread, as if you're a film editor putting together scenes for a movie. What happened first, and what happened after that? What happened at the end of this "scene"? What background image will lend the emotion you want to evoke in viewers?

Move the images into folders in the page order in which you want them to appear in the album. Images which don't necessarily fit into a specific category will be backgrounds and details that you'll place where they fit best.

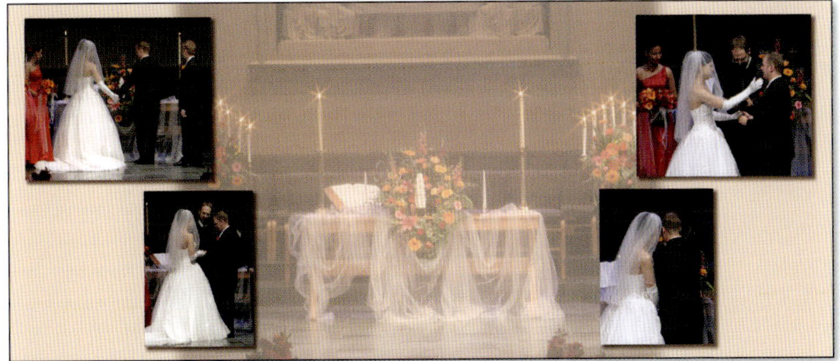

Think of the background image as the musical score. It should enhance the enjoyment of the scene, but not overpower it or become distracting.

When you begin placing images in a page spread window, you'll place background images on the page first because the background image will help determine where the other images will go. Look in each folder and figure out where the remaining images will fit best as backgrounds. After you're familiar with the images in each page folder, look back through the proofs that *weren't* selected for inclusion in the album, to see if anything else might be useful for backgrounds or to round out the images on a page.

Design issues to keep in mind

You want to move quickly through the design process. Of course you can lay out the images on each page in an infinite number of ways, but you can't try them all. You need to be decisive. Choose an arrangement, place the images on the page, and move on.

I usually fly through a series of page spreads in a day without adding background colors or layer styles. (Layer styles are edge effects you can add to each image in Photoshop. These are covered in detail in Chapter 4.)

The design you choose depends upon many variables:

- How many images need to fit on the page?
- Because of the order that events occurred, how must the images be ordered on the page?
- Did the bride or groom simply love one of the images, and would they like to see it large?
- Are all the images clear and sharp? Is there a grainy or a soft one that needs to be small on the page?
- Would the individual images crop best as a square or as a rectangle?
- How many portrait and how many landscape images are there on a particular page?
- Is one of the images stunning and worthy of being set off on its own page?
- What do you want to be able to see in the background?

If you keep these variables in mind when deciding on a design, the images themselves will often tell you exactly what design will work best.

Look at the designs again from a fresh perspective the next day. Make sure you like what you see and that the pages look good in sequence. Then you'll be ready to add background colors and layer styles.

Graphic design principles

As a photographer, you already recognize good composition when you see it. You may be able to explain in words why a particular image works well and why another doesn't, or you may just "know."

When you're capturing an image, you have some choices about how to frame the composition in the viewfinder at the moment you click the shutter, and then you have a few more choices about how to frame it differently through cropping in Photoshop.

With page design, however, the choices for composition are limitless. You will constantly be making decisions about where to place each image, and it's important not to place an image on the page solely based on where there's an empty space. Each image needs to have a reason for being exactly where it is. You'll also have a wide range of choices for altering the appearance of the images and the background. It helps to have some principles in mind that will provide good reasons for the choices you make.

Alignment

The most effective principle you can use in page design is alignment. Aligning images provides the viewer's eye with a pattern that's comfortable to look at, even when those images are separated by some distance. Use the guides in Photoshop, and choose Snap on the View menu. Make sure images that can be aligned are perfectly aligned. Crop and scale images so that they line up precisely with other images.

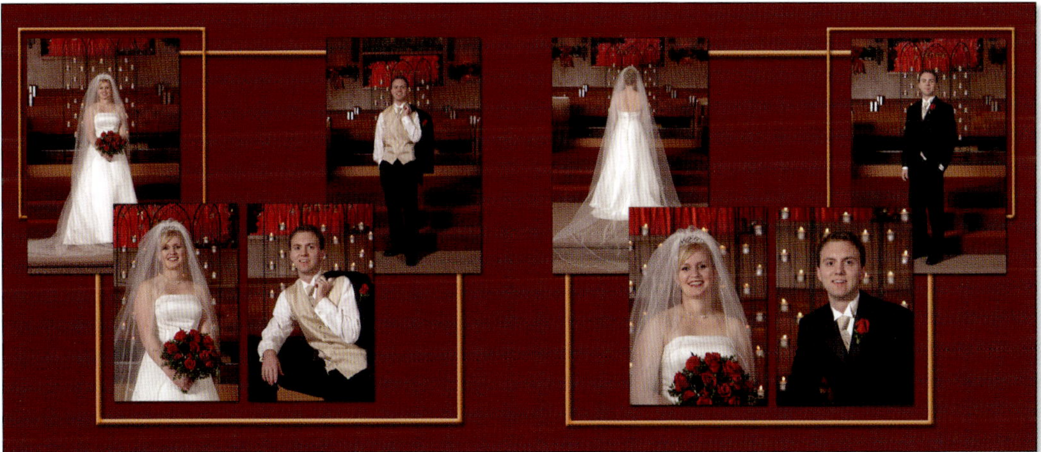

Repetition

The use of repetition ties different images together. You can help provide a sense of continuity by adding similar design elements with layer styles. It's a good idea to use only one layer style on each page spread, and to use that style on just about every image on the page. This gives images the appearance of belonging together. Say, for example, you have four small images in a page spread, and one large image that the clients loved. You'll do one layer style for the four small images, and then you might add a different effect to the larger image, to set it apart.

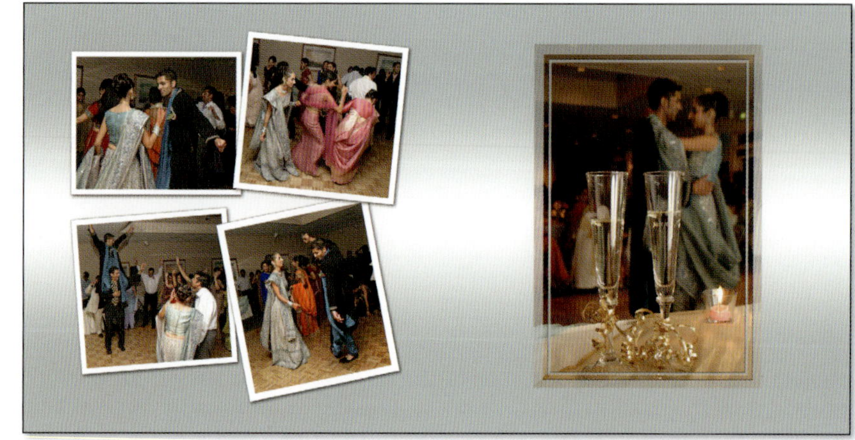

You can use repetition in other ways too.

- Make two images exactly the same size and shape.
- Include a three-quarter view of the bride and a matching view of the groom.
- Sample a color from an image and use it for a wide stroke or an outer glow.
- Sample a color from an image and use it to fill the Background layer. Even a lighter or darker shade helps bring coherence.
- Use uniform spacing between images.

Proximity

Just as layer styles can make images seem part of a cohesive group, proximity helps the viewer see which images belong together. When images are related because they were part of the same event, lay them out close together on the page, or on a page of their own.

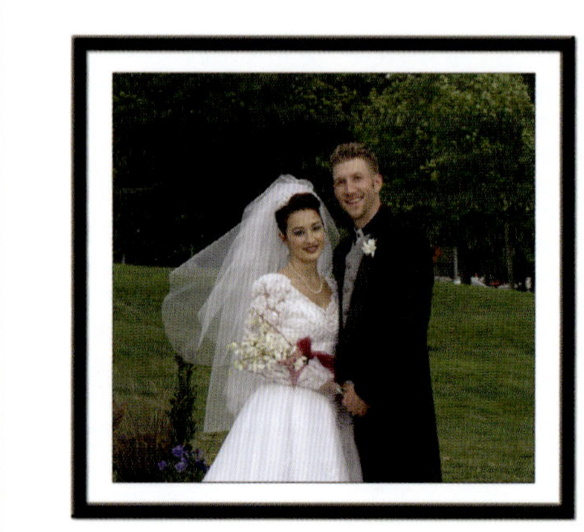

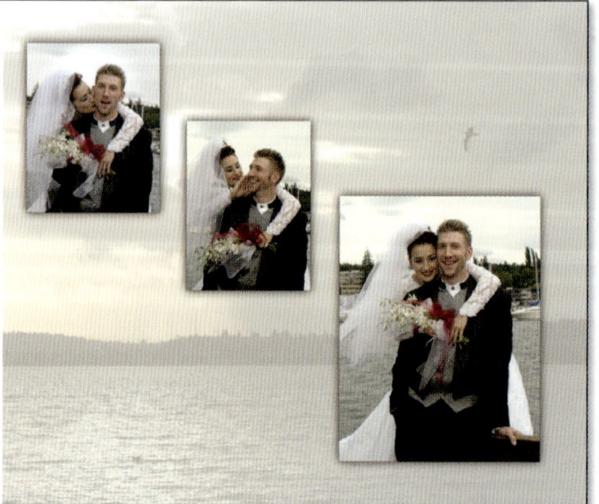

Contrast

One way to judge the effectiveness of your use of contrast is to look at the page through squinted eyes. Do the images blend into the background, with no apparent pattern for the eye to follow? Maybe you need to lower the opacity of the background image. Or you might add a high-contrast layer style to the images to help them stand out.

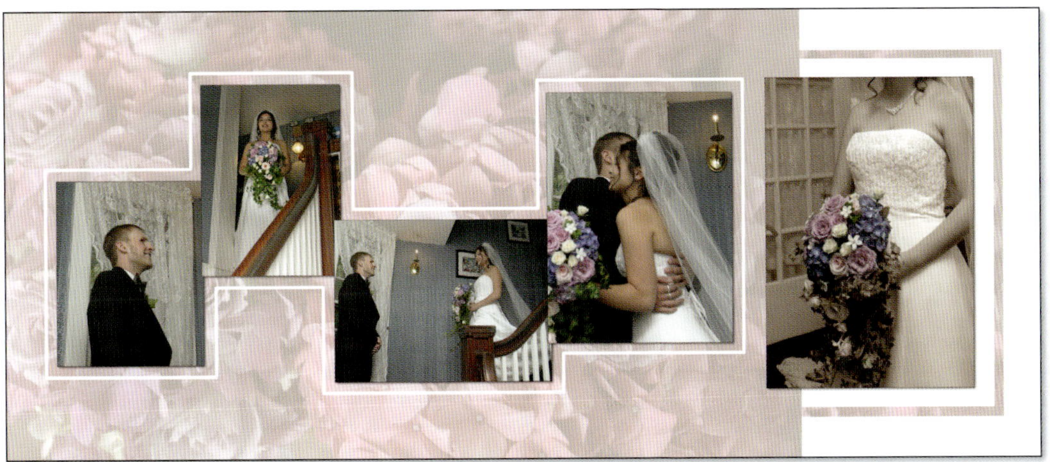

Do you see a blended mass of small images, like a hastily thrown-together collage? It's too much work for the eye to pick out what to look at in a composition like that. Some of those images are more important than others. Give the viewer a restful composition with visual clues about where to look first and where to look next. Make some images larger, or add more pages to the album if necessary to make room for compositions with more contrast and more white space. The areas you've left blank on the page are just as important as the images in creating an effective composition.

Experimenting with design ideas

Now we'll look at how to easily try out various layout options. You'll create a two-page spread, and then move the image windows around over it to get a preliminary idea of where you'll want to place each image, and how large you might want it on the page. After you've added some images to this page spread, you can try the Photoshop features explained in the rest of this chapter.

Creating the first two-page spread

After you've chosen an album company and decided on a page size, it's time to create your first blank page spread. Remember that you'll be designing in two-page spreads (except for the first and last pages, usually), regardless of whether you need to submit separate files to the lab for an album with split pages. You want to be able to see how the entire composition works for each double-page spread.

For instance, with the Renaissance Soho Book, you'll need to submit a 12 x 24 print for every page spread including the first and the last. For the Classic Album flush mount book, you'll submit a 10 x 12 print, for example, for each individual page.

I chose 256 pixels per inch for our 10 x 12 horizontal albums because at this size I can paste a full-length image on the page (shot with a 6.3 megapixel Canon 10D), and it fills the page from top to bottom without the need to scale up. For a 10 x 12 horizontal album, we create a Photoshop file that's 6,144 x 3,072 pixels. This creates a 256 pixels per inch document at 10 x 24. We save each two-page file in layered .tif format under the number of the page (01.tif, 02 03.tif, 04 05.tif, and so forth). Always save the layered version so you can go back and make revisions as necessary.

It's important to ask your lab representative what resolution they recommend for digital album pages.

When you create a new document for the first page, you'll save these settings as a preset, enabling you to quickly create each new page spread file without retyping the settings.

Saving default settings for new files

1. In Photoshop, choose New from the File menu.
2. In the New dialog, type a name for the document, such as 02 03.
3. For Width, choose Inches, and type the width of a double-page spread (such as 24).
4. For Height, type the page height (such as 10).
5. For Resolution, type the number your lab recommends (H&H Color Lab recommends 250–300 pixels per inch.)

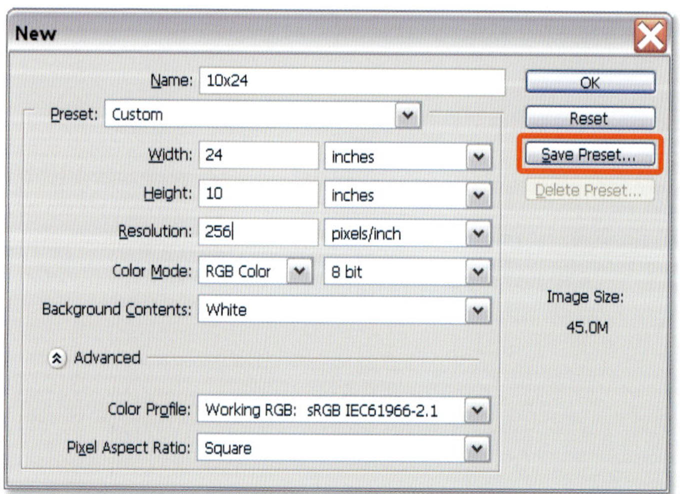

6. For Color Mode, choose RGB Color.
7. For Background Contents, choose White.
8. Click the Save Preset button, and type a name for this type of page, for instance "10 x 24." Click OK in both dialogs.

Now that you've saved a preset, the next time you're ready to create a new double-page spread, you can choose New from the File menu and choose your 10 x 24 preset from Preset in the New dialog.

It's also a good idea to create a preset for a single page (in this case the size would be 10 x 12), because that's also a size you'll be using often.

Adding guides

It's a good idea to add a vertical guide in the center of your page spread, so you won't put someone's face right where the fold or the cut will be.

1. If rulers are not visible at the top and left side of your image window, press Ctrl+R (⌘-R).
2. No matter what tool is selected, you can move your cursor over a ruler and drag a guide out of the ruler and onto the page.

   If you want to move a ruler later, you can drag it using the Move tool.

It's also a good idea at first to add a guide at approximately three-quarters of an inch in from each outside edge. During the mounting process, the album company will trim some amount around the outside of the pages and then sand off a little more. You don't want important parts of the design cut off or uncomfortably close to the edge of the finished page.

This trimming is even more dramatic for the parent album: an element that's three-quarters of an inch from the edge in the large album becomes half that in a 5 x 6 album.

Moving images around over the page

1. In Photoshop, open all the images from one of the page folders.

   You can open images by dragging them from the File Browser into the Photoshop main window. (If you're not working on a sample album yet, open four or five good images.)

2. Move the blank page spread window to the top of the screen.
3. Press Z for the Zoom tool and check the Resize Windows To Fit option in the options bar.
4. Holding Alt (Option), click each image several times to make the windows very small.

   This way you can move them around over the page spread window to get a preliminary idea of how the images will work together on the page.
5. Move the image windows into the order that best tells the story.
6. Make the best images (or images the couple loved) larger than the others.

You often will find that you need to see the selection handles of an image that's larger than your canvas. For this reason it's helpful to drag out the window boundary to make the window larger than the canvas. This makes it especially easy to resize large background images.

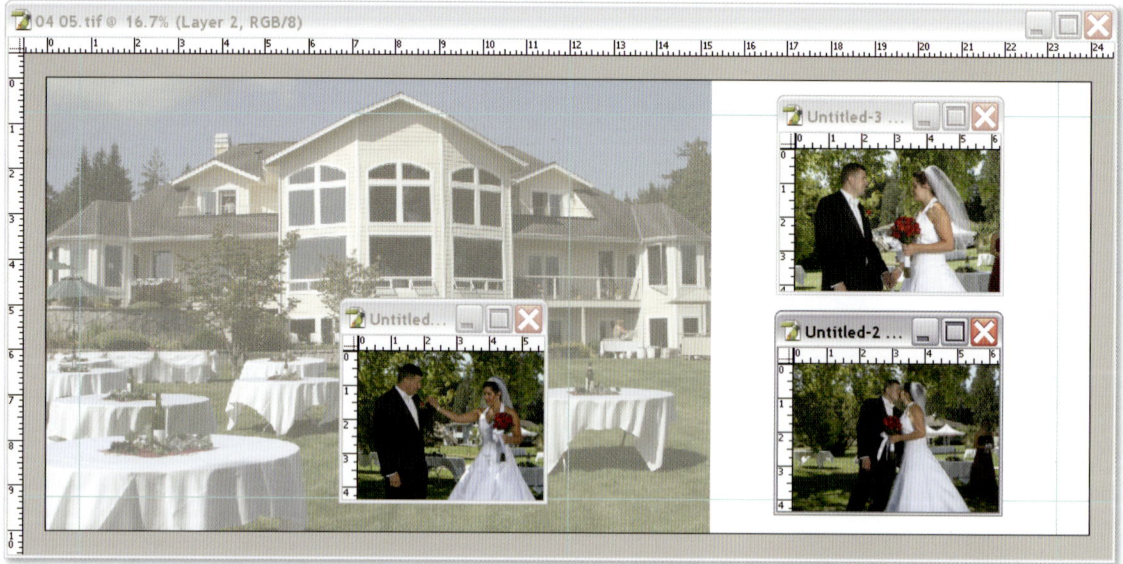

Move small image windows around over the page spread window to decide how images will work best on the page.

Adding images to the page

After you've decided roughly where each image will go and the approximate size you'd like it to be, it's time to place the images on the page. The first image you'll place is the background image, because this will determine to some extent where the other images can be placed.

1. Move the page spread window to the top of the screen.
2. If you'll be using a background image, click that window.
3. In the Layers palette, drag the image layer into the page spread window and drop it there.

   The background image is pasted in on its own layer.

4. Press Ctrl+T (⌘-T) for Free Transform. Holding Shift, drag a corner handle to resize the background image so that it fills the area you want to fill.

   If you also hold Alt (Option), the image resizes out from the center.

5. Drag the opacity slider to about 30% to reduce the opacity of the background image.

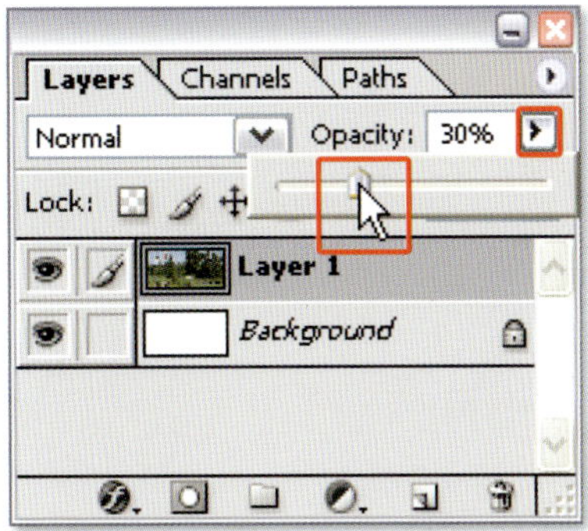

Next, paste each image into the page spread window and resize them the way you resized the background image in the last procedure.

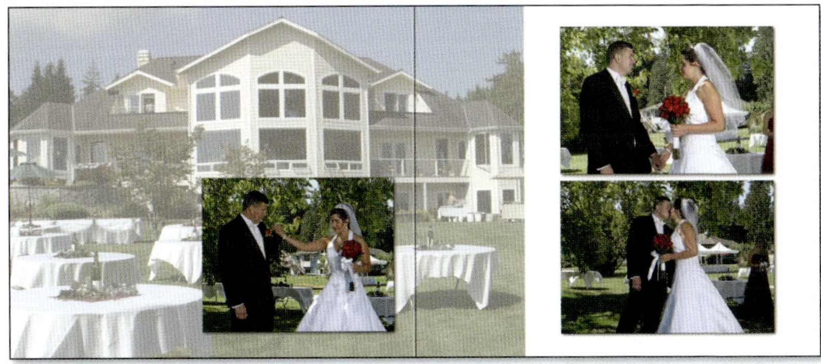

For your first album, you might consider arranging images in patterns you've seen in matted albums.

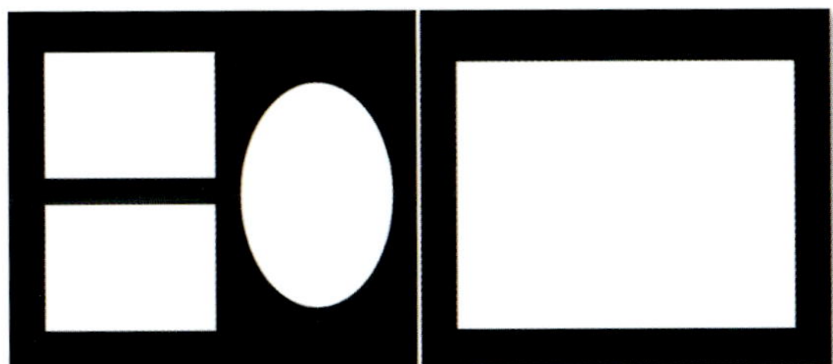

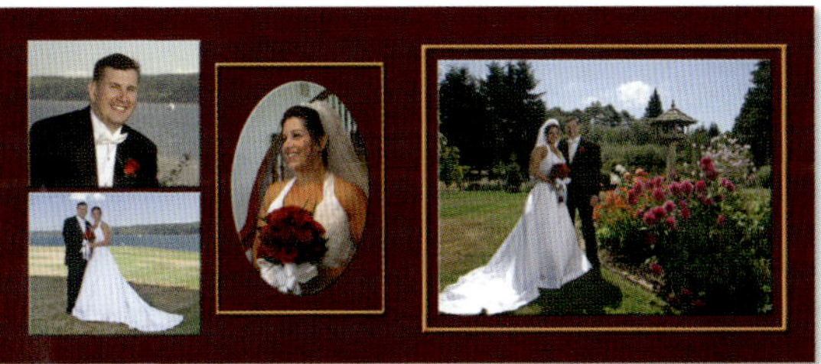

As you look at more examples of digital page layouts that you like and build your own, you'll soon have a collection of design ideas at your fingertips, ready to apply to new pages. In fact, I print thumbnail images of each set of album pages, so I can easily glance through them for inspiration when designing a new album.

Thumbnail pages (or contact sheets) are easy to create using the Contact Sheet II command under Automate on the File menu.

So far in this chapter, you've learned how to select the images for proofs and the album, how to arrange the album images into page folders, and how to experiment with design ideas. Next, you'll learn which Photoshop features you'll use in creating digital albums.

Using Photoshop

Many books have been written about Adobe Photoshop, books which attempt to provide readers with information about every feature they might need for every kind of project. In this section, however, you'll learn about only the features you need to know to design album pages.

The design samples you'll see in Chapter 4 were created using these Photoshop features and techniques. Once you've become familiar with everything in this chapter, the procedures in Chapter 4 will be much easier to follow.

A great resource for learning more about Photoshop in-depth is the *Total Training* DVD series by Deke McClelland. You'll learn an amazing number of useful techniques. And Deke makes the experience as fun as watching twenty hours of training videos can possibly be. You'll find Deke's training products at www.dekemc.com.

Learning the keyboard shortcuts

You want to design pages as quickly as possible. For this reason, it's worth your time to spend a few minutes familiarizing yourself with the keyboard shortcuts for the most common tools and commands.

For each keyboard shortcut used in the design techniques, the PC key combinations are shown first, followed by the Mac equivalents in parentheses, like this:

- Ctrl+J (⌘-J)

For Mac users, when you see the ⌘ symbol, hold down the Command key while you press any additional keys indicated.

For instance, you'll be changing the size of every image you add to a page spread window. To prepare to scale every image, you could click the Edit menu, click Transform, and then click Scale. But think how much time you could save every time by pressing Ctrl+T (⌘-T) instead!

Here are some other keyboard shortcuts you'll find useful in speeding your design work.

Tools

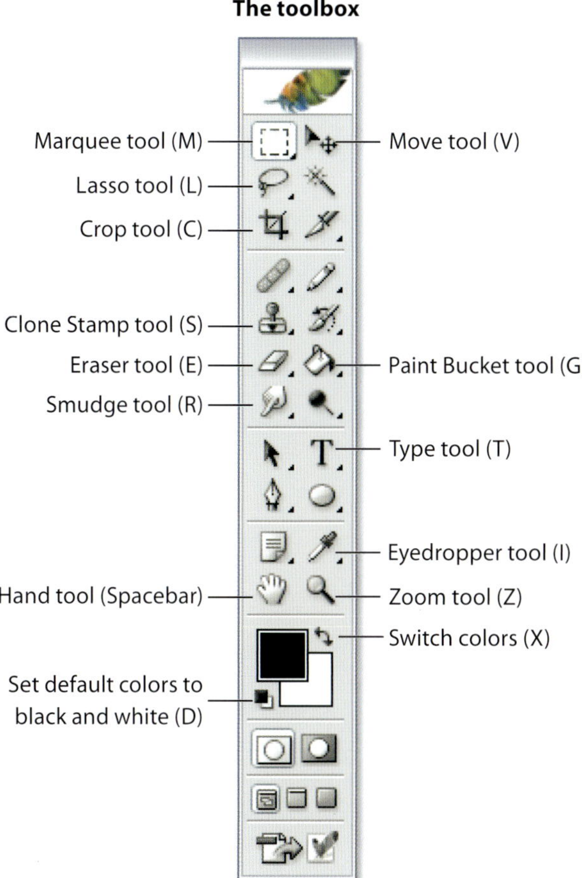

Layers

New layer	Ctrl+Shift+N (⌘-Shift-N)
Copy image and paste on a new layer	Ctrl+J (⌘-J)
Cut selection and paste on a new layer	Ctrl+Shift+J (⌘-Shift-J)
Bring layer to front	Ctrl+Shift+] (⌘-Shift-])
Send layer to back	Ctrl+Shift+[(⌘-Shift-[)
Select next layer up	Alt+] (Option-])
Select next layer down	Alt+[(Option-[)

Editing

Copy	Ctrl+C (⌘-C)
Copy merged	Ctrl+Shift+C (⌘-Shift-C)
Cut	Ctrl+X (⌘-X)
Fill with background color	Ctrl+Backspace (⌘-Delete)
Fill with foreground color	Alt+Backspace (Option-Delete)
Free transform	Ctrl+T (⌘-T)
Paste	Ctrl+V (⌘-V)
Undo	Ctrl+Z (⌘-Z)
Back a step in History	Ctrl+Alt+Z (⌘-Option-Z)
Forward a step in History	Ctrl+Shift+Z (⌘-Shift-Z)
Toggle between two History steps	Ctrl+Z (⌘-Z)
Change cursor size	[(smaller) and] (larger)

Views

Show/hide all palettes	Tab
Fit to screen	Ctrl+0 (⌘-0)
Toggle grid	Ctrl+' (⌘-')
Toggle guides	Ctrl+; (⌘-;)
Toggle Snap	Ctrl+Shift+; (⌘-Shift-;)
Zoom in	Ctrl++ (⌘-+)
Zoom out	Ctrl+- (⌘--)

Selections

Deselect	Ctrl+D (⌘-D)
Reselect	Ctrl+Shift+D (⌘-Shift-D)
Invert selection	Ctrl+Shift+I (⌘-Shift-I)
Move selection (while creating it)	Spacebar
Select all	Ctrl+A (⌘-A)

Optimizing your workspace

Here are a few ways to optimize your workspace for the tasks you'll be doing. The reasons for these settings will be clear as you become more familiar with Photoshop.

- Make sure you have the Info palette, the History palette, and the Layers palette on-screen. Once in a while you'll also want the Actions palette and the Channels palette. To view any of these palettes, check them on the Window menu.
- Make sure Rulers is checked on the View menu.
- Try leaving Snap checked on the View menu. If at times you find that snapping is not helpful, uncheck it temporarily.
- From the Edit menu, choose Preferences.
    - Under Display and Cursors, choose Brush Size for Painting Cursors, and Standard for Other Cursors.
    - Under Units and Rulers, set Rulers to Inches, Type to Points.
    - Under Transparency and Gamut, set Grid Size to None.
    - Under Guides, Grid & Slices, choose Dots for Grid Style, and set Gridline to every 0.25 inches and four Subdivisions.

In CS2, choose Normal Brush Tip for Painting Cursors, and Standard for Other Cursors.

Zooming in and out

Being able to navigate quickly in Photoshop will save time when you're designing pages.

Here are some handy tips about zooming.

- Press Ctrl++ (⌘-+) and Ctrl+- (⌘--) to zoom in and out.
- Press Z to select the Zoom tool.
- Drag in the image with the Zoom tool to specify the area you want to fill the window.
- In the options bar, check Resize Windows to Fit. Thereafter, Photoshop does its best to fit the window to the size of the image.
- In the options bar, uncheck Ignore Palettes. This way, part of your zoomed image window won't be hidden behind the palettes.
- Click the area of the image you want centered in the window when you magnify the view with the Zoom tool.
- Holding Alt (Option), click the image to zoom out.
- Hold the spacebar and drag to move a zoomed image within the window (unless you're currently typing in a text block!).

You'll find that the fastest way to magnify an area is to drag with the Zoom tool to define that area. If you haven't tried this method yet, try it. You'll wonder how you ever lived without it.

- To maximize screen real estate, press Tab to hide the palettes. Press Tab again to show them. Pressing Shift+Tab hides the palettes while leaving the toolbox on-screen.

Selecting and deselecting

You will most often use the Marquee tool to select portions of an image. If you want to select an area that extends from one edge of the canvas to the other, first drag out the window border to make it larger than the canvas. This way you can begin and end the selection outside the boundaries of the canvas.

When dragging out a selection:

- To constrain the selection to a square (or a circle with the Elliptical Marquee tool), hold Shift while dragging.
- To move the entire selection as you drag, hold the spacebar.

After a selection has been created, you can make the selection larger or smaller:

- To add more areas to the selection, hold Shift while dragging in a new area with the Marquee or Lasso tool.
- To make the selection smaller, hold Alt (Option) while dragging inside the selection with the Marquee or Lasso tool.

To trim off everything outside the selection, choose Inverse from the Select menu and press Delete.

You'll find the Lasso tool useful for selecting uneven areas. Zoom in so you can select edges precisely. Again you can use Shift to add to the selection and Alt (Option) to remove parts of the selection.

If you've created a complicated selection, you might want to save it. From the Select menu, choose Save Selection, and give the selection a name. The selection is saved in a separate channel. When you open the document later, you can reapply the selection by choosing Load Selection from the Select menu.

To select everything in multiple stacked layers, drag out a selection and then choose Copy Merged from the Edit menu. The image you then paste is a flattened version of all the stacked sections that were copied.

To select everything on the layer currently selected in the Layers palette, press Ctrl+A (⌘-A).

To select just the image on a layer (and not the whole canvas), hold Ctrl and click the image icon for that layer in the Layers palette.

To deselect (clear a marquee), press Ctrl+D (⌘-D). To reselect, press Ctrl+Shift+D (⌘-Shift-D).

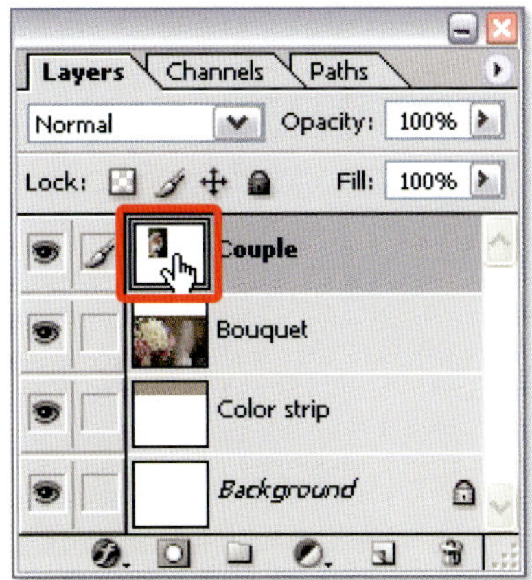

Hold Ctrl and click the image icon to select an image on the page.

Cropping images

When you're preparing images for loose prints, you probably use the Crop tool. You specify the dimensions of the print, such as 5 x 7 or 4 x 5, and crop for those dimensions. However, for digital album pages, an image can have any size and aspect ratio (the relationship between height and width) that you'd like. Therefore most of the time you'll want to use the Crop tool without specifying dimensions.

Cropping using the Crop tool

1. In the individual image window, press C to select the Crop tool.
2. In the options bar, delete any dimensions set for height and width.
3. Drag a crop box around the image.
   - Hold the spacebar to move the entire selection as you drag, if necessary.
   - Hold Shift to constrain the image to a square if appropriate.
   - After releasing the mouse button, drag a corner to resize and change the aspect ratio.
   - Hold Shift and drag a corner to resize while retaining the same aspect ratio.
   - Drag inside the crop box to move it.
   - Drag outside the crop box to rotate it.
   - If you want to cancel the selection, press Esc.
4. When you're satisfied with the crop box location and size, press Enter to accept it.

Cropping using the Marquee tool

You can use the Marquee tool for cropping if you prefer. Use the Elliptical Marquee tool when you want to create a round or oval image. To select the Elliptical Marquee tool, click and hold on the Marquee tool and drag to select the Elliptical Marquee tool. You can also press

Shift+M to switch between the Marquee and Elliptical Marquee tools.

1. Press M or Shift+M to select the Marquee or Elliptical Marquee tool.
2. In an image window, drag out a selection.
   - To constrain the selection to a square (or a circle), hold Shift while dragging.
   - To move the entire selection as you drag, hold the spacebar.
3. From the Image menu, choose Crop.

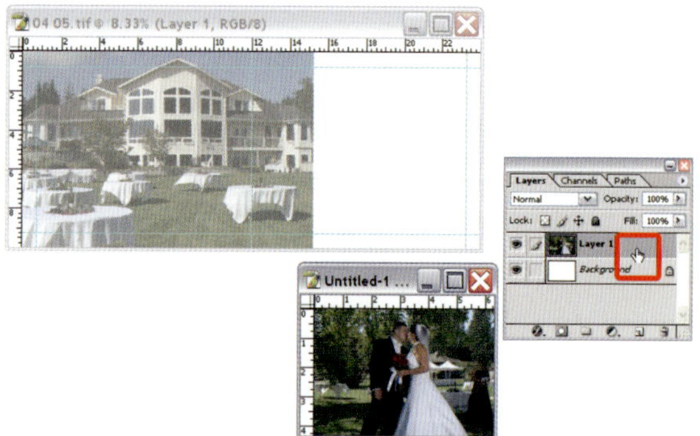

1. Click the layer for the image you want to add to the page.

Placing images on the page

This procedure is how you'll copy each image from its own window into the page spread window. When an image is copied into a window, it appears on a new layer there.

1. Crop each image in its own window the way you think you'll probably use it (see "Cropping using the Crop tool," above).
2. Save the cropped file over this file in the page folder. (You can always go back to the Originals folder if you find that you need the uncropped version again later.)
3. Create a blank page spread and move it to the top of the screen.
4. In the Layers palette, drag the layer containing the image into the page spread window and drop it there. After each image is placed, you'll resize it.

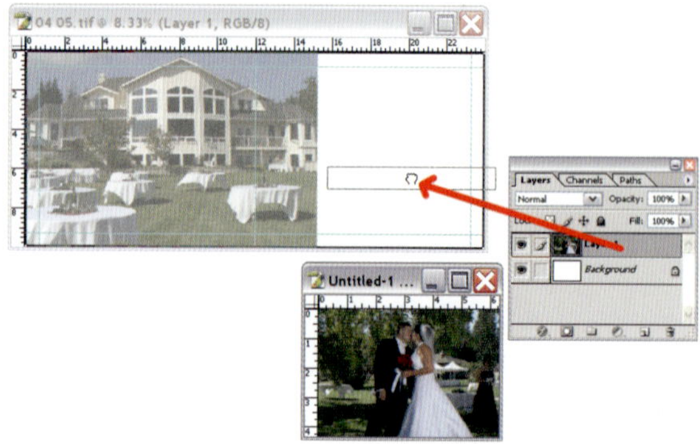

2. Drag the layer into the page spread window.

If you have part of an image selected in a window, you can also use the Move tool and drag from within the selection into the page spread window.

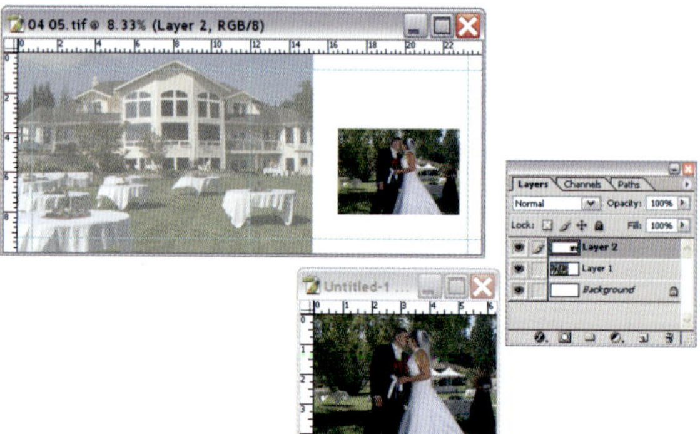

3. The image is copied and pasted.

Resizing images

You sometimes may be tempted to stretch an image—that is, to change the aspect ratio so that it fits in a tall, narrow location. I realize this makes people look taller and thinner, but resist this temptation! For clients, it would be like looking in a fun house mirror, and there's a good chance they won't like it. To maintain the original aspect ratio of an image, always hold Shift while dragging a resizing handle.

1. In the Layers palette, select the layer containing the image.
2. Press Ctrl+T (⌘-T) for Free Transform.

   If the image is on the Background layer, you'll need to drag a selection around the image with the Marquee tool first, and then press Ctrl+T (⌘-T).
3. Holding Shift, drag one corner of the image to scale it. This constrains the image as you resize it so you don't get the fun house mirror effect. When you're through resizing, always release the mouse button first, and then the Shift key.

   You can drag in the middle of the image to move it before you finish scaling it. You'll want to do this most of the time when you're resizing, so you'll be able to see what size will fit best in exactly the location you've chosen for the image.
4. Press Enter to accept the new size.

Always hold Shift when dragging a resizing handle to scale an image.

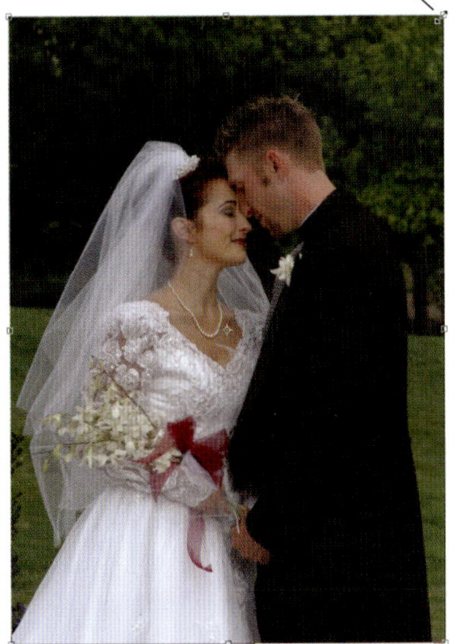

A word about scaling up

Here's why you'll want to save the cropped version of each image in its own window. If you paste the image onto the page spread and resize down to try out various design ideas, many of the pixels it once had are now gone. Scaling an image down means that you've thrown away pixels. You can't size up again and recover the original quality. So resize down conservatively, and ideally leave the image that size or smaller.

If you find, after pasting all the images onto the page and scaling them down, that the design requires one of the images to be larger, you'll need to place the high-resolution version in the page spread again. Open the image in its own window and place it in the page spread window, scaling down more conservatively this time.

While you're scaling an image by dragging a resizing handle, you can make the image frame very small and then larger (but no larger than its original size) without loss of quality. It's only after pressing Enter to accept the transformation that scaling up again will result in a loss of quality.

One instance where you can safely scale up is when you'll be lowering the opacity of an image for a background. You can enlarge an image considerably for this use, and the lower quality won't show because of the transparency you'll apply.

Moving images around on the page

When using the Move tool, you'll usually want the Auto Select Layer option checked in the options bar. This allows you to simply click each image on the page to select that layer.

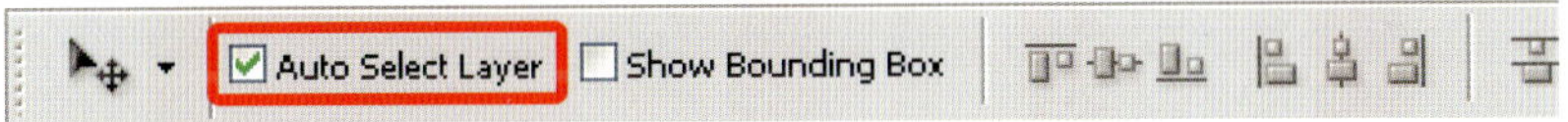

However, when you have an image with an opacity of less than 50%, Photoshop can no longer "see" that image, so if you click it, the layer below it is selected. In this case, you'll want to uncheck Auto Select Layer and instead click a layer in the Layers palette to select it. The same thing sometimes happens with text layers, where clicking a text block with the Move tool may select right through the text layer to the layer beneath it.

Two more handy tips about moving images:

- When dragging an image with the Move tool, hold Shift to constrain movement horizontally or vertically (depending upon which direction you begin to drag the image).
- With the Move tool selected, you can use the arrow keys on the keyboard to nudge the image on the layer currently selected in the Layers palette.

Using the Layers palette

The Layers palette allows you to separately modify and move each image in a page spread. Each image pasted onto the page spread creates its own layer, and you'll want to leave the images on separate layers. This allows you to move and resize images independently, to change their stacking order, and to apply layer styles to them individually.

When you want to move or modify an image, you need to select that image layer in the Layers palette.

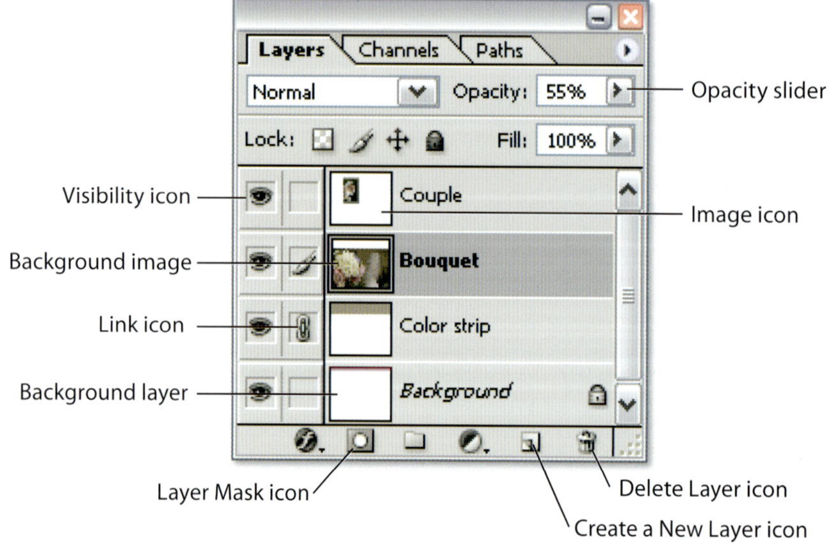

Creating a new layer

Create a new layer by clicking the Create a New Layer icon at the bottom of the Layers palette. (The keyboard shortcut for this is Ctrl+Alt+Shift+N [⌘-Option-Shift-N].) You probably won't find that you need to do this very often, as each image you add to the page spread is automatically pasted in on a new layer.

Renaming a layer

If you have many layers in a page spread, it's handy to rename each layer to indicate what's on it. This makes it easier to later select the layer on which you want to modify images.

1. Double-click the layer name in the Layers palette.
2. Type a new name that indicates what's on the layer.

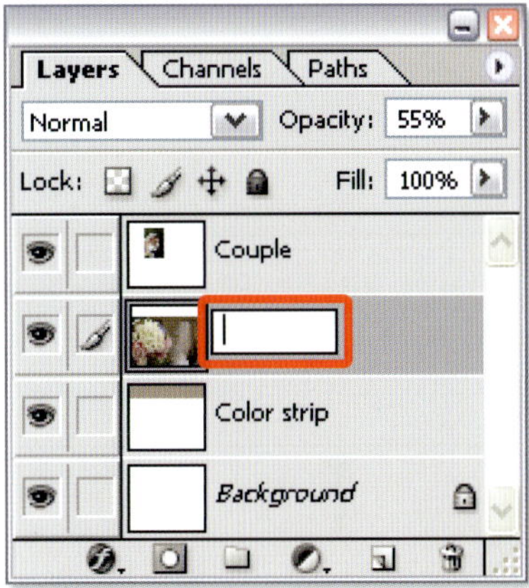

To rename a layer, double-click the layer name and type a new name.

Deleting a layer

Delete a layer by dragging the layer name to the Delete Layer icon at the bottom of the Layers palette. You can also right-click (Ctrl-click) the layer name and click Delete Layer.

Selecting the image on a layer

If the image on the layer is smaller than the canvas size, you can select the boundaries of the image by holding Ctrl (⌘)and clicking the image icon in the Layers palette.

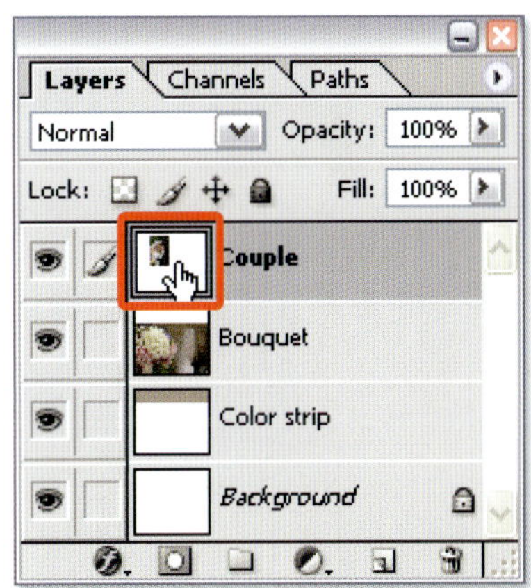

To select an image on a layer, hold Ctrl (⌘)and click the image icon.

Changing the stacking order of layers

To change the stacking order of layers, drag a layer name to a new location in the Layers palette.

Merging layers

Most of the time, you'll want to leave every element of your design on its own layer so you can easily change individual items later. But every now and then you'll know that you never again want to modify the elements on a particular layer separately. For instance, you may add a new head for a subject, and after you've blended it into the image, you want to make it permanently part of that image.

1. In the Layers palette, drag the layer so that it's just above the layer you want it to merge into.
2. Press Ctrl+E (⌘-E) for Merge Down.

Hiding a layer

Hide the contents of a layer by clicking the Visibility icon in the Layers palette. Show the contents again by clicking to replace the Visibility icon.

To quickly hide or show adjacent layers in the Layers palette, drag with the mouse down the Visibility column.

Duplicating a layer

Click the layer in the Layers palette, press Ctrl+D (⌘-D) to make sure nothing is selected, and press Ctrl+J (⌘-J). You can also drag the layer name to the Create a new layer icon in the Layers palette. (If part of the image is selected with a selection tool, pressing Ctrl+J [⌘-J] copies just the selected portion onto a layer of its own.)

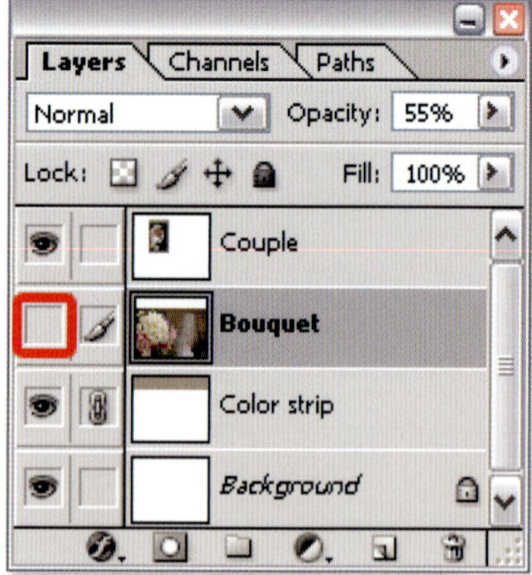

To hide or show a layer, click the Visibility icon.

Cutting an image and pasting it onto a new layer

This is a handy keyboard shortcut when you want to lower the opacity of an image that's currently on the Background layer. Or you may want to select an element that shares a layer with other elements, and put it on a layer of its own.

1. Press M for the Marquee tool, then drag a marquee around the image to select it.
2. Press Ctrl+Shift+J (⌘-Shift-J).

This cuts the image from the layer, creates a new layer, and pastes the image onto the new layer.

In CS2, hold Shift or Ctrl to select multiple layers in the Layers palette, and then click the Link icon at the bottom of the palette to link them.

Moving or resizing layers together

You'll often have images perfectly aligned with one another and then decide to move the whole block of them to a slightly different location on the page. Or you might want to make the entire block of images a little smaller without resizing each individual image.

1. Press V for the Move tool, and select one of the layers in the Layers palette.
2. Make sure Auto Select Layer is checked in the options bar.
3. Click to place a Link icon on related layers. Or drag the mouse cursor down the link column if you want to quickly link several adjacent layers.
    - You can link layers by clicking in the Layers palette to place a link icon on each additional layer, or you can simply hold Shift and click each image on the page spread to link its layer with the layer selected first.

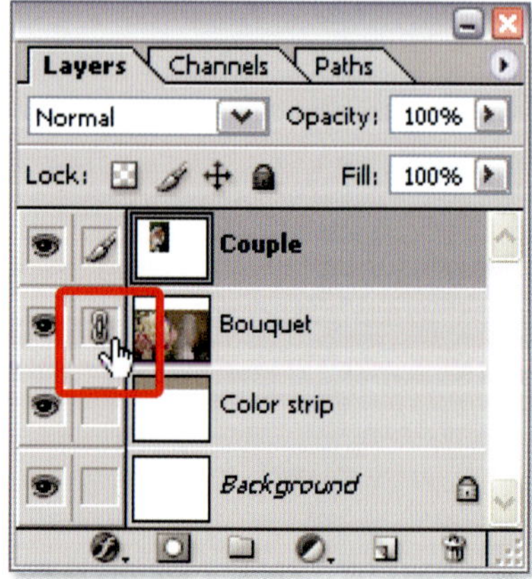

To link another layer with the selected layer, click the Link icon.

- To move layers together, drag the linked block of images to a new location on the page or use the arrow keys to nudge it.
- To resize images on different layers together, press Ctrl+T (⌘-T) for Free Transform. Holding Shift, drag a corner of the linked block of images. Press Enter to accept the transformation.

To quickly link or unlink adjacent layers in the Layers palette, drag with the mouse down the Link column.

Any moving or resizing changes you make are applied to all images linked together. To unlink layers, click the Link icons in the Layers palette to remove them, or drag down the Link column with the mouse.

To unlink layers in CS2, click to select one of the linked layers in the Layers palette, and then click the Link icon.

Saving layered versions

You'll want to save layered versions of the album pages you design, even after you've received the album and delivered it to your clients. Imagine, for instance, the parents of the bride deciding months later that they want a parent album, but that they'd like different images on two of the pages. If you still have the layered files, making these changes will be easy.

You might consider saving the layered versions on DVDs and keeping only the flattened .jpgs on your computer to save hard disk space. This way you'll be able to look through the .jpgs to be reminded of your favorite designs as you're laying out subsequent albums.

The "Background layer" and "background images"

Throughout the design procedures, you'll see references to the "Background layer" and to "background images." When "Background" is capitalized, it's referring to the bottom layer in the Layers palette. A "background image" is an image usually made semitransparent, and it's used as a design element behind the other images on the page.

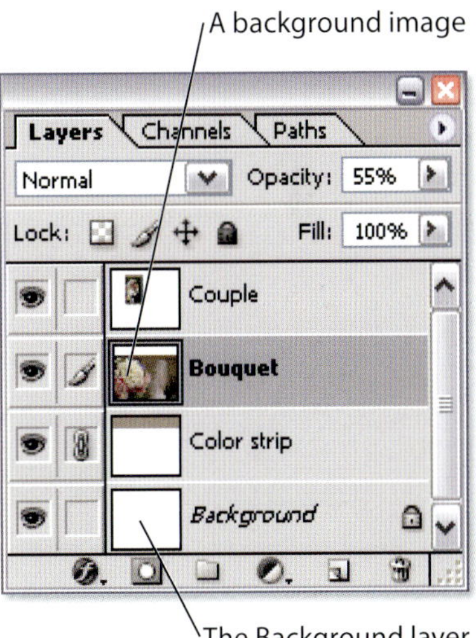

The Background layer in the Layers palette has a couple of unique qualities that are useful to know.

- If you merge an image down to the Background layer, you'll no longer be able to move that image without first selecting it using a selection tool such as the Marquee or the Lasso, or by pressing Ctrl+A (⌘-A) to select everything on the layer.
- You can't lower the opacity of an image on the Background layer without first renaming the layer.

Lowering the opacity of a background image

To lower the opacity of an image, select the image layer in the Layers palette and drag the Opacity slider until you like what you see.

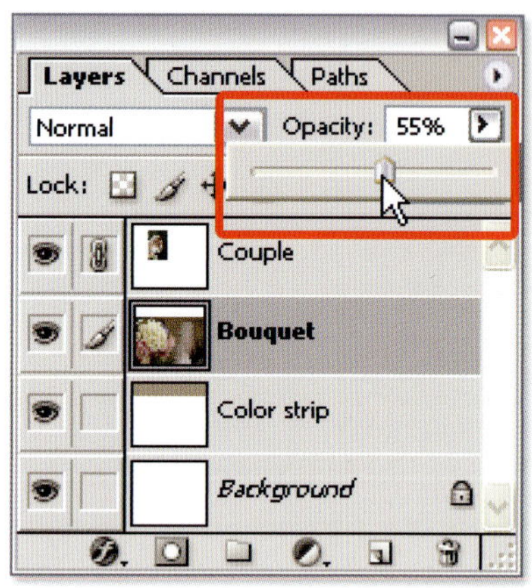

To lower the opacity of an image on the Background layer, you first need to rename the Background layer.

1. In the Background layer, double-click the layer name.
2. Type a new name for the layer.

Now you'll be able to lower the opacity of the image on this layer by dragging the Opacity slider.

Making a semitransparent image opaque

You'll often want the screened-back look of a background image, but then you'll want that image to be opaque so that you can't see the images or colors beneath it.

1. Drag the semitransparent image to just above the Background layer in the Layers palette.
2. Hold Ctrl (⌘) and click the image icon in the layer to select the image.

   It's important that the image remains selected through the next two steps.
3. Press Ctrl+E (⌘-E) to merge that layer down to the Background layer.

   The image should still be selected with a marquee.
4. Press Ctrl+Shift+J (⌘-Shift-J) to cut the selected image and place it on its own layer.

Now you have a screened-back image that's no longer transparent.

Filling an area with color

You can quickly fill either a selection or an entire layer with color.

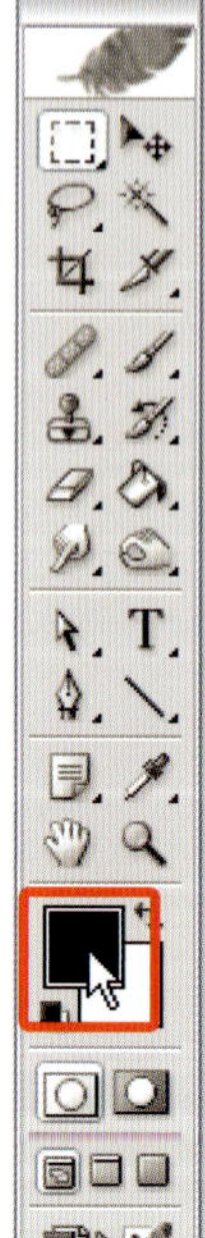

Click here to set the foreground color.

1. Click the Set Foreground Color box in the toolbox.
2. Select a color in the Color Picker, and click OK.
3. Specify the area to fill with color:
   - To fill an entire blank layer with color, first click that layer in the Layers palette.

- To fill a selected area, use the Marquee tool to make a selection, and then select the appropriate layer in the Layers palette.

4. Press Alt+Backspace (Option-Delete) to apply the color. This fills the area with the foreground color.

   You can also press Ctrl+Backspace (⌘-Delete) to fill the area with the background color.

Using layer styles

Layer styles are design elements you can add to image borders. In the page samples included in this book, only five Photoshop layer styles were used.

Drop shadow

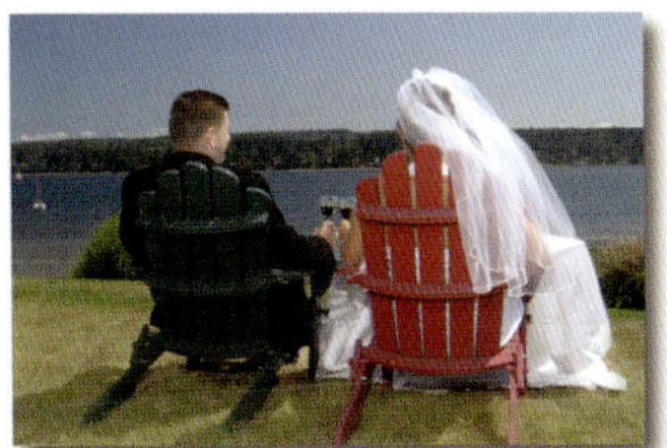

Outer glow

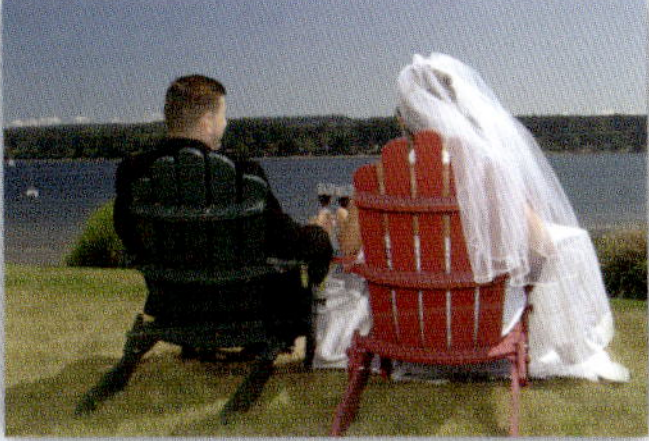

Bevel and emboss

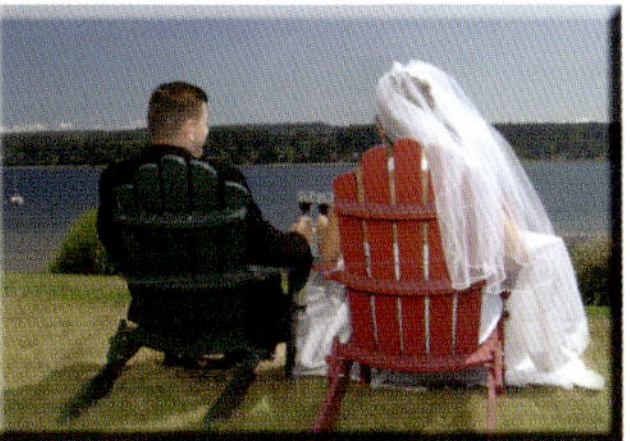

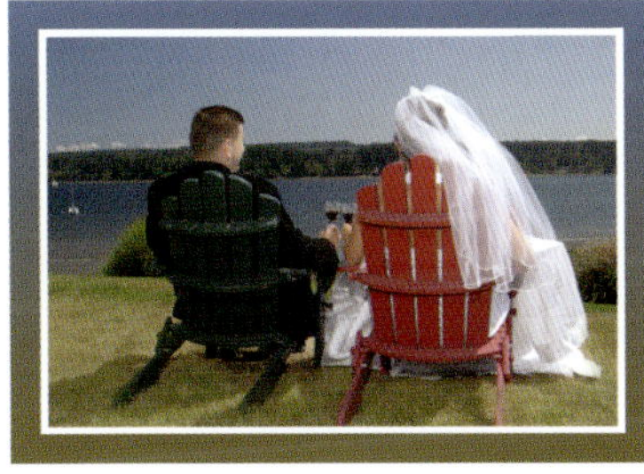

Gradient fill

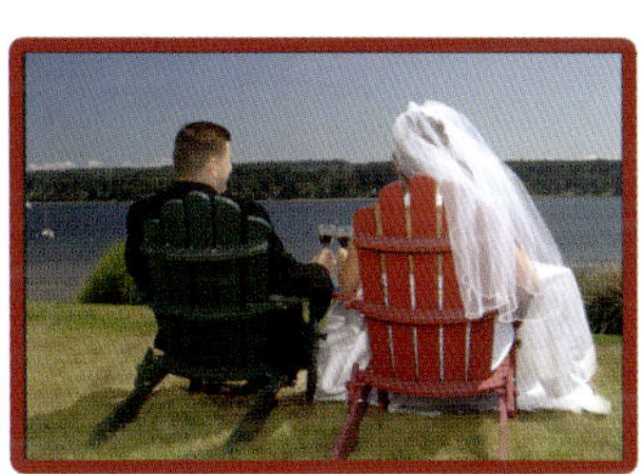

Stroke

Because you can adjust the settings for each layer style to match the images on the page, the same style can look very different depending upon the settings you choose.

Once you have the Layer Style dialog open, you can select any combination of styles to apply to the image on the selected layer, and set the options for each of them before closing the dialog. For the various sample designs in Chapter 4, you'll learn specific settings used to achieve the effects in the illustrations there.

Adding layer styles

The easiest way to add a layer style to an image border is to double-click the image icon for that layer in the Layers palette. This opens the Layer Style dialog, where you can add and define one or more layer styles for the image.

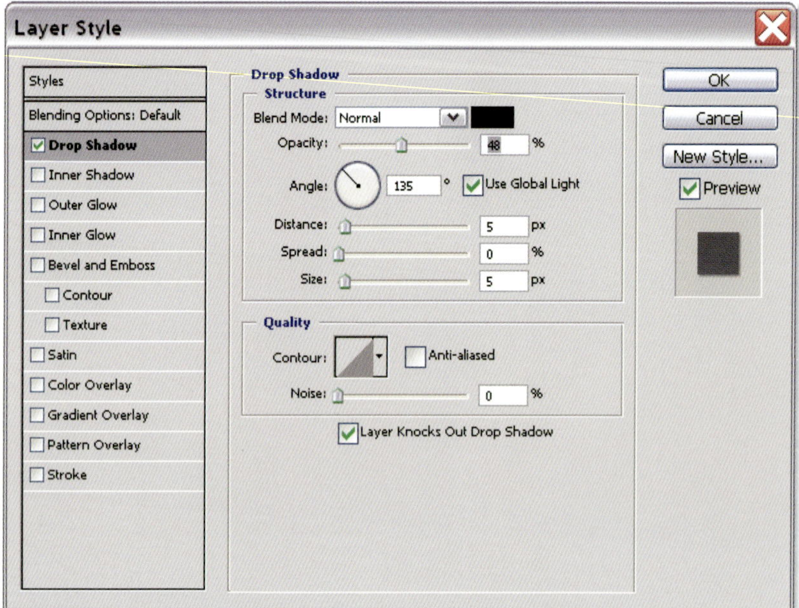

Copying layer styles

It's easy to copy layer styles from one layer to another. If you have just one style applied, such as a stroke (a line around the image), you can drag that style name in the Layers palette to another layer name in the palette, copying the style to the new layer.

But if you have two styles applied to one image, such as a stroke and a drop shadow, you'll need to drag them one at a time. In this case you'll want to copy the entire layer style and paste it onto the other layer.

1. In the Layers palette, right-click (Ctrl-click) a layer name and choose Copy Layer Style.
2. Right-click (Ctrl-click) another layer and choose Paste Layer Style.

Here's a quick way to copy layer styles to every related image on the page spread.

1. Double-click the image icon for one of the layers in the Layers palette.

Copying layer styles

1. Right-click (Ctrl-click) a layer, and choose Copy Layer Style.

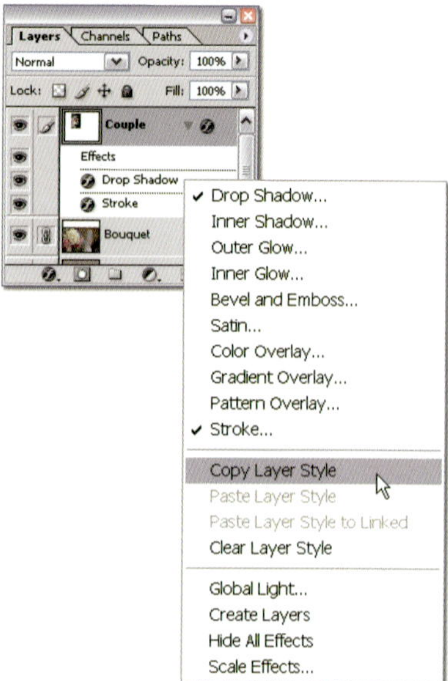

2. Add a Link icon to all other layers that need this style. (In CS2, Shift+click in the Layers palette to select the layers needing the style, and then click the Link icon.)

2. Apply the layer styles to this layer. Click OK.
3. Click in the Layers palette to place a Link icon for every layer where you want this style applied.

   If you want to apply the style to multiple adjacent layers, drag the mouse through the Link column to quickly place all the Link icons.
4. Right-click (Ctrl-click) the first layer style in the Layers palette and choose Copy Layer Style.
5. Right-click (Ctrl-click) one of the linked layers, and choose Paste Layer Style to Linked.

The layer style is applied to every linked layer.

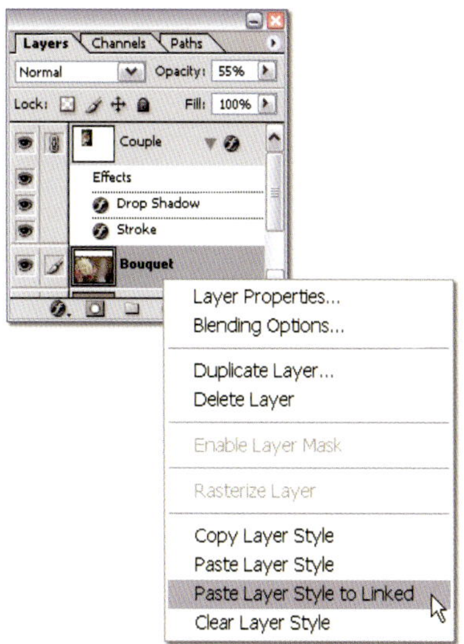

3. Right-click (Ctrl-click) another layer, and choose Paste Layer Style to Linked.

Hiding layer styles

If you have many layers with styles applied, it's handy to hide the style details in the Layers palette so you can see more layer names. In the Layers palette, click the triangle next to the Style icon to toggle hiding or showing style details.

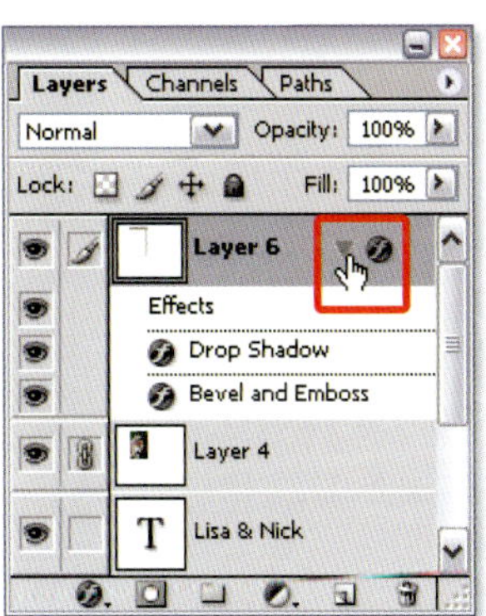

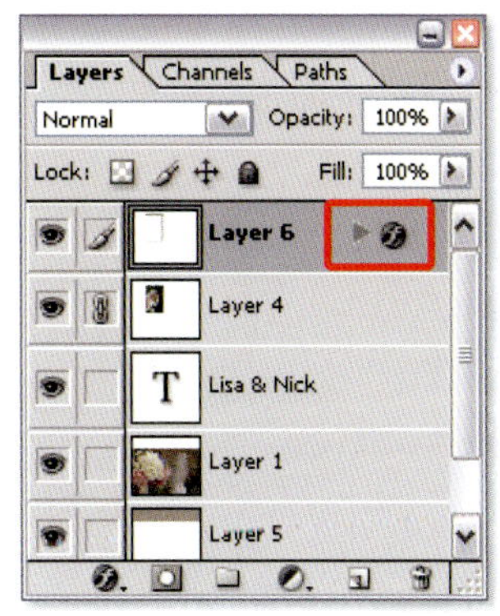

Using the History palette

The History palette stores a list of the changes you make in each open document. Once you become accustomed to using it, you'll find that you'll often want to select a previous step to undo a series of changes.

Here are a few useful things to know about the History palette.

- To show the History palette, choose History from the Window menu.

- As you make each change in your document, the changes are listed as separate steps in the History palette.
- To revert to a previous document state, click the step in the list. All the steps below the selected step appear grayed, indicating that if you make a change now, those grayed steps will be discarded.
- If you click a previous step and make one change, you can choose Undo to restore the steps that were discarded by the change. However, if you click a previous step and make two changes, you cannot restore the discarded steps.
- You can drag the pointer in the History palette to scroll through and view a series of changes.
- At any time, you can click the top entry in the History palette to view the image in its original state. You can make changes to the document, in effect "starting over." Or, without making changes to the original state, you can click the last step in the History palette again to return to the last state.
- When you close the document and open it again, the History palette is cleared of previous entries.
- To move back a step in History, press Ctrl+Alt+Z (⌘-Option-Z).
- To move forward a step in History, press Ctrl+Shift+Z (⌘-Shift-Z).

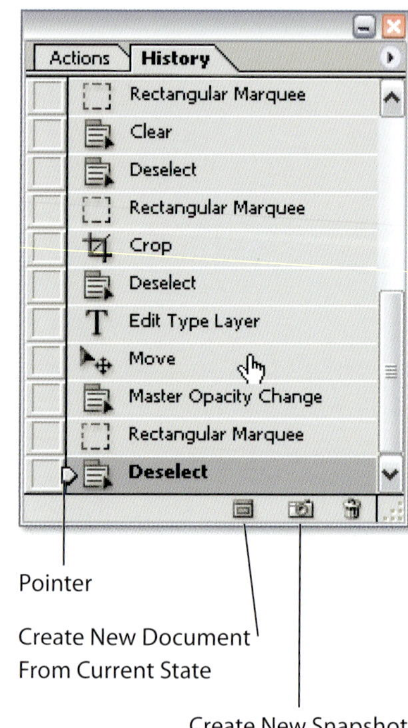

Changing the number of History states

By default, Photoshop saves only twenty steps in the History palette. When you're modifying an image using a tool like the Eraser or the Clone Stamp tool, you might quickly make twenty edits which will wipe out any of your previous state changes in the History palette.

You can increase the number of History states to make it easier to undo a great many changes, however, you may pay a price in performance. If Photoshop needs to save a large number of comprehensive changes in the file, it can slow down considerably. Try setting the History states to a large number if you want to, and then you can lower it again if performance is unacceptably slow.

Change the number of History states in General Preferences.

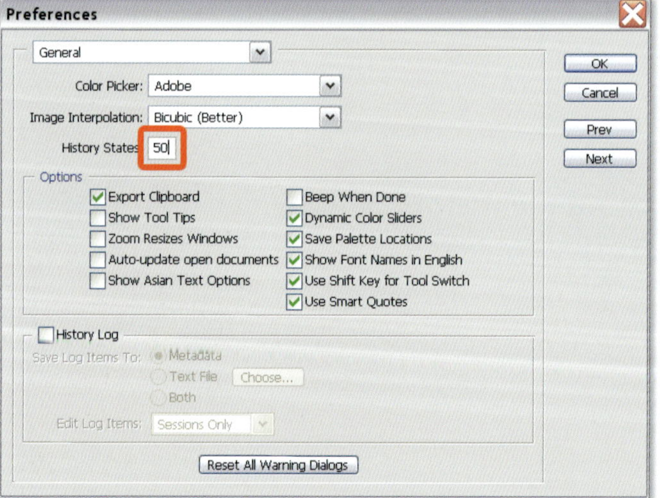

1. From the Edit menu, choose Preferences.
2. In the General section, change History States to a larger number, such as 50.

Snapshots

Even if you increase the number of History states, making snapshots is a good idea. Snapshots allow you to save specific states of the document so you can revert to one of them at any time.

Snapshots are saved only as long as the document is open. Once you close a document and re-open it, the snapshots are gone. If you want to save a particular snapshot before closing the document, right-click (Ctrl-click) the snapshot name (you'll find it if you scroll to the top of the History palette) and choose New Document. That snapshot state appears in its own window and you can then save it as a separate document.

If you want to save any particular state of the document, select the step in the History palette and click the Create New Document from Current State icon at the bottom of the History palette.

To create a snapshot:

1. Click the Create New Snapshot icon at the bottom of the History palette.

   You'll see the new snapshot at the top of the History palette.
2. If you want to give the snapshot a name, double-click the snapshot title and type a name.

About layer masks

Understanding a little bit about how layer masks work will help you understand what's happening in the techniques that use them.

Layer masks are a powerful feature that can be used to achieve a variety of effects. For digital album page design, one way we use layer masks is to hide and reveal parts of images on different layers. One advantage to using a layer mask instead of simply deleting part of the image is that you can easily "paint" the image back in later if you change your mind or make a mistake. Another advantage is that you can move the layer mask, thus moving the area that hides or reveals the image beneath it.

Because you probably work in RGB mode, your images are made up of three channels: Red, Green, and Blue. (Photoshop shows a fourth channel in the Channels palette, but this is simply a composite of the other three channels.) When you add a layer mask, you're adding an additional channel that holds only grayscale values. The grayscale values you apply to different areas in this channel determine the transparency or opacity of those areas of the image. Photoshop uses the convention that black indicates complete transparency and white indicates complete opacity. (Intermediate gray values indicate partial transparency.)

In a layer mask, black indicates transparency, and white indicates opacity.

This convention is arguably backward, and here's why. When you have an image selected in the Layers palette and you press D to set the default foreground and background colors, Photoshop sets the foreground color to black and the background color to white. If you paint in your image with the Paintbrush tool at this point, you'll see a black line in the image.

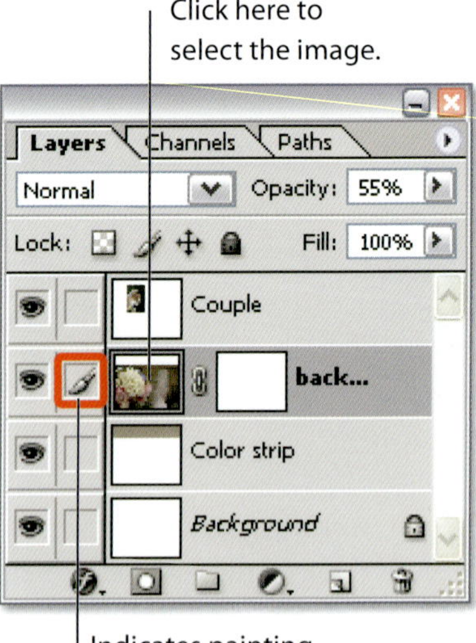

But if you have a layer mask selected in the Layers palette and you press D, Photoshop switches the foreground and background colors, setting the foreground color to white and the background color to black. If you then paint with the Paintbrush tool, you won't see a change because by "painting with white," you're telling Photoshop that you want those areas of the image opaque—and they're already opaque. To hide part of the image, you would need to press X to switch the foreground and background colors so that you're "painting with black." Everywhere that you paint with black, the image becomes completely transparent, showing whatever is on the layer underneath it.

After you've painted with black to make part of the image transparent, you can always press X to switch the foreground and background colors, and then paint with white in the layer mask to bring parts of the image back to full opacity.

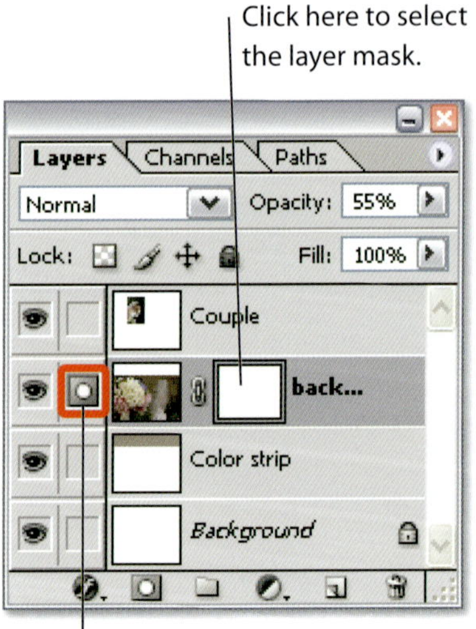

You need to be aware that after you've added a layer mask, there are two ways to select the layer.

- If you simply click the layer name in the Layers palette, the image is selected, and any edits you make affect the image itself.
- If you want to make changes to the layer mask, you need to click the layer mask icon to select the mask before editing.

It's also useful to note that you can unlink the mask from the image by clicking the Link icon between the image and layer mask icons. This allows you to use the Move tool to move the mask relative to the image.

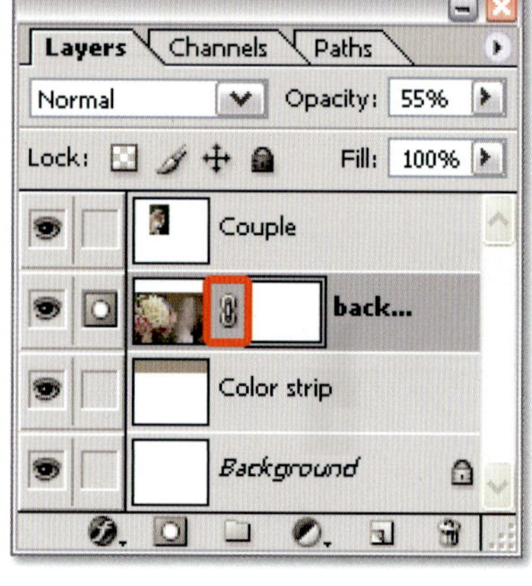

Click to unlink the mask from the layer so you can move the mask independently.

See Design 15 for an example of how to create a particular effect precisely by using a layer mask, and then less precisely (but more quickly), without using a layer mask.

Aligning images

It's important that you line up image edges precisely on the page whenever possible. On some pages you design, there will be a lot going on, and having edges line up on a grid provides a pattern that gives a sense of organization and coherence.

It's also a good idea to create precisely the same spaces between images in most cases. Paying attention to this kind of detail is what gives an album the most professional look.

Be sure to align images before applying any styles. Some layer styles (such as an outside stroke) make it difficult to see the actual edge of the image.

To align images in CS2, hold Shift or Ctrl and click in the Layers palette to select multiple layers. Then choose a command from Align Linked on the Layer menu.

The easiest way to align images is by making sure Snap is checked on the View menu, and dragging guides out of the rulers and placing them where you want images to line up. To learn about aligning image blocks precisely, see Design 5.

It's also easy to align images on different layers using the Align Linked commands on the Layer menu.

1. Select one of the layers containing an image you want to align.
2. Click to show the Link icon on the other layers.
3. From the Layer menu, choose Align Linked, and then choose the command that works best for the images being aligned.

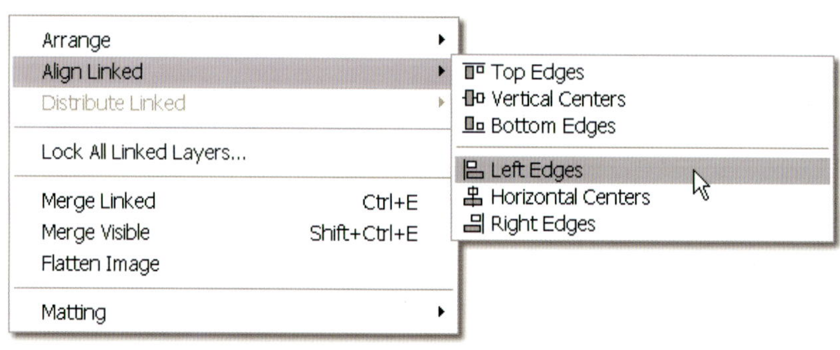

Sending a test page to the lab

You may be perfectly happy with the individual prints ordered from your professional lab. However, as I've mentioned before, once you've flattened numerous images onto a page spread, the lab can no longer color correct the individual images.

Ordering an entire set of prints for album pages is expensive. Before you design a whole set of pages and place the first print order, you want to make sure your color-correction techniques are working well. I recommend creating a test page and sending it to your lab using images that, for whatever reason, were a challenge to color correct.

Select five or six hard-to-correct images from one session. These may be a little dark or they may have a color cast that needs correcting. Open them all in Photoshop and make them look as perfect as you can on the screen, especially in relation to one another.

Before you create a test page, ask your lab representative these three questions:

- What resolution do they recommend for digital album pages?
- What file type do they prefer—.jpgs, .tifs, something else?
- What is the price difference between having the lab color correct the images and having them print the images exactly the way you submit them?
- Do they have an ICC profile you can download and use?

If you're not already using an ICC profile from your lab, you need to talk with a lab representative about how to obtain and use this file.

Creating a test page

1. In Photoshop, choose New from the File menu.
2. Set these parameters:
    - Width: 14 inches
    - Height: 11 inches
    - Resolution: the resolution your lab recommends (we use 256 pixels/inch)
    - Color Mode: RGB Color
3. Click OK.

Copying images onto the test page

1. Open the image files you've color-corrected and position them so you can also see part of the test page window.
2. In the Layers palette for one of the image windows, click to select the layer containing the image.
3. Drag that layer into the test page window and drop it. This pastes it into the test page window.
4. Press Ctrl+T (⌘-T) for Free Transform.
5. Holding Shift, drag a corner of the image to scale it down enough so the rest of your images will fit on the page.
6. Place all the other images on the page in the same way and scale them.

   The layout of this page is not important. You simply want to see what the images will look like when printed as one image.
7. From the File menu, choose Save and save the file as "Corrected.jpg."
8. After saving, press T for the Text tool, click somewhere on the page, and type "Uncorrected."
9. From the File menu, choose Save As and save this file as "Uncorrected.jpg."

Send these images to your lab and order two prints: one that they color correct, and one that they print exactly the way you submit it.

When the prints come back, examine them carefully. You'll know when you see the resulting prints whether you need to learn more about color correction. Do all the skin tones look the same between images? Do the whites all look white? Are light areas that used to contain detail now blown out by corrections made by the lab? Has detail been lost in any shadows? If you're not happy with the results for any reason, talk with your lab about how to resolve the problem.

Also look at how the two prints compare. It's possible that your lab offers a less expensive service option in which they do no color correction at all. If you're happy with the way the print looks that wasn't color corrected, you can save costs by requesting no color correction.

Preparing separate pages for the lab

After you've read this book and designed your first set of album pages, you'll want to divide the double-page spreads into separate, flattened images so they're ready to send to the lab. If the album you're creating will have full panoramas on every page, you won't need to split the pages. But you may need to add white space to create the correct aspect ratio for a print size offered by your lab.

We work with H&H Color Lab, and the closest size they offer to a 10 x 12 is a 10 x 13. So we add white space to each image and submit each page as a 10 x 13. For a 5 x 6 parent replica album, we submit images that are 5 x 7. The following steps explain how to add extra space to the canvas to provide the correct aspect ratio for the prints. You'll trim the extra white space off later.

Ideally you'll select an album size that requires print sizes your lab offers! When we do the 12 x 12 panoramic Soho Book by Renaissance, no trimming of the 12 x 24 prints is necessary.

Of course you can automate this process by using actions. Nonetheless, for purposes of illustration, the procedures below show all the steps involved in the process.

When you're creating flattened pages for the lab, be sure to have the Channels palette visible so you can see if any extra channels remain from masks you've created. Sometimes, even when you flatten an image, you'll still see a mask channel, and your lab may not accept image files with extra channels.

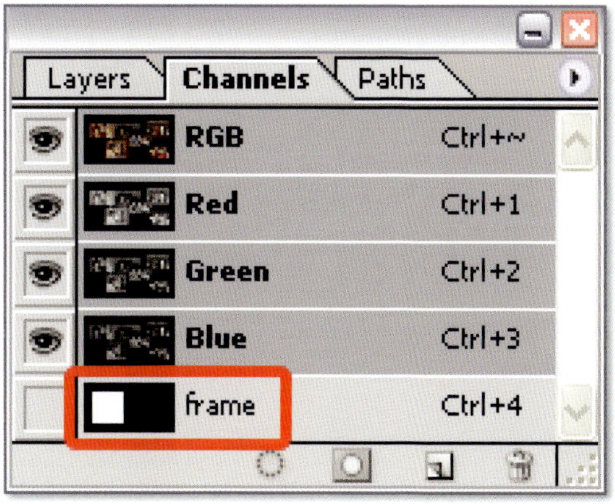

If mask channels remain after flattening, delete them.

If you see extra channels after flattening, simply delete them. This has no effect on the appearance of the flattened image.

Crop down to one page

1. Open a double-page spread.
2. Press D for default foreground and background colors.
3. Choose Flatten Image from the Layer menu.
4. Drag the window out a little larger than the canvas.
5. Make sure Snap is checked on the View menu, and drag a vertical guide precisely to the middle of the pages (if you don't already have one there).
6. With the Marquee tool, begin dragging outside the canvas edge and then drag out to precisely select the left half of the image.
7. From the Image menu, choose Crop.

Be careful not to save the flattened version with the same name! You'll need the layered version in case you need to make changes for any reason later.

Resize it for the large album

1. From the Image menu, choose Canvas Size.
2. For Width, change the 12 to 13 (or whatever dimension is needed to create a size offered by your lab).
3. Because you're working with a left-hand page, for Anchor, click the arrow pointing left and click OK.

   This adds the new white space to the right side of the image only. You'll be trimming this later, and this allows you to trim one side instead of two. (If you don't change the anchor, Photoshop applies half the amount of additional white space on each side of the image, and then you'd have to trim both sides of the print.)

Always add the white space to the inside of the page, the edge next to the album core. This way, if you have a panoramic image across two pages, a little extra trimming by the lab won't affect the center of the panorama. You'll do a precise job of cutting off the extra white strip yourself when the prints arrive.

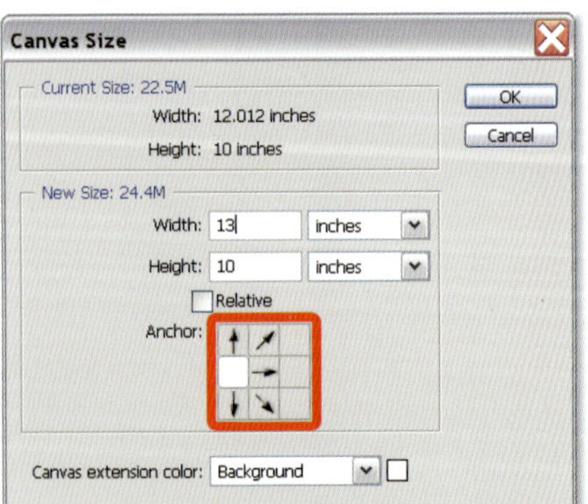

For even-numbered pages (left pages), click this anchor point to add white space next to the core.

For odd-numbered pages (right pages), click this anchor point to add white space next to the core.

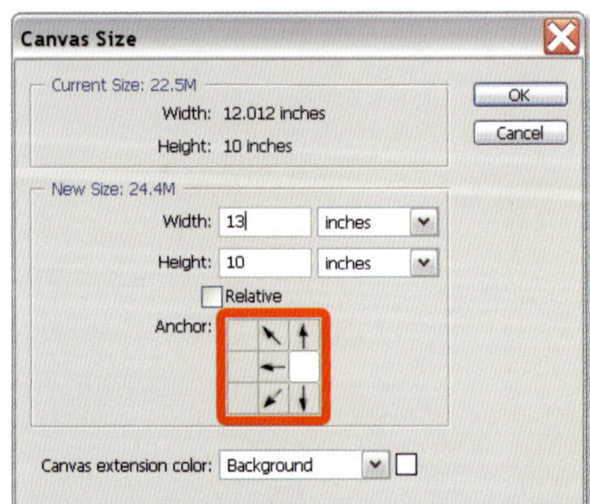

4. Save the image in a different location with the name of that page (e.g. 02.tif).

Resize again to create a parent replica album

1. From the Image menu, choose Canvas Size.
2. For Width, change 13 to 14.

   This gives you a 10 x 14 image, which of course is the same aspect ratio as a 5 x 7. When you place your order with the lab, you'll specify that you want 5 x 7 prints for this set of images.
3. For Anchor, click the arrow pointing left to add more white space to the same edge (if this is an even-numbered page) and click OK.
4. Save this image in a new folder called Parent.

Now do the facing page

1. In the History palette, click the step where you first selected the left-hand page (the Rectangular Marquee step).
2. From the Select menu, choose Inverse.
3. Now start again with the directions in "Resize it for the large album" above, but click the opposite Anchor arrow to add white space to the other side for the right-hand pages.

A tip for dealing with your lab

If your lab balances your images, it's important to indicate to them that the images need to be balanced in pairs because they're facing album pages. In the Comments section of the print-ordering software for H&H Color Lab, I always write, "Please balance image pairs together (i.e., 02 & 03, 04 & 05), as they are facing album pages." Otherwise, a background color might appear differently on facing pages if the lab is color correcting.

Alternately, specify that you do your own color correcting and that you wish the lab to print your images exactly as submitted.

Sending the images to the lab

If you have an account set up with H&H Color Lab, they'll send you a program called eZprint. Add your images to it, and specify the size, quantity, and effect for each image. Then eZprint creates a zip file containing each image file with the print order information.

The easiest way to get your images to the lab is to upload this zip file to their website: www.hhcolorlab.com. As a customer, you'll have a user

name and password. Log in on the studio homepage, choose "upload orders," add the zip file, and click to upload it. With a large order such as an album, this upload may take many hours, even with a high-speed Internet connection. The prints will arrive on your doorstep in a matter of days.

Trimming prints

When you receive the prints, you may need to trim off the extra white border. We use a 24-inch RotaTrim; you can find this excellent cutter at www.bhphotovideo.com. When it's time to trim prints, cut a corner from a small, thin piece of cardboard and tape it to the cutter table as a guide. (You can also order a RotaTrim Side Guide, a measuring accessory that locks into place to ensure identical print sizes.) You want to make sure every print is trimmed to exactly the same size.

Putting your ideas to work

You've learned the theory behind all the issues of producing digital albums. Now it's time to learn the practical aspects. In the next chapter you'll find the information you need to create all the design examples shown.

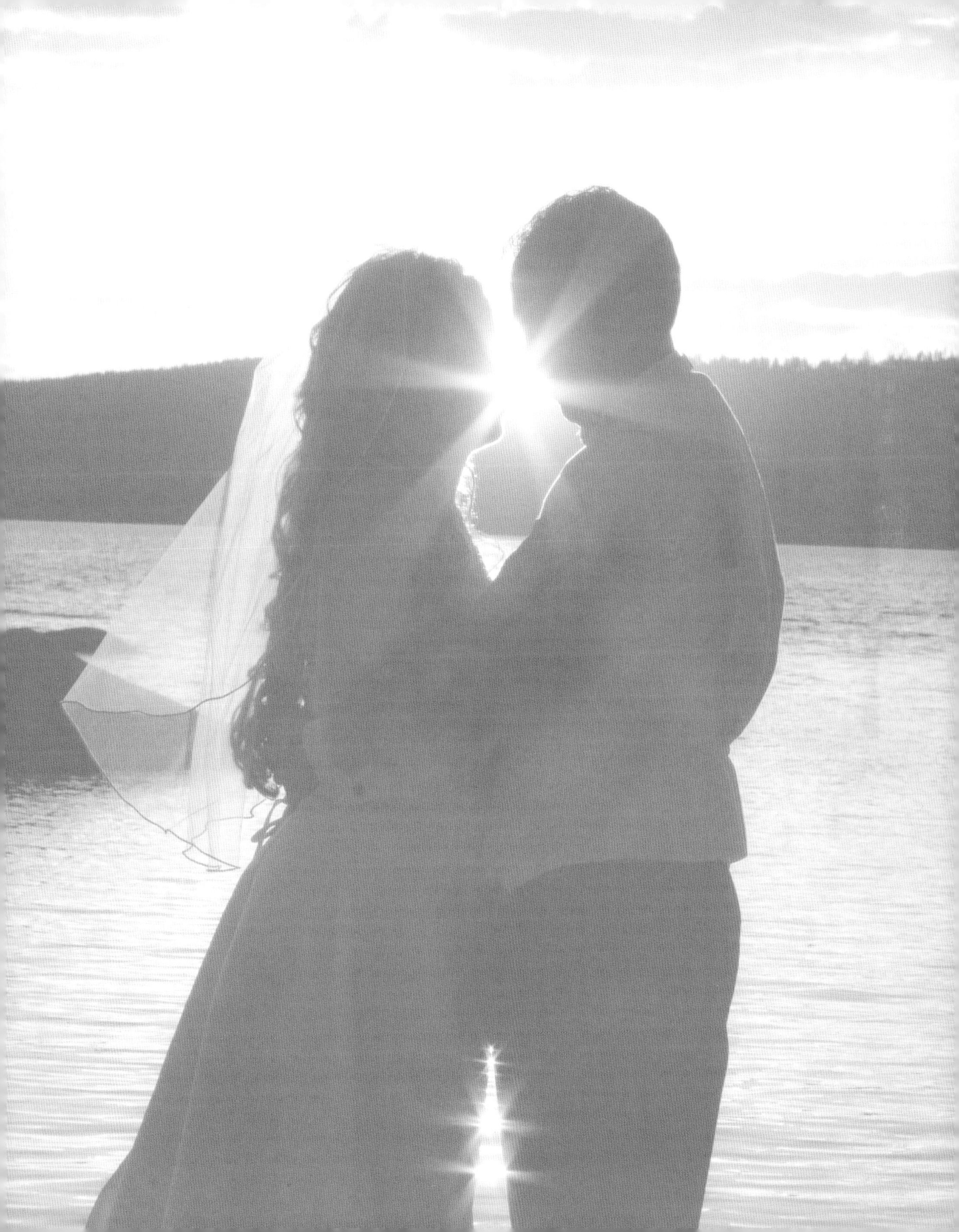

3. Press Ctrl+T (⌘-T) for Free Transform.
4. Holding Shift, drag a corner handle to scale down the image.

   When you scale down, do so conservatively. You can always scale down a little more later, but after you've pressed Enter to accept the transformation, you can't scale up again without loss of sharpness in the image.
5. Press Enter to accept the transformation.

Double-click the image icon to open the Layer Style dialog.

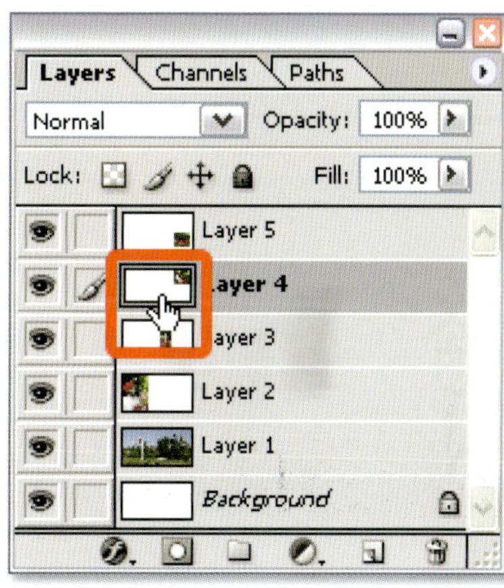

Adding a black stroke

1. In the Layers palette, double-click the image icon to open the Layer Style dialog.
2. Choose Stroke.
3. For Size, type 1.
4. Click the red square and set the color to black by setting the R, G, and B values to 0.

Adding a shadow

1. On the left side of the Layer Style dialog, click Drop Shadow.
2. For Blend mode, choose Normal.
3. For Opacity, choose 75%.

   If the image is in front of a white background instead of in front of an image, you might want a lighter shadow, such as 40%.
4. For Angle, choose 135.
5. Move the Distance and Size sliders until you like the appearance of the shadow. In this example, Distance was set to 16 pixels, and Size was set to 18 pixels.

   If you don't want the shadow showing at the top or left side of the image, increase the distance or decrease the size.

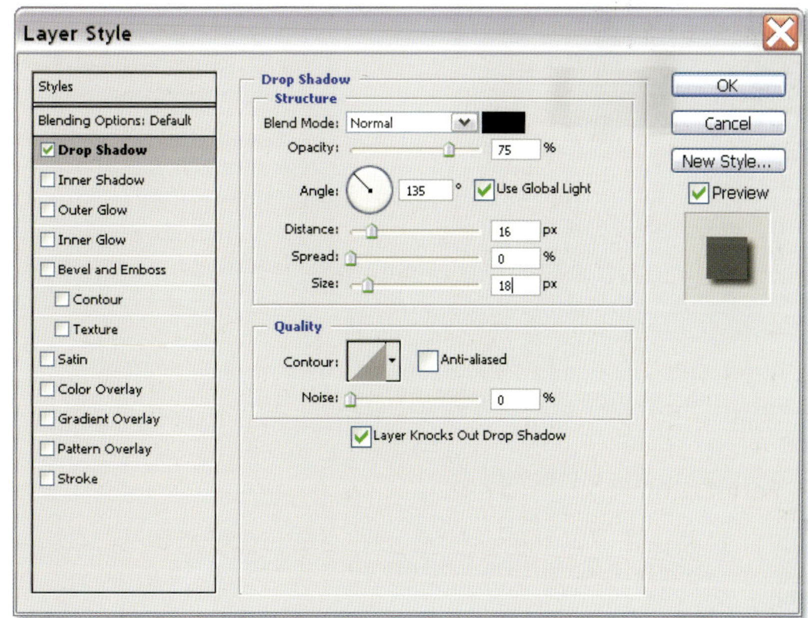

Design 3: Designing the first page

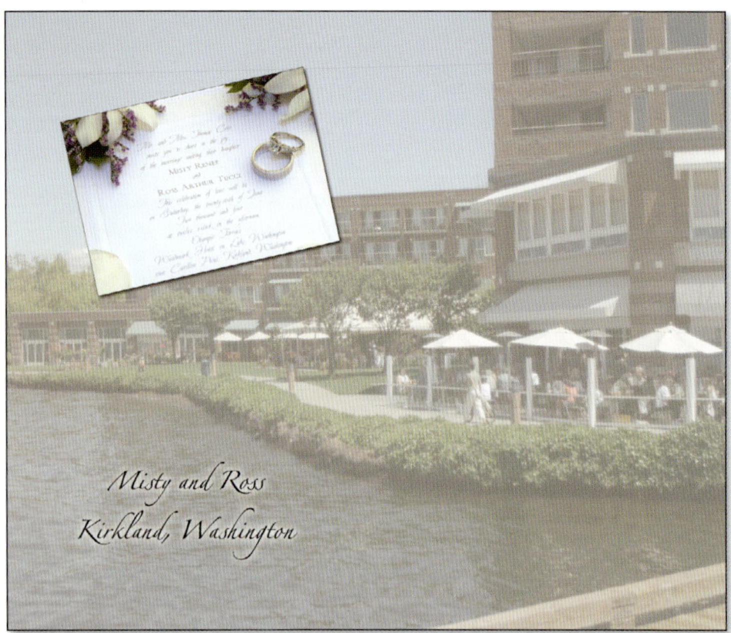

Design notes

This image was obtained by walking a considerable distance from the reception site. Wide views of a lovely outdoor location make great background images, especially for the first page. Another nice way to start the album is with "getting ready" pictures or with portraits from an engagement session.

If you use medium-toned text on a dark background, you can give it a light outer glow to make it easy to see. Or you can use light text and give it a dark outer glow. Either way, make sure the text is clearly set off from the background and is easy to read.

The invitation was rotated and given two styles: stroke and drop shadow. The text font is Zapfino with an outer glow style applied.

Formatting the invitation

1. Select the invitation layer in the Layers palette, and press Ctrl+T (⌘-T) for Free Transform.

   If you'd like the invitation smaller on the page, you can hold Shift and drag a corner handle.

2. Drag outside the image to rotate it and then press Enter to accept the transformation.
3. Double-click the image icon for that layer to open the Layer Style dialog and click Drop Shadow.

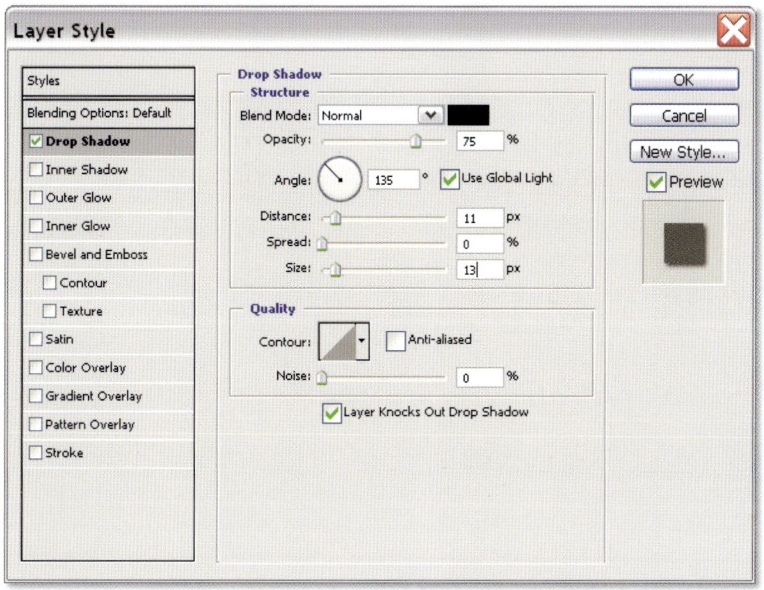

4. Set Blend mode to Normal, Distance to 11 pixels, Size to 13 pixels, and Angle to 135.
5. In the Layer Style dialog, click Stroke.
6. Set the Size to 1 pixel and the Color to black, as described in Design 2.

Adding text

1. Press T for the Text tool.
2. In the options bar, specify a font, size, alignment, and color.

Commit Current Edits

Adobe Photoshop
File Edit Image Layer Select Filter View Window Help
LTZapfino One | Regular | 48 pt | Strong

3. Click the page to create a new text layer, and then type the clients' names.

4. Click the Commit Current Edits check mark in the options bar to deselect the new text block.
5. Click the page again to create another text layer.
6. Type an additional line of text, if needed.
7. Click the check mark in the options bar to deselect the text block.

Selecting text

You can always select text again later and change any of the options specified, such as font, size, or color. But in some instances, selecting an existing text block can be difficult. Photoshop sometimes has a tendency to create a new text layer when you're trying to click in an existing text block with the Text tool (you'll see the new blank text layer in the Layers palette).

If this happens, you can press Esc to cancel the creation of the new text layer, and then double-click the image icon in the text layer in the Layers palette. This selects the entire text block. You can then use the arrow keys to move the cursor.

When you're moving text layers around on the page, it's a good idea to have Auto Select Layer unchecked in the options bar. It's easiest to select text layers by clicking the layer name in the Layers palette.

If you want to make text bolder and you don't have a bold version of the font, you can add a 1-pixel black stroke by holding Alt (Option), double-clicking the image icon for the text layer in the Layers palette, and adding a stroke in the Layer Style dialog.

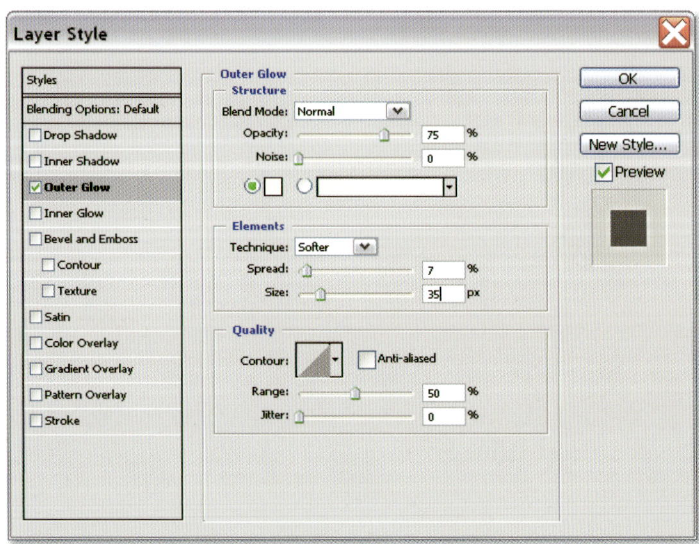

Adding outer glow to text

1. Hold Alt (Option) and double-click the image icon on the text layer in the Layers palette.
2. In the Layer Style dialog, click Outer Glow.
3. Set Color to white and Opacity to 75%. Set Spread to 7%, and set Size to 35%.

Design 4: Adding a decorative border

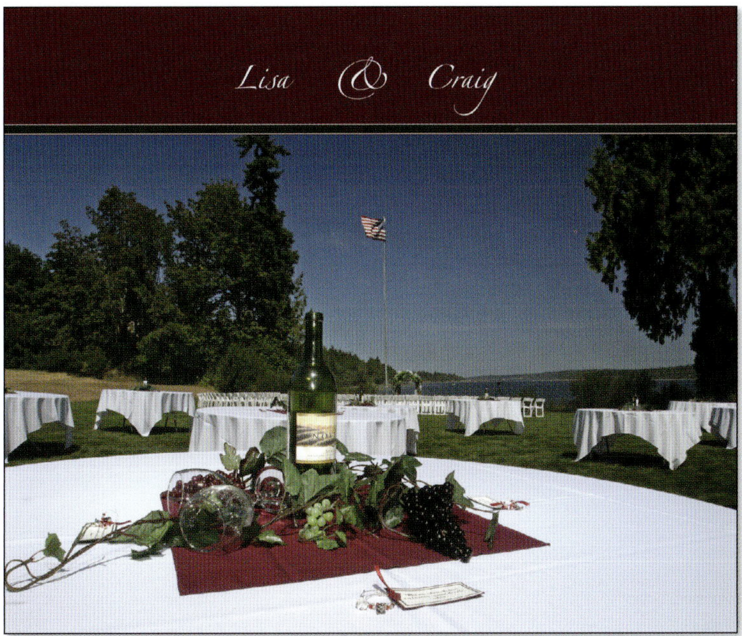

Design notes

The couple decided on a wine theme for this wedding, using the colors burgundy and evergreen. If you can find a way to highlight their theme and use their colors, clients are guaranteed to love those pages. The text font used is Zapfino and the ampersand was set in a larger point size than the words.

Creating the first color block

1. Paste the background image onto the page, and resize it to fill the page. (See Design 1.)
2. Drag out the border of your window to add space around the canvas so you can create a selection from edge to edge.
3. Select the top layer in the Layers palette and press Ctrl+Alt+Shift+N (⌘-Option-Shift-N) to add a new layer (this allows you to add a layer without being asked to give it a name).
4. Press M for the Marquee tool and drag out a selection on this new layer for the burgundy rectangle.
5. Press I for the Eyedropper and click an area in the image to pick up something close to the color you want for the rectangle.

Create a new layer above the background image layer.

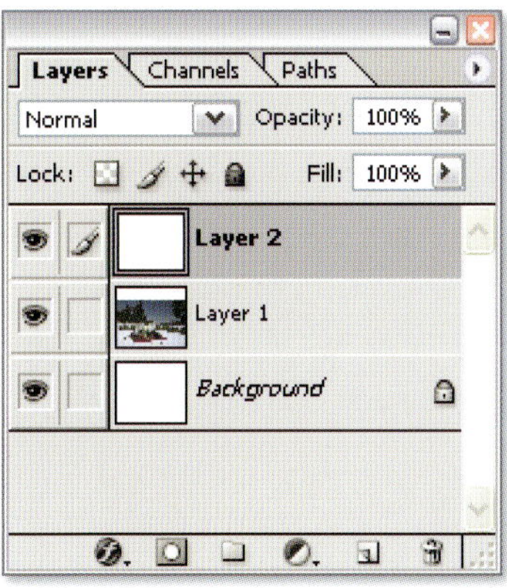

6. Press Alt+Backspace (Option-Delete) to fill the selection with color.

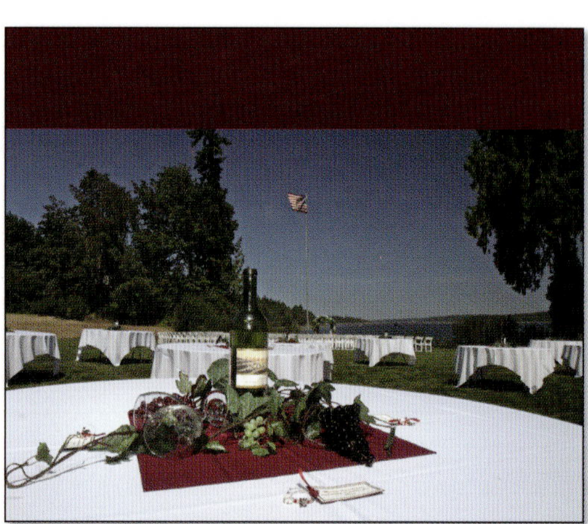

Creating the second color block

1. Press Ctrl+Alt+Shift+N (⌘-Option-Shift-N) to add another new layer above the layer with the first color block.
2. Press M for the Marquee tool and drag out a selection for the dark green strip between the image and the color block.
3. Press I for the Eyedropper and click an area in the image to pick up something close to the color you want for the strip.
4. Press Alt+Backspace (Option-Delete) to fill the selection with the sampled color.
5. Double-click the image icon for this layer in the Layers palette.
6. Choose Stroke and give the strip a 5-pixel white stroke.

   It's easy to set the stroke color to white in the Color Picker dialog by setting the R, G, and B values to 255.

7. If you see the white stroke at the edges of the page, press Ctrl+T (⌘-T) to select the strip of color. Then hold Shift and drag the handles at the sides of the strip to make it longer, so the white strokes at the sides are positioned off the canvas and out of sight.

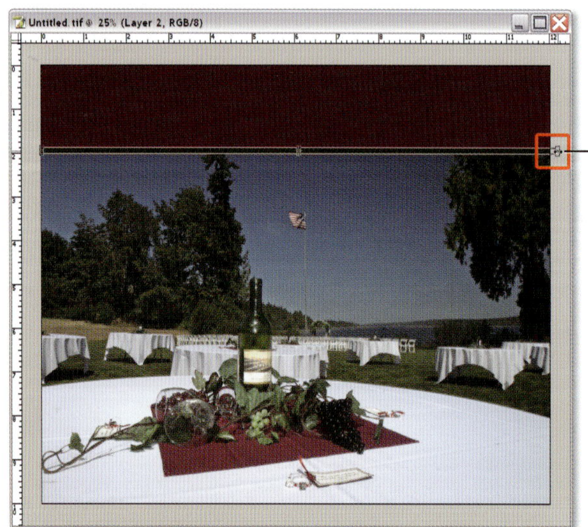

Press Ctrl+T (⌘-T) for Free Transform, and drag the ends of the color strip outside the edge of the canvas to hide the white stroke at the sides.

Design 5: Aligning image blocks precisely

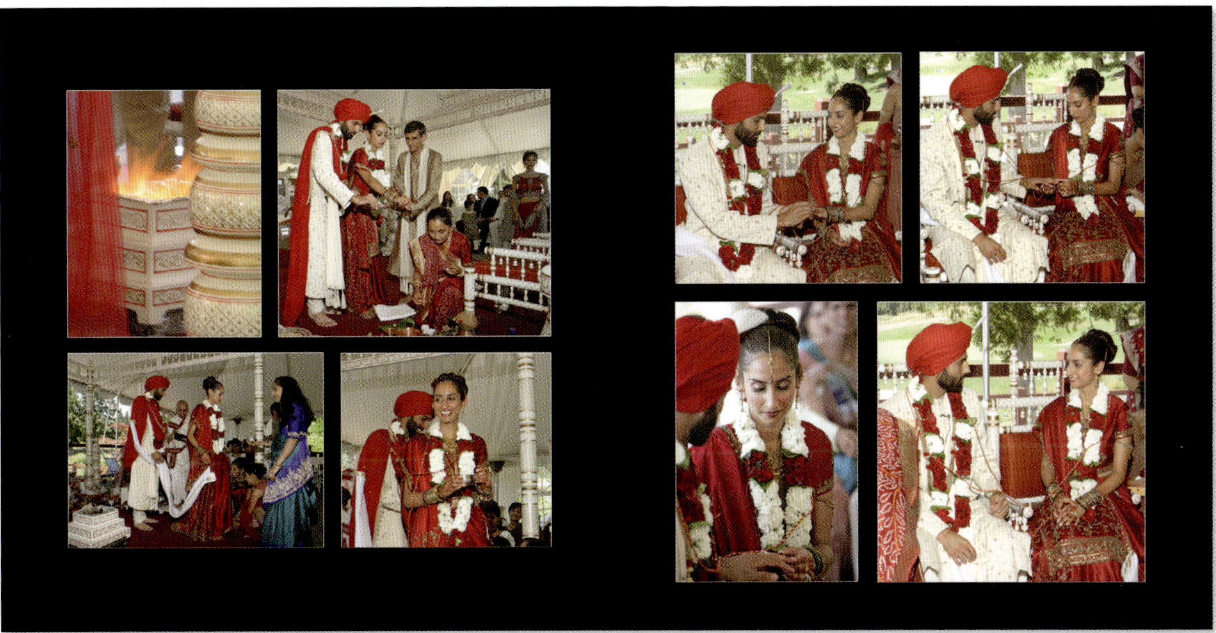

Design notes

In creating a page like this, you'll be selecting the various layers frequently to do the moving and trimming. After you've copied all the images into the page spread window, you'll find that it's useful to drag their layer names in the Layers palette so all the images on the left page are at the top, followed by the images on the right page.

Drag the layers in the list to place the images on the left page at the top, followed by the images on the right page.

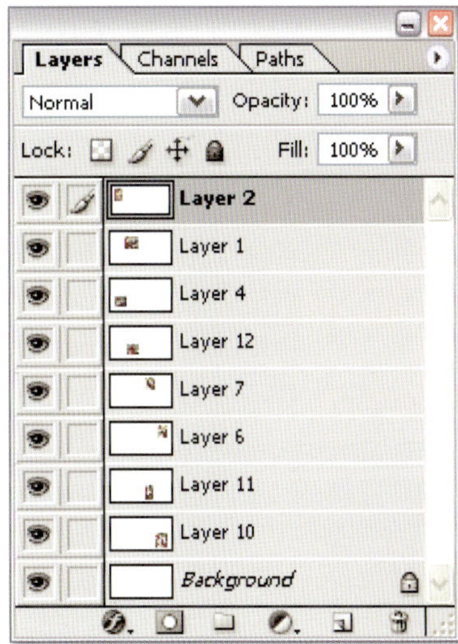

You won't want to put eight images in a page spread very often. With so many images, there isn't room to display one of them in a large size and draw attention to it. But when you do have this many images on a page, think about alignment and repetition to create a restful composition. The pattern created by the spaces between images is just as strong an element of the design as the images themselves.

The images in this example each have a 3-pixel white stroke applied, to set them apart from the black background.

Creating a block of four images

1. Each in its own window, crop every image to approximately the right shape.

2. Drag each of these layers from the Layers palette into the page spread window.
3. For each image, press Ctrl+T (⌘-T), hold Shift, and drag a corner handle to resize down to approximately the right size, leaving the images just a little too large (so you have room to trim them later).
4. With the Move tool, align the images so they're close to creating a square block, with approximately the right amount of space between images.

As you place images in a block, be aware that the largest space currently between images is the space you'll need to use between all of them. This is because you'll be trimming the inside edges to create even spacing. If you think one of the spaces between images is a little too big, move the images to create a smaller amount of space.

Now you're ready to align the edges precisely, and you'll do this by trimming the images.

Creating perfect outside edges

1. Press M for the Marquee tool and drag out a selection along the outside edge of one side of the block, exactly where you'd like the images to line up.

   Be sure to slightly overlap each image on that edge with the selection.
2. Press V for the Move tool.
3. Make sure the Auto Select Layer option is checked in the options bar.

   This allows you to click images on the page to select their layer in the Layers palette.
4. Click an image along that edge to select it and press Delete to trim it.
5. Click any other images along that edge and press Delete to trim them.
6. Press M for the Marquee tool and drag out a selection along another outside edge of the block. Again use the Move tool to click each image and Delete to trim. Repeat this for the top and the bottom edges of the block.

Drag out a selection along the outside edge of the image block, slightly overlapping each image.

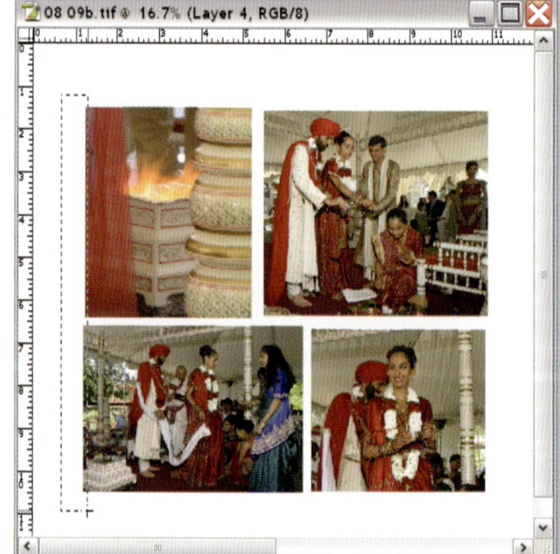

Creating perfect spaces between images

Look carefully at the spaces between the images and determine which amount of spacing is largest.

1. Press M for the Marquee tool and drag out a selection between the images with the largest spacing between them, making sure to overlap each image a little.

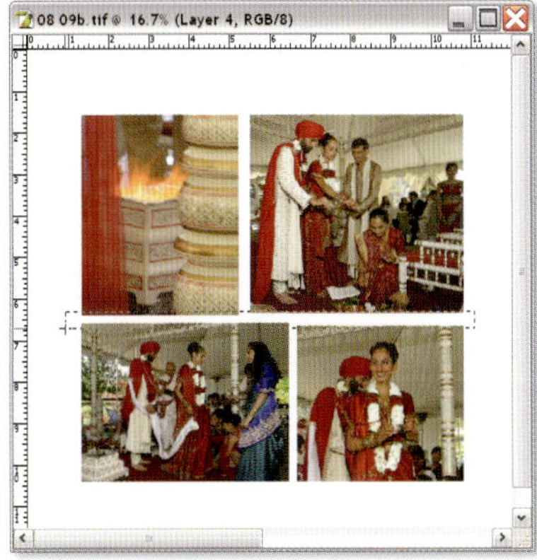

1. Drag out a selection between the images.

2. With the Move tool, click each image, and then press Delete.

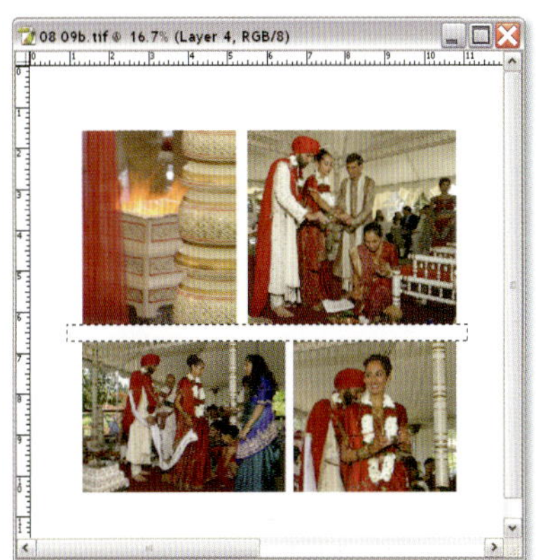

2. Press V for the Move tool. Click each image overlapped by the selection, and press Delete to trim it.

   Now you're going to rotate this selection 90 degrees so you can create the same amount of spacing in the other direction.

3. Rotate the selection so you can trim the same amount for the vertical spaces.

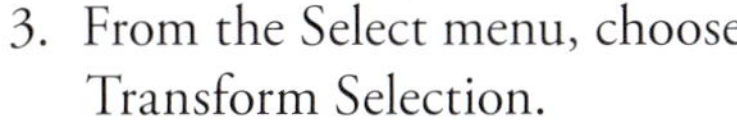

3. From the Select menu, choose Transform Selection.

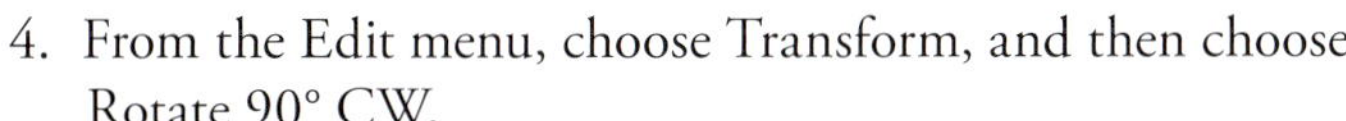

4. From the Edit menu, choose Transform, and then choose Rotate 90° CW.

5. Drag an end sizing box on the selection if you need to make it shorter or longer (but don't adjust the selection width by dragging a corner sizing box). You can drag in the middle of the selection to move it, if necessary. Press Enter to accept the transformation.

6. Again line up the selection between the images (overlapping the edges), press V for the Move tool, click each image to select it, and press Delete to trim it.

   If you need to move the selection to another location, press M for the Marquee tool and then drag the selection. Press V for the Move tool again, and click each additional image to trim it.

4. After trimming, move the selection to another location with the Marquee tool, and trim again.

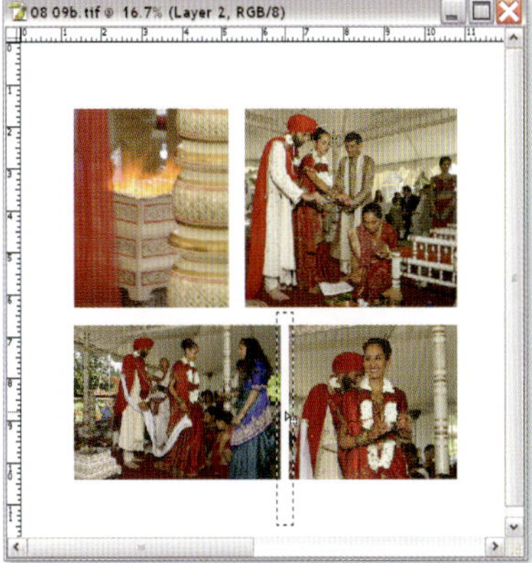

Design 6: Creating a stroke in a coordinating color

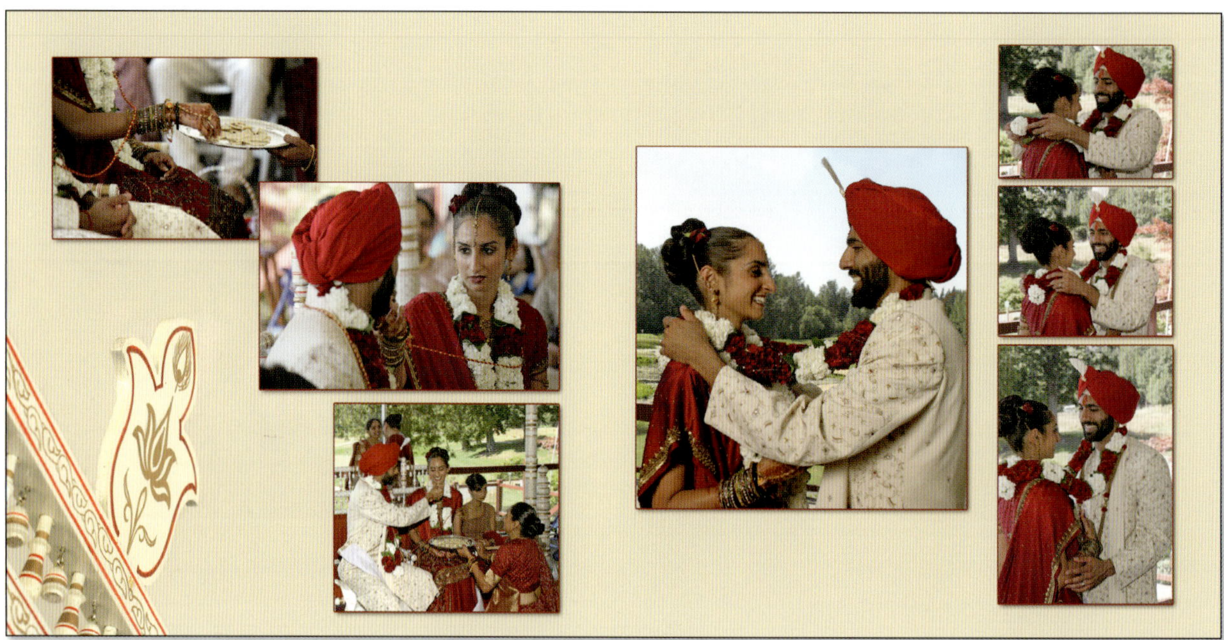

Design notes

The red stroke around these images helps to tie them in with the red outline around the background image. After the decorative background image was pasted onto the page spread, the edges of that image were erased, and then the eggshell color in the image was sampled with the Eyedropper tool and used to fill the background for both pages.

Creating a coordinating stroke

1. Double-click the image icon for an image layer in the Layers palette.
2. In the Layer Style dialog, choose Stroke.

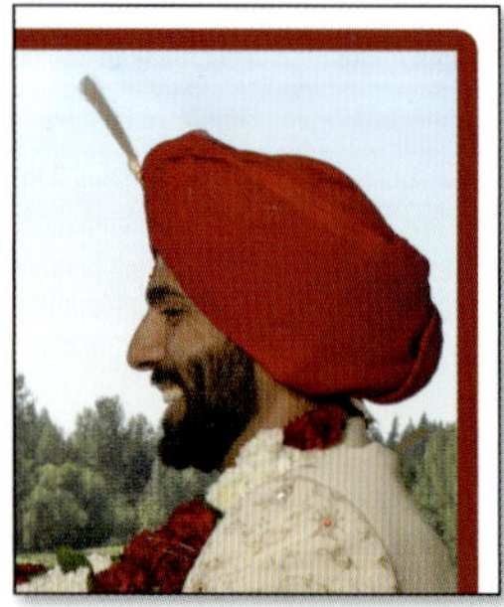

Outside stroke

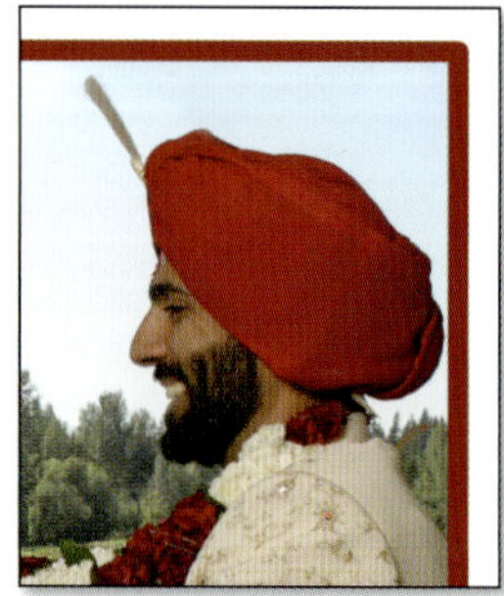

Center stroke

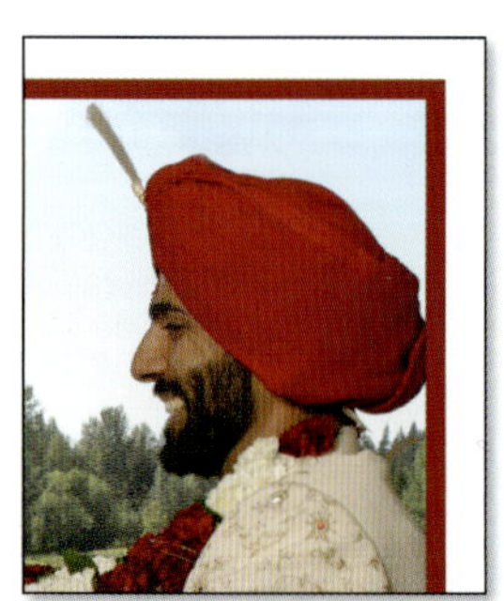

Inside stroke

3. For position, choose Outside.
    - "Outside" applies the stroke outside the boundaries of the image and appears with obviously rounded corners.
    - "Center" applies the stroke equally inside and outside the boundaries of the image (obscuring part of the image) and appears with slightly rounded corners.
    - "Inside" applies the stroke inside the boundaries of the image (obscuring more of the image, depending upon the stroke size) and appears with square corners.
4. Click the Color box. With the eyedropper, click in an image to select a color. Or select a color in the Color Picker. Click OK.
5. For Size, move the slider until you like the appearance of the stroke.
6. Choose Drop Shadow and add a shadow to the image. Click OK.

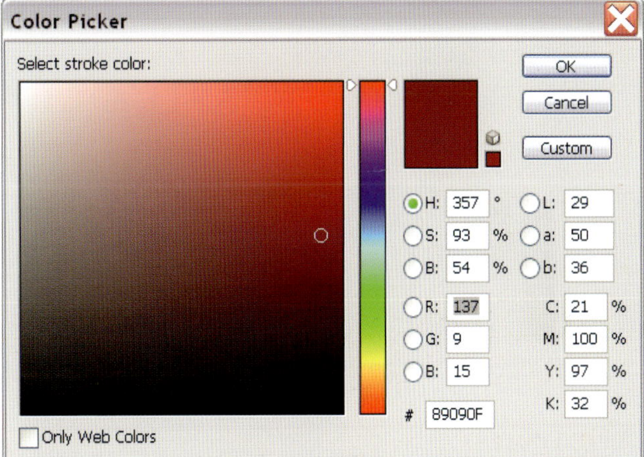

Applying the layer style to another image

1. In the Layers palette, right-click (Ctrl-click) the layer name and choose Copy Layer Style.
2. Right-click (Ctrl-click) another layer and choose Paste Layer Style.

For CS2, see the note on page 62 about applying layer styles to multiple layers.

Here's a quick way to copy layer styles to every related image on the page spread.

1. Click in the Layers palette to place a Link icon for every layer where you want the style applied.
2. Right-click (Ctrl-click) the first layer style in the Layers palette, and choose Copy Layer Style.
3. Right-click (Ctrl-click) one of the linked layers and choose Paste Layer Style to Linked.

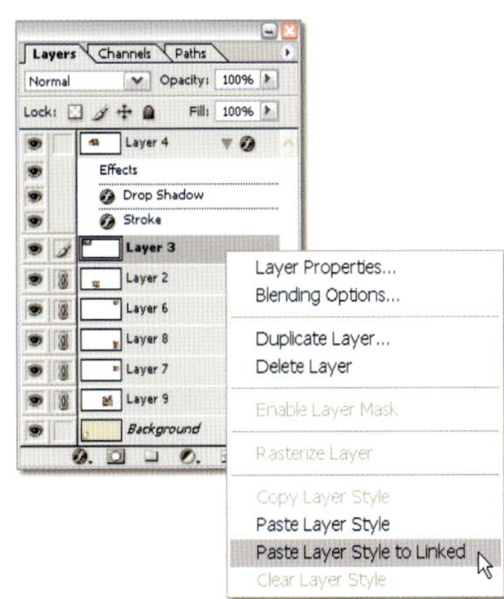

The layer style is applied to every linked layer.

Design 7: Creating an outer glow

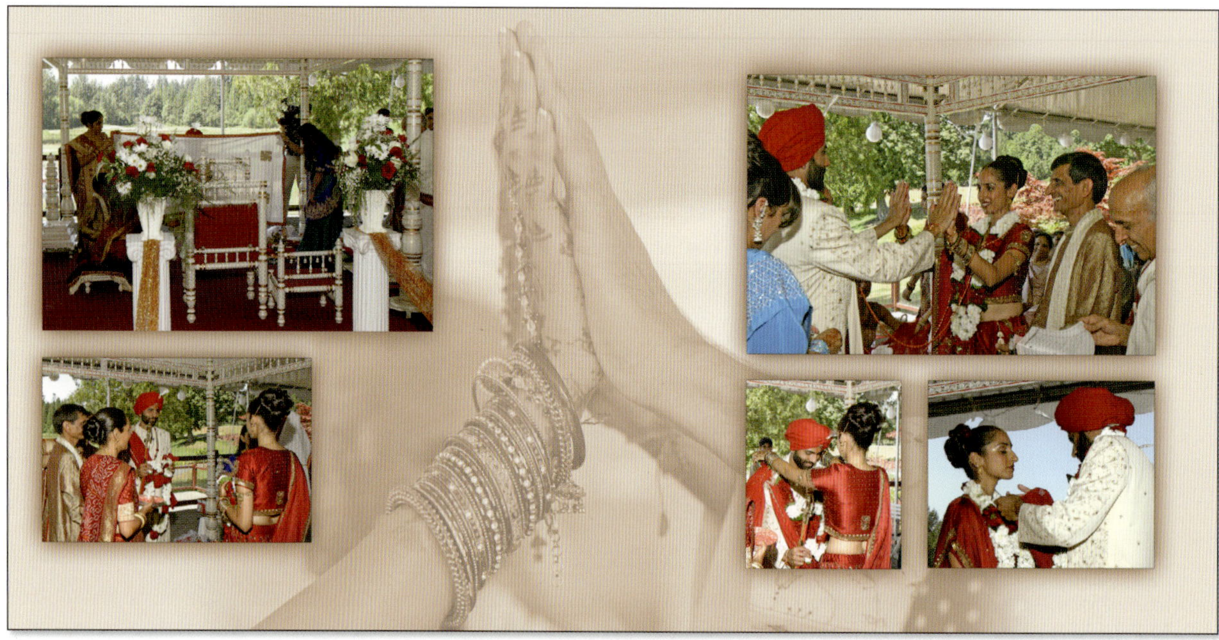

Design notes

The coordinating color of the lovely glow around these images helps to tie them in with the background image.

Creating an outer glow

1. Double-click the image icon for the layer in the Layers palette.
2. In the Layer Style dialog, choose Outer Glow.
3. For Opacity, choose 100%. For Noise, choose 0.
4. Click the yellow square to set the color of the glow.
5. Click in an image to select a color, or select a color in the Color Picker. Click OK.
6. For Spread, choose 0. For Size, move the slider until you like the appearance of the glow.

Applying the layer style to another image

1. In the Layers palette, right-click (Ctrl-click) a layer name and choose Copy Layer Style.
2. Right-click (Ctrl-click) another layer and choose Paste Layer Style.

Design 8: Adding a bevel

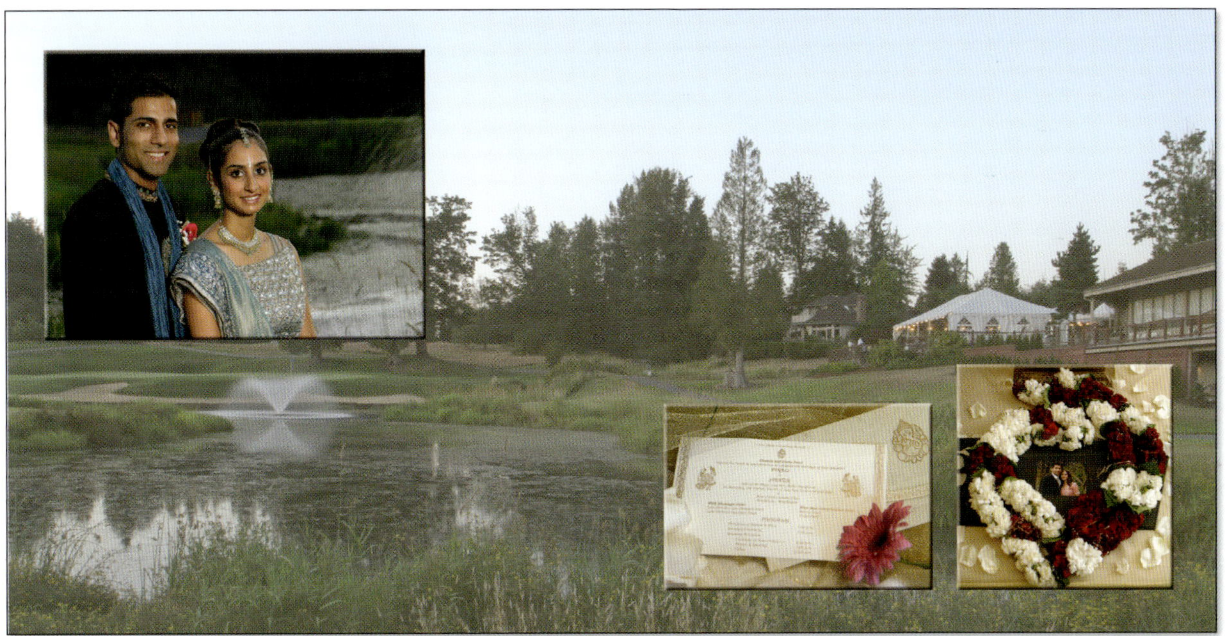

Design Notes

A bevel looks nice applied to images or applied to text. In this example, an inner bevel gives the images a dimensional appearance. You can use an outer bevel to create a virtual mat, as you'll see in Design 21.

Adding a bevel

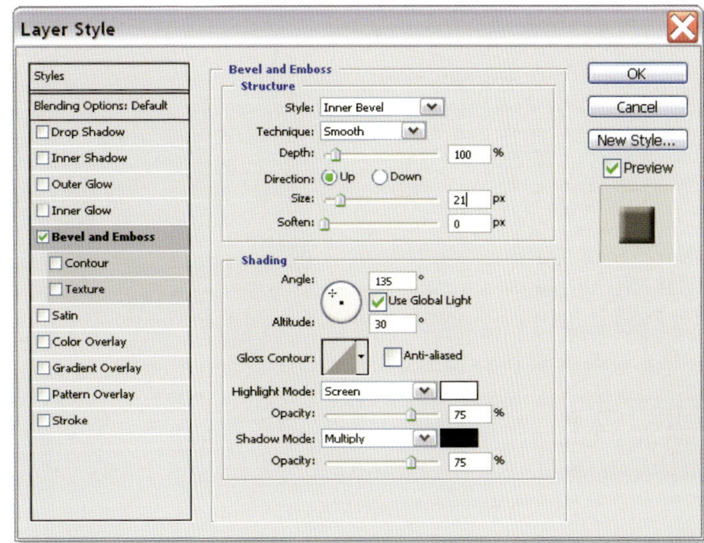

1. Double-click the image icon for the layer in the Layers palette.
2. In the Layer Style dialog, choose Bevel and Emboss.
3. For Style, choose Inner Bevel.
4. For Technique, choose Smooth.
5. For Direction, choose Up.
6. For Depth and Size, move the sliders until you like the appearance of the bevel.

   In this example, Depth is set to 100% and size is set to 21 pixels.

Design 9: Designing with "first glance" images

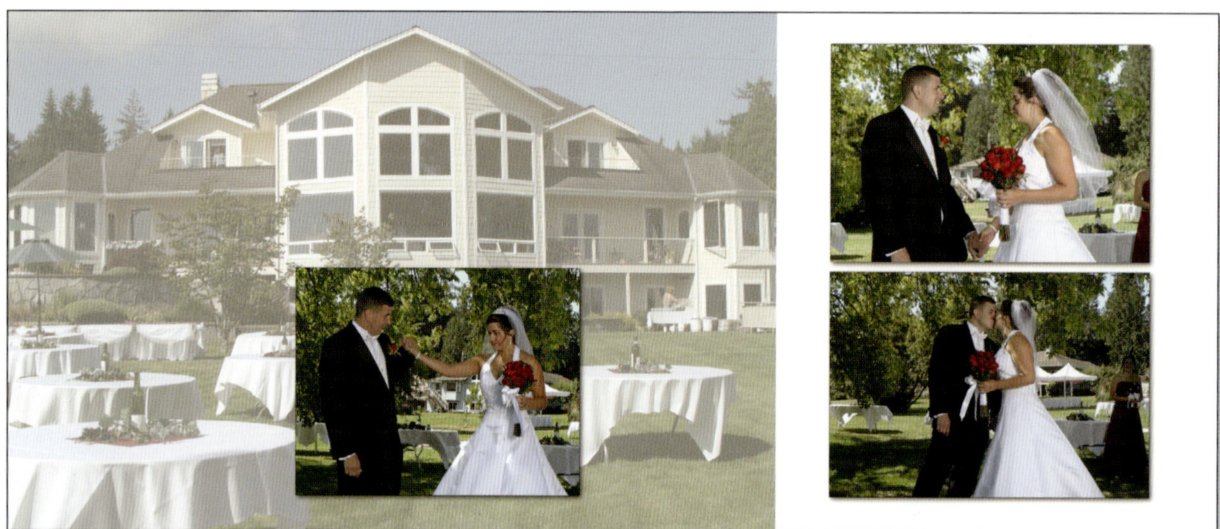

Design notes

We like to talk with couples about taking all the formal portraits before the ceremony. Some brides are reluctant at first to have the groom see them before they walk down the aisle. However, when I tell them about how we set up the "first glance" moment (and about how they will go straight from the ceremony to the reception and begin enjoying the party right away!), they can see the benefits.

For the First Glance moment, we always carry walkie-talkies. My husband waits with the groom while I stay with the bride and capture the last few "getting ready" pictures.

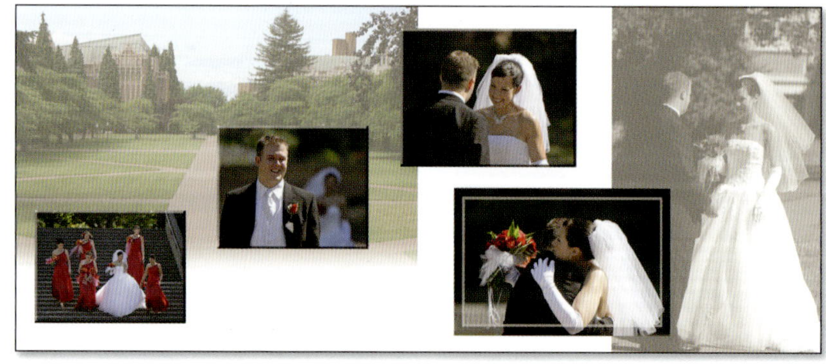

When the bride is about to arrive where the groom is waiting, we have the groom turn his back. Those images of the groom's smiles when the bride comes up behind him are often some of the bride's favorites.

We use a long lens so we can capture images unobtrusively as they greet each other and share their feelings.

Design 10: Setting the mood for the ceremony

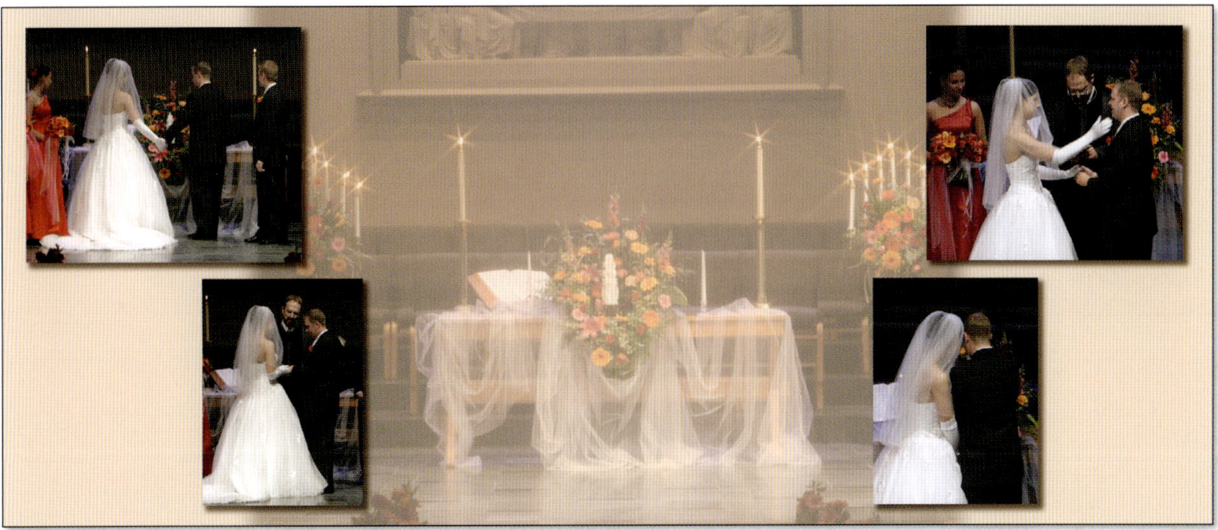

Design notes

This image in the sanctuary was taken with a six-point star filter. It makes a beautiful background for the special moments during the ceremony. The flowers and the décor meant a great deal to the bride because she is a florist and did all the arrangements herself.

In this design, the color on the Background layer was allowed to show through the semitransparent background image, adding a warm glow to the scene.

Scaling the background image

1. With the Zoom tool, adjust the window until you can see all four sides of the page spread, holding Alt (Option) to zoom out, if necessary.
2. Drag out the window border to make it larger than the canvas.
3. Add a background image to the page spread and press Ctrl+T (⌘-T) for Free Transform.
4. Holding Shift, drag one corner of the image to enlarge it.

   You can drag within the image (without holding Shift) to move it before you're finished scaling. Hold Alt (Option) while dragging to scale outward from the center.
5. Press Enter to accept the transformation.

Lowering the opacity of the background image

- With the background image selected in the Layers palette, lower the opacity by dragging the Opacity slider to approximately 50%.

Adding a soft edge to the background image

1. Press M for the Marquee tool and drag out a selection that remains inside the image on both sides.
2. Press Alt+Ctrl+D (Option-⌘-D) for Feather and type a number around 80. Click OK.
3. Press Shift+Ctrl+I (Shift-⌘-I) for Inverse.
4. With the background image layer selected in the Layers palette, press Delete.

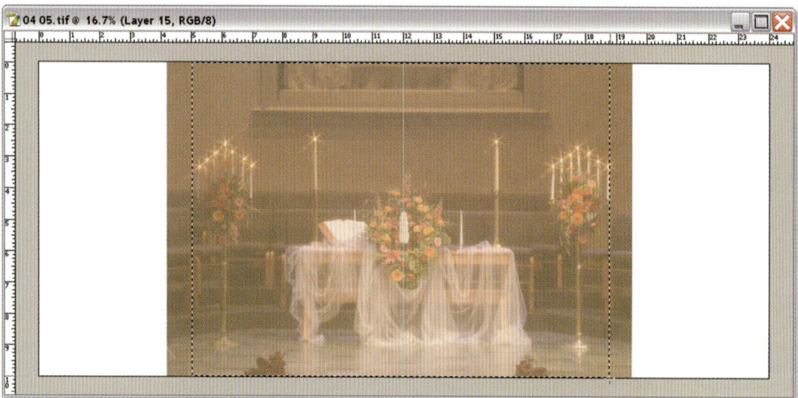

Zoom in and check to make sure you can't see where the edge of the background image was before you pressed Delete. If you can see it, you have two options for fixing this.

For the most professional look, be careful not to leave the original image edge visible.

Fixing problems with soft edges

When you use a large amount of feathering to delete and create a soft edge, you may sometimes see the original edge of the image faintly. This looks less than professional, and you'll want to fix the problem.

Option 1: Making the feathering amount smaller

If the original edge of the image shows after deleting, making the feathering amount smaller is one way to fix the problem.

1. In the History palette, select the Rectangular Marquee step.

2. Press Alt+Ctrl+D (Option-⌘-D) for Feather and enter a smaller number than the one you just tried.
3. Press Shift+Ctrl+I (Shift-⌘-I) for Inverse.
4. Press Delete.

Option 2: Making the selection farther inside the image

The other way to get rid of the original image edge is by making a selection that's farther inside the image.

1. In the History palette, click the step before the Rectangular Marquee step.
2. Drag out a selection that stays farther away from the image edge (closer to the center of the image).
3. Press Alt+Ctrl+D (Option-⌘-D) for Feather and enter the same number you used before.
4. Press Shift+Ctrl+I (Shift-⌘-I) for Inverse.
5. Press Delete.

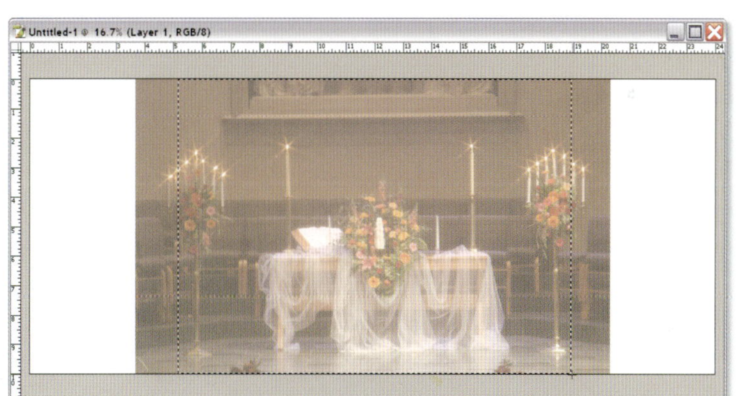

Adding a background color

In this example, the background image was left semitransparent. This way, when a background color is added, it will show through the image.

1. Press Ctrl+D (⌘-D) to clear any selections, if necessary.
2. Click the Background layer in the Layers palette.
3. Press I for the Eyedropper.
4. Click a color in the image to specify a coordinating color for the background.
5. Press Alt+Backspace (Option-Delete) to fill the Background layer with color.
6. If necessary, press Ctrl+L (⌘-L) for Levels and adjust the color and brightness of the background color.

Design 11: Creating a center glow background

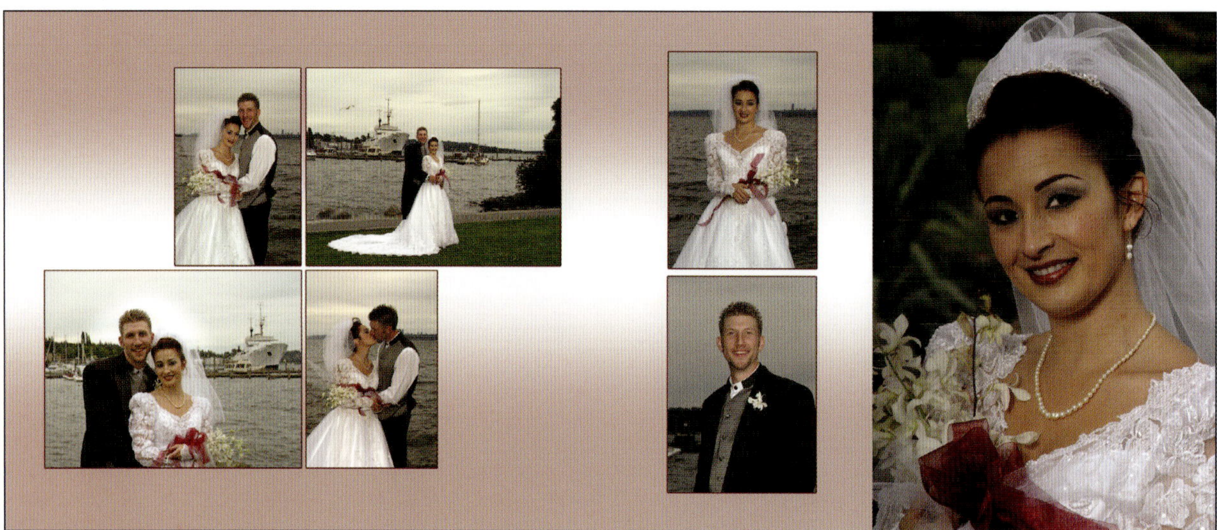

Design notes

This type of graduated background is easy to create by deleting a feathered selection. You'll want to create a new layer for the graduated effect, because if you add the color to the Background layer, you won't be able to easily lower the opacity if you want to later. You can create the same effect using a gradient fill, but this way is faster and easier.

Instead of grouping images by orientation, with the portrait images together on the page and the landscape images together, try lining up the inside corners and see what happens. In this case, it created a more interesting layout.

Adding color on a new layer

1. In the Layers palette, select the blank Background layer, and press Ctrl+Alt+Shift+N (⌘-Option-Shift-N) to create a new layer.
2. With this new layer selected in the Layers palette, click the Set Foreground Color swatch in the toolbox.
3. Set the color to something close to what you want in the background for this page.

   It's not critical that you get the color exactly right at this point, and it's okay if it's too dark.
4. Click OK.

5. Press Alt+Backspace (Option-Delete) to fill the layer with this color.

Creating a horizontal center glow

1. Zoom the window out and resize the frame so you have empty space around the canvas.
2. Drag a rectangle across the middle of the page spread, starting and ending your selection outside the edges of the canvas so it fills the entire page.
3. Press Alt+Ctrl+D (Option-⌘-D) for Feather.
4. Type a large number, such as 200, and click OK.
5. Press Delete.

Changing the feathering amount

It's easy to change the look of this effect. Click the Rectangular Marquee step in the History palette to undo the feathering and deleting. Again press Ctrl+Alt+D (⌘-Option-D) for Feather, type a new value, and click OK. Then press Delete.

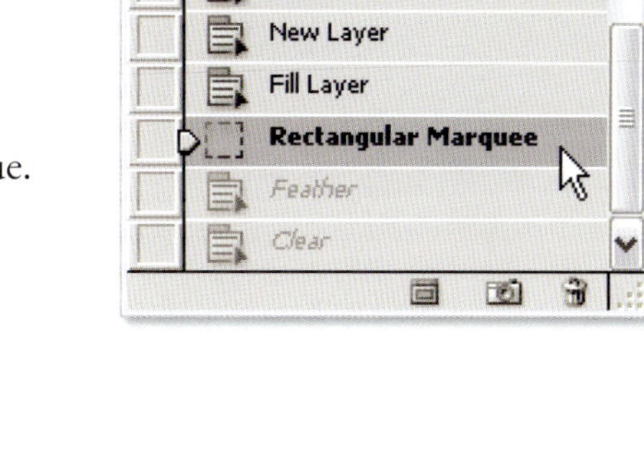

You can also create a vertical center glow by using the same technique.

Modifying the background color

Now adjust the color of the background so it works well with the images placed on the page.

1. Press Ctrl+D (⌘-D) to clear any selections, if necessary.
2. Press Ctrl+L (⌘-L) for Levels.
3. Choose the Red channel and adjust the middle slider as necessary to achieve a good color.
4. Choose the Green and Blue channels and adjust the middle sliders as necessary. Click OK.
5. In the Layers palette, dial down the Opacity to fade the background color, if necessary.

Design 12: Creating a mirror image for the background

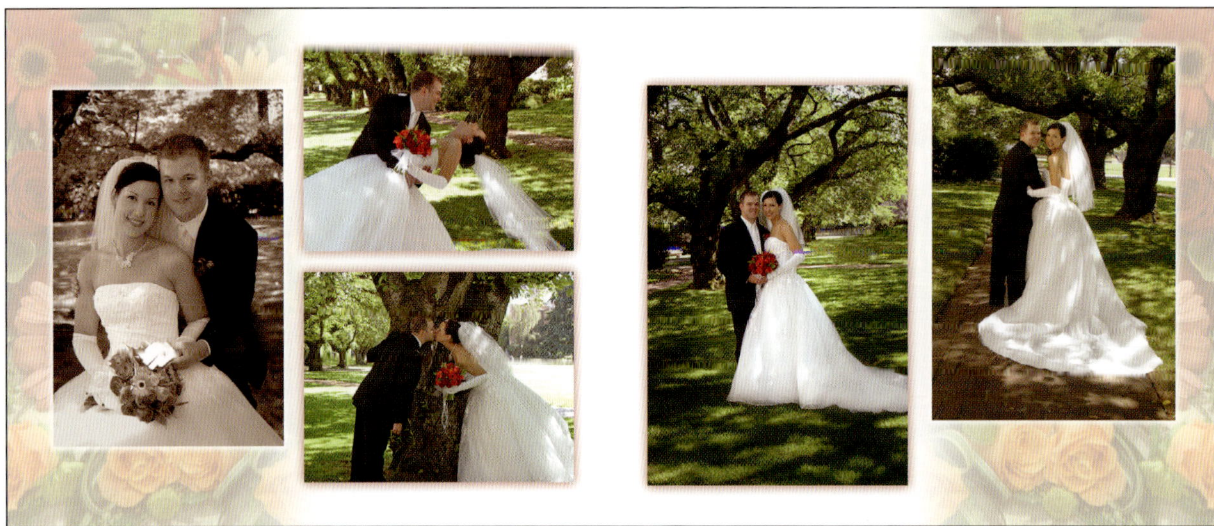

Design notes

This background image was shot just after the florist had delivered all the bouquets. It was copied and flipped horizontally to make two mirror images of the flowers.

1. Crop a nice background image in its own window to make it relatively tall and narrow.
2. In the page spread window, drag out the window border to make it larger than the canvas.
3. Paste the image into the page spread, press Ctrl+T (⌘-T) for Free Transform, and scale the image until it's tall enough to fill the page from top to bottom. Press Enter to accept the transformation.
4. Press Ctrl+D (⌘-D) to deselect the image.

   If the image is selected when you do the next step, the duplicate image will be created on the same layer as the original. This would make it more difficult to flip and move the duplicated image.
5. Press V for the Move tool and, while holding Alt+Shift (Option-Shift), drag a copy of the image to one side, leaving space between the two. This creates a duplicate of the image on a new layer.

6. From the Edit menu, choose Transform and then choose Flip Horizontal. This creates a mirror image of the first image.
7. Holding Shift, drag the flipped version to the correct location on the opposite page.

   Holding Shift constrains the movement horizontally.
8. Press Ctrl+E (⌘-E) to merge the two layers.
9. Lower the opacity of the images by dragging the Opacity slider in the Layers palette.

Giving the mirror images a soft edge

After you have created the mirror images, you can easily create a soft inside edge for both of them. Before doing the following procedure, drag the window border out to create space around the canvas.

1. Using the Marquee tool, drag out a selection in the background image layer that overlaps the inside edge of each background image by the same amount.
2. Press Alt+Ctrl+D (Option-⌘-D) for Feather, and enter a large number such as 80. Click OK.
3. Press Delete.

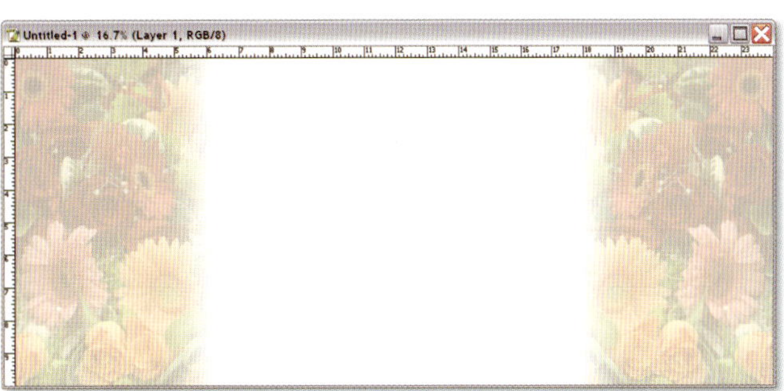

Make sure the formerly straight edges are no longer visible. If you can see the straight edges faintly, use one of the techniques in Design 10 to fix the problem.

Design 13: Creating a bubble effect

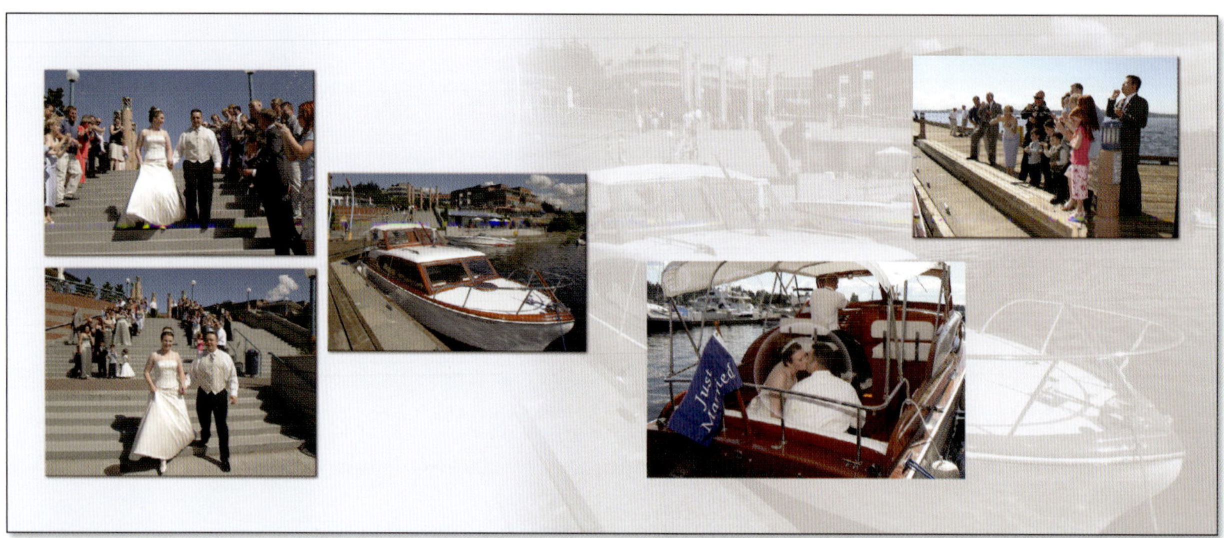

Design notes

I don't recommend using this kind of fabricated design element if it's not in keeping with what's happening in the moment portrayed. I like to keep designs simple and elegant. But some clients do enjoy playful touches like the bubble in this example, and I think it works here because bubbles filled the air as the couple departed from the reception.

1. In the individual image window, press Ctrl+A (⌘-A) and Ctrl+Shift+J (⌘-Shift-J) to select the image, cut it, and paste it onto its own layer.
2. Click the Set Foreground Color swatch in the toolbox and set the foreground color to:
   - R: 220
   - G: 220
   - B: 250
3. In the Layers palette, click the blank Background layer and press Alt+Backspace (Option-Delete) to fill it with color.
4. With the Elliptical Marquee tool, hold Shift and drag a circular selection around the subjects.

   Hold the spacebar if you need to move the circle as you drag.
5. Click the image layer to select it in the Layers palette.

After step 6, the Layers palette will look something like this.

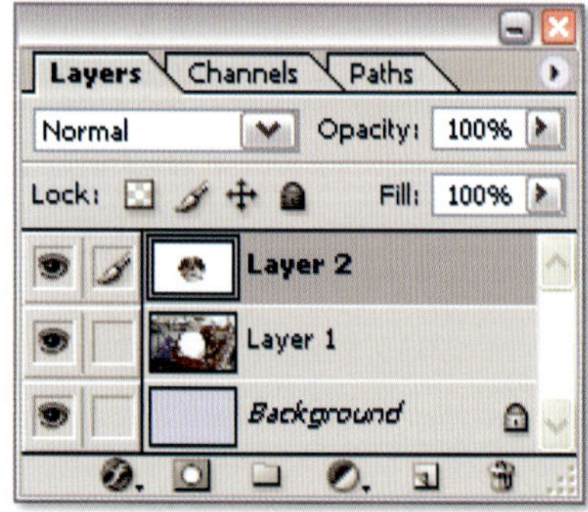

6. Press Ctrl+Shift+J (⌘-Shift-J) to cut and paste the circle onto its own layer.
7. Hold Ctrl (⌘)and click the image icon in the Layers palette to select the circle.
8. Press Alt+Ctrl+D (Option-⌘-D) and give it a feather of 25.
9. Press Shift+Ctrl+I (Shift-⌘-I) to invert the selection.
10. Press Delete.

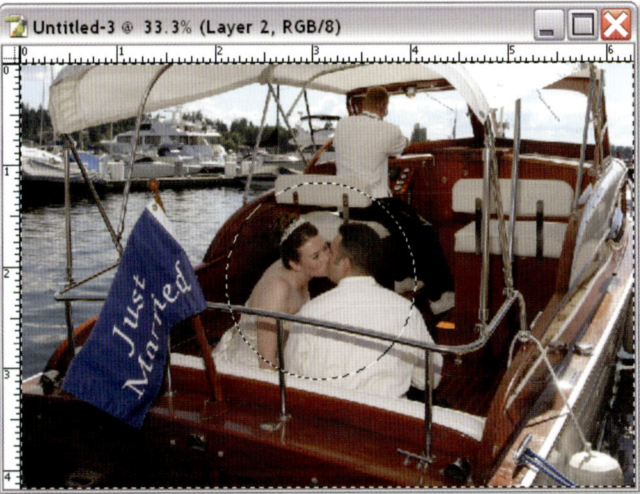

You may want to add one or two more bubbles for a more realistic effect. After you're finished, flatten the image and paste it into the page spread window.

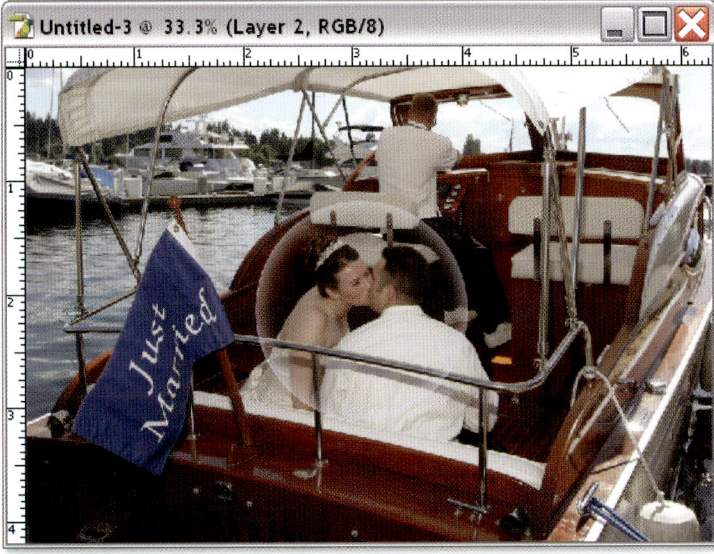

Design 14: Adding decorative bars

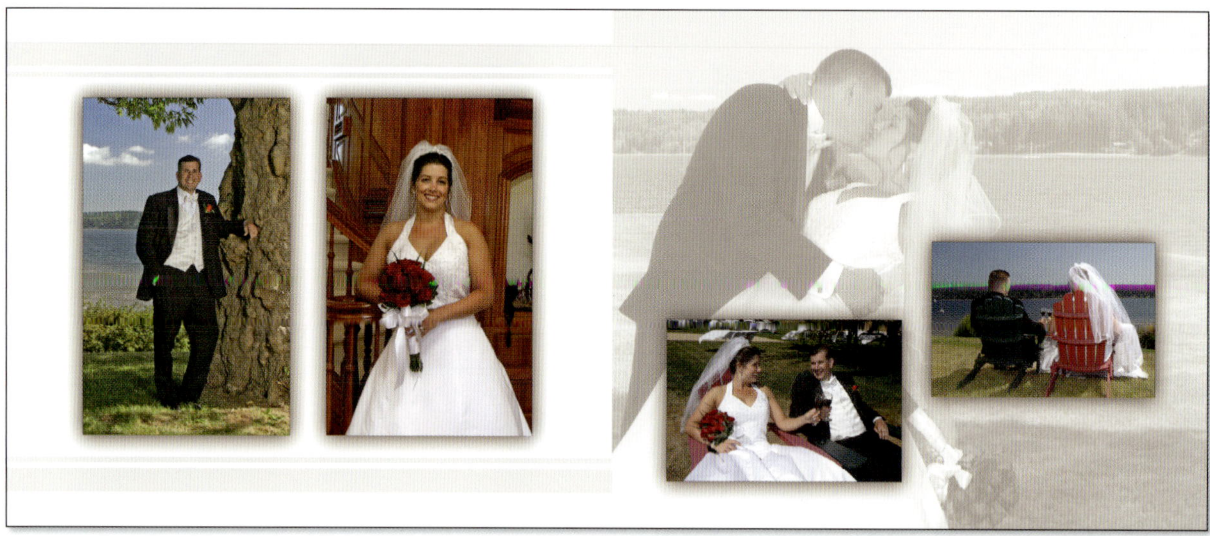

Design notes

One tricky part of this design is making sure there's a clean transition where the semitransparent background meets the bars. You don't want a gap there, nor do you want the right edge of the bars showing under the background image. The best way to make this look perfect is to create bars going all the way across the page and then put a screened-back opaque image over one side, hiding the bars on the right page.

Remember to keep design elements such as these at least three-quarters of an inch from the edge of the page, especially if you plan to produce a parent album, too.

Before beginning, drag the window frame open to provide space around the canvas. We'll create the background image first so we can sample color from it for the bars. Paste an image on the page, scale it up to fill half the page, and lower the opacity, as explained in Design 1.

Making a background image opaque

1. Drag the image layer to just above the Background layer.
2. Hold Ctrl (⌘) and click the image icon in the image layer.

   This selects the image. Leave the image selected through the next two steps.

3. Press Ctrl+E (⌘-E) to merge the semitransparent image into the Background layer.
4. Press Ctrl+Shift+J (⌘-Shift-J) to cut the image and paste it onto its own layer.

Now the screened-back image is no longer transparent, and you're ready to add the horizontal bars.

Creating the first set of decorative bars

1. In the Layers palette, select the Background layer and press Alt+Shift+Ctrl+N (Option-Shift-⌘-N) to create a new empty layer.
2. Press I for the Eyedropper and click inside the left edge of the background image to sample the color nearest the edge.
3. Press M for the Marquee tool and drag out a selection for the wide bar at the top, all the way across the top of the page. For selections such as this, you can drag from outside one edge of the canvas to outside the other.

   The portion of the bar on the right side will eventually be hidden behind the background image.
4. Press Alt+Backspace (Option-Delete) to fill the selection with the sampled color.
5. Drag out a selection for the narrow bar and again fill it with color using Alt+Backspace (Option-Delete).

Creating the second set of decorative bars

1. Press V for the Move tool, hold Shift+Alt (Shift-Option), and drag down to create a duplicate set of bars on a new layer.
2. From the Edit menu, choose Transform, and then choose Flip Vertical.
3. With the Move tool, hold Shift to constrain the movement vertically, then drag the new bars to the appropriate location near the bottom of the page.
4. Press Ctrl+E (⌘-E) to merge the two layers of bars.

You can now drag the opaque image layer over the bars layer in the Layers palette (if necessary) to hide the bars on one side of the page.

Design 15: Creating a screened-back frame

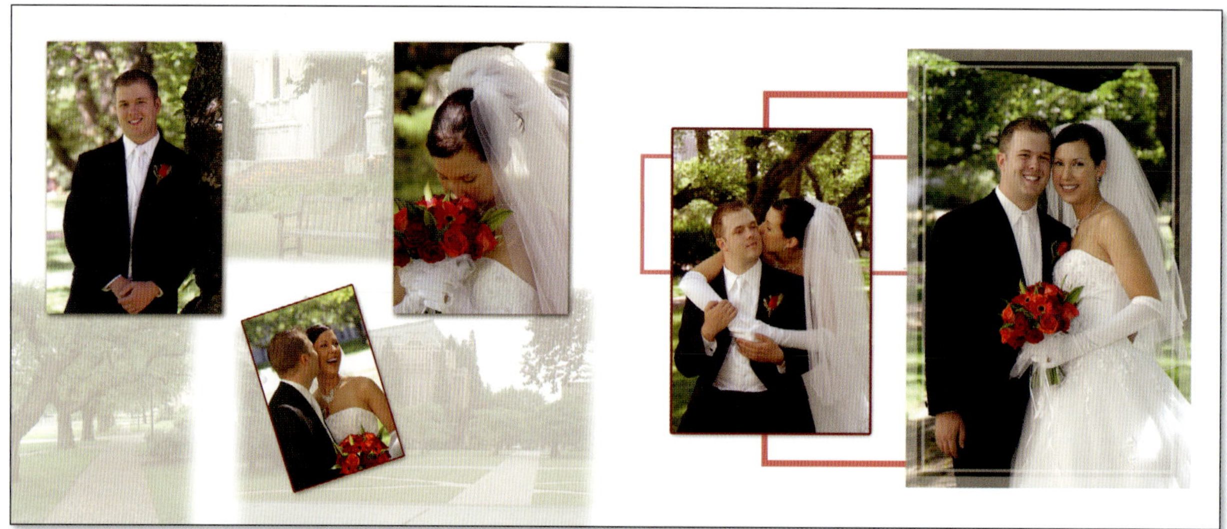

Design notes

A screened-back frame is one in which you've taken the outside border of the image itself and lowered the opacity to create an interesting frame effect.

For the most professional look, it's important that the selections in this technique are precise, with exactly the same amount of space on all sides. The best technique for achieving that precision involves using a layer mask and contracting selections. After you learn this method, you'll learn a second method that's faster but less precise.

The slower, precise method

1. In the Layers palette, select the image layer and press Ctrl+J (⌘-J) to create a duplicate layer.
2. Click the original image layer in the Layers palette to select it, and drag the Opacity slider down to approximately 50%.

   You won't see a change at this point because the opaque image hides the semitransparent one beneath it.
3. Again click the top layer in the Layers palette to select it.
4. Hold Ctrl (⌘) and click the image icon to select the image.
5. Click the Add Layer Mask icon at the bottom of the Layers palette.

6. Hold Ctrl (⌘) and click the image icon again to select the image.
7. Click the layer mask icon to select the mask if it's not selected.
8. Press D for default foreground and background colors and press Ctrl+Backspace (⌘-Delete) to temporarily hide all of the opaque image.
9. From the Select menu, choose Modify and then choose Contract. Enter a number such as 60. Click OK.
10. Press Alt+Backspace (Option-Delete) to show the selected part of the opaque image.
11. From the Select menu, choose Modify and then choose Contract. Enter a number such as 15. Click OK.
12. Press Ctrl+Backspace (⌘-Delete) to temporarily hide the selected portion of the opaque image.
13. From the Select menu, choose Modify and then choose Contract. Enter a number such as 8. Click OK.
14. Press Alt+Backspace (Option-Delete) to once again show the selected portion of the opaque image.

For another variation, add a Bevel and Emboss style to the top layer or to both layers (see Design 8). And if you want to be able to add other design elements or colors behind the semitransparent frame without having them show through it, you'll need to make that layer opaque. You can do this by following the instructions in Design 14.

The faster, "eyeballing" method

Follow steps 1 through 4 above, so you have two versions of the image, with the one on the upper layer selected. Then do the following.

1. From the Select menu, choose Modify and then choose Contract. Enter a number such as 40. Click OK.
2. From the Select menu, choose Inverse. Press Delete.
3. Press M for the Marquee tool, and drag out a selection inside the remaining opaque image.
4. Holding Alt (Option), drag out a second selection inside the first, to create a thin double selection.

   Hold the spacebar to create even spacing between the two selections, if necessary.
5. Press Delete.

Click to select the layer mask.

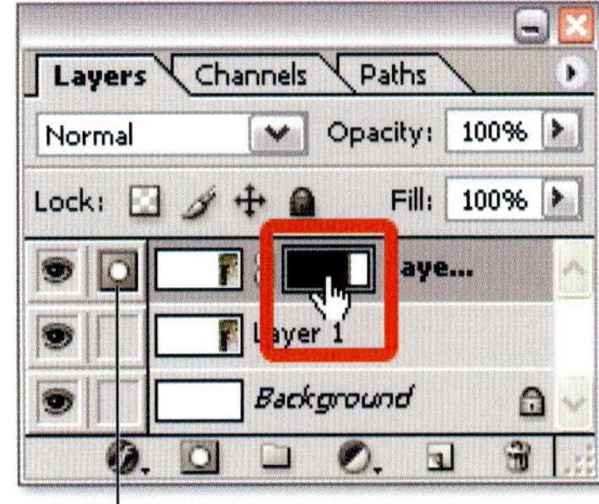

Indicates the layer mask is selected.

Pressing Ctrl+Backspace (⌘-Delete) fills the selection with the background color. When you're working with a layer mask and using default foreground and background colors, filling the selection with black means "make this area completely transparent."

Pressing Alt+Backspace (Option-Delete) fills the selection with the foreground color. When you're working with a layer mask, filling the selection with white means "make this area completely opaque."

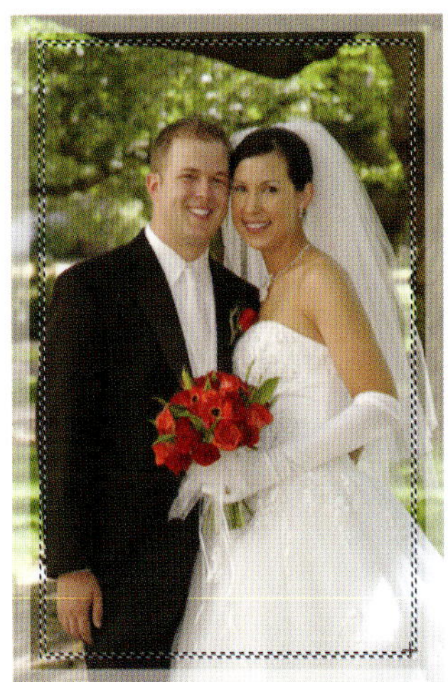

Design 16: Creating "snapshots"

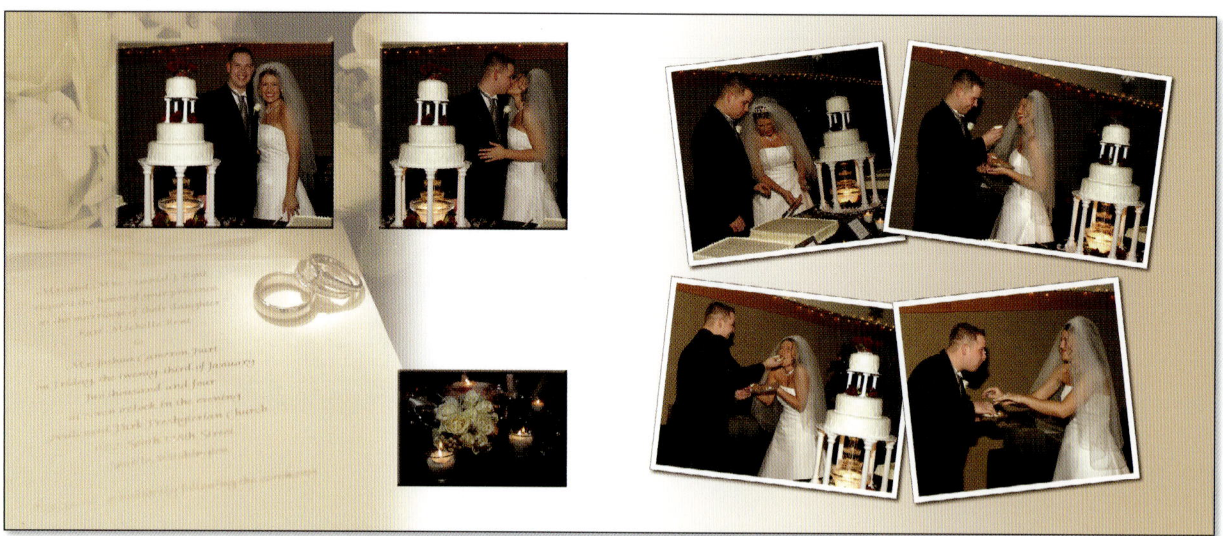

Design notes

The images on the left page were not rotated because they convey a more formal feeling; a playful design would be less appropriate there. But when the fun began on the right page, the images were given borders and were rotated to give them the feeling of candid snapshots. Notice that a coordinating background color was used in a gradient fill on the right page to balance out the background image on the left. This helps keep the focus within the page spread. To learn how to do a gradient fill, see Design 23.

You might wonder why a wide white stroke wasn't used to create the white frame. If you use an Outside stroke or a Center stroke, the corners would be rounded. And if you use a wide Inside stroke (in order to get square corners), it would probably obscure an unacceptably large portion of the image because Inside strokes are added inside the border of the image.

Creating the appearance of snapshots

1. Crop an image in its own window. If there's more than one layer, press Ctrl+E (⌘-E) to flatten the image.
2. Press D to set the foreground and background colors to their defaults of black and white.
3. From the Image menu, choose Image size.

4. Making sure Resample image is unchecked, type something like 4 inches for width. Click OK.

   This number doesn't affect the pixels in the image. It only changes the appearance of the rulers and makes it easier for you to guess a reasonable amount to add for the white border.

5. To add the white border, choose Canvas Size from the Image menu.
6. Check the Relative option.
7. Type a number, such as 0.25 inches for both Width and Height, and click OK.

   If you'd like the border to be larger or smaller, click the previous step in the History palette, and try a different relative size.

8. Drag this image from the Layers palette to the page spread window.

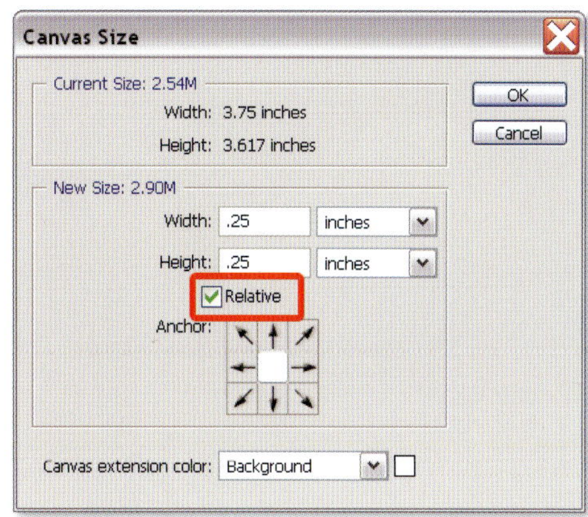

If the image is pasted in without the white border, this means it wasn't flattened in its own window. To fix this, in the page spread window, drag this image layer to the Delete Layer icon in the Layers palette. In the individual image window again, press Ctrl+E (⌘-E) to flatten the image, and then redrag the image layer into the page spread window.

After pasting the image into your page spread, add a 1-pixel black stroke and a drop shadow (see Design 2). Now rotate a few for a fun and casual look.

Rotating an image

1. Select the appropriate layer in the Layers palette.
2. Press Ctrl+T (⌘-T) for Free Transform.
3. Drag anywhere outside the image to rotate it.

   You can drag inside the image to move it on the page before applying the rotation. You can also hold Shift and drag a corner handle to scale down before completing the transformation.

4. When you're finished rotating, press Enter to apply the change.

After pressing Ctrl+T (⌘-T), drag outside the image to rotate it.

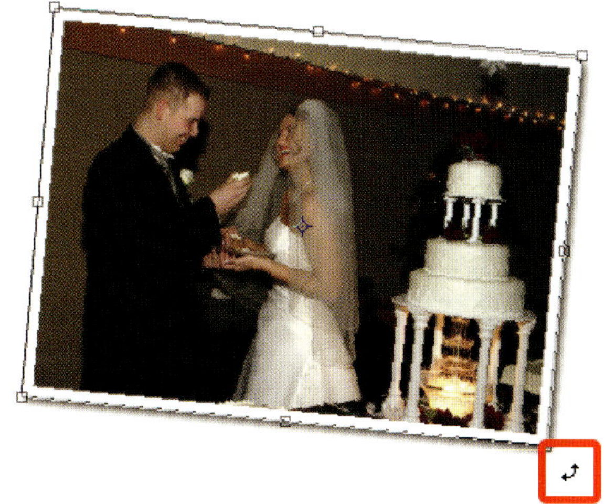

Design 17: Creating a gold frame

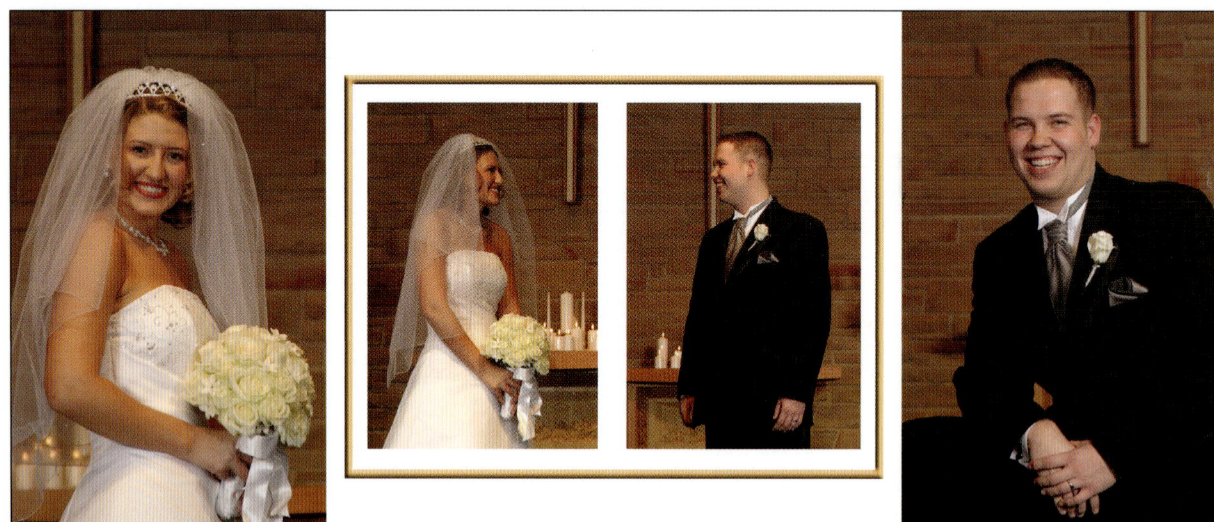

Design notes

Adding a gold frame is a nice way to draw attention to an image or a set of images. It also serves to establish a relationship between similar images.

When you're photographing the bride and the groom separately, consider asking them to face a certain way for a few of the individual images. Keep in mind to ask the groom to face left, for instance, and then later, to ask the bride to face right. You can even say, "Imagine you're looking at your gorgeous bride over there." This gives you the opportunity to lay out images as you see on this page spread, with the subject in every image directing attention toward the other images.

Creating the frame

Before you begin, make sure you have a blank Background layer, and make sure Grid is checked under Show on the View menu.

1. Press M for the Marquee tool and drag out a selection around the outside of the image or images.
2. Holding Alt (Option), drag out a second box inside the first one.

   Hold the spacebar, too, if you need to move the selection to make the space between the two selections even all the way around.

3. Click the blank Background layer in the Layers palette.
4. Click the Set Foreground Color swatch in the toolbox.
5. In the Color Picker, set these values for a nice gold tone:

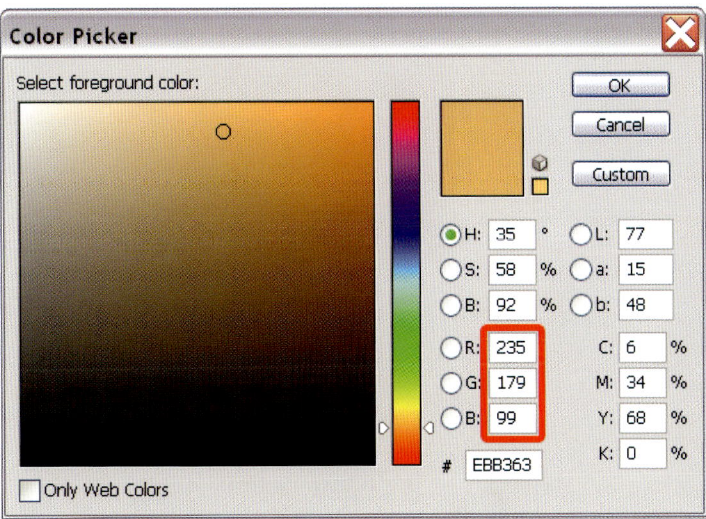

6. Click OK.
7. Press Alt+Backspace (Option-Delete) to fill the selection with gold.
8. Press Ctrl+Shift+J (⌘-Shift-J) to cut the frame and paste it onto its own layer.

Giving the frame a beveled edge

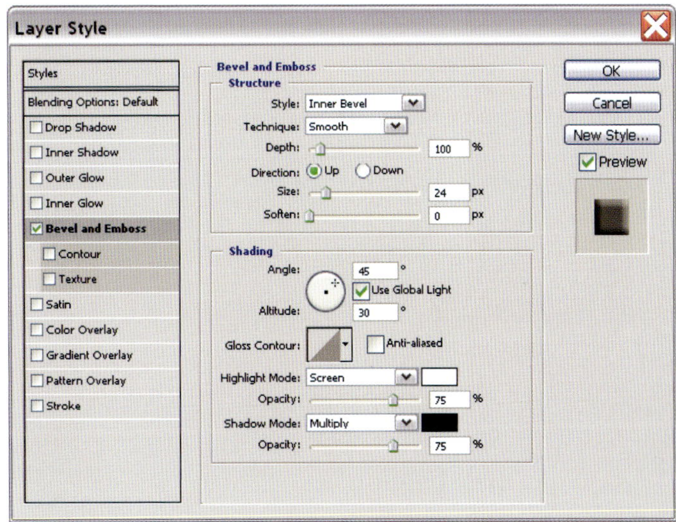

1. Double-click the image icon for the layer in the Layers palette.
2. For Style, choose Inner Bevel.
3. For Direction, choose Up.
4. For Depth and Size, move the sliders until you like the appearance of the bevel.
5. Set the Shading Angle to 135 degrees.

   Applying the same shading angle throughout the album, including in the drop shadows, makes the most sense to the eye.

Design 18: Creating multiple images with the same sepia tone

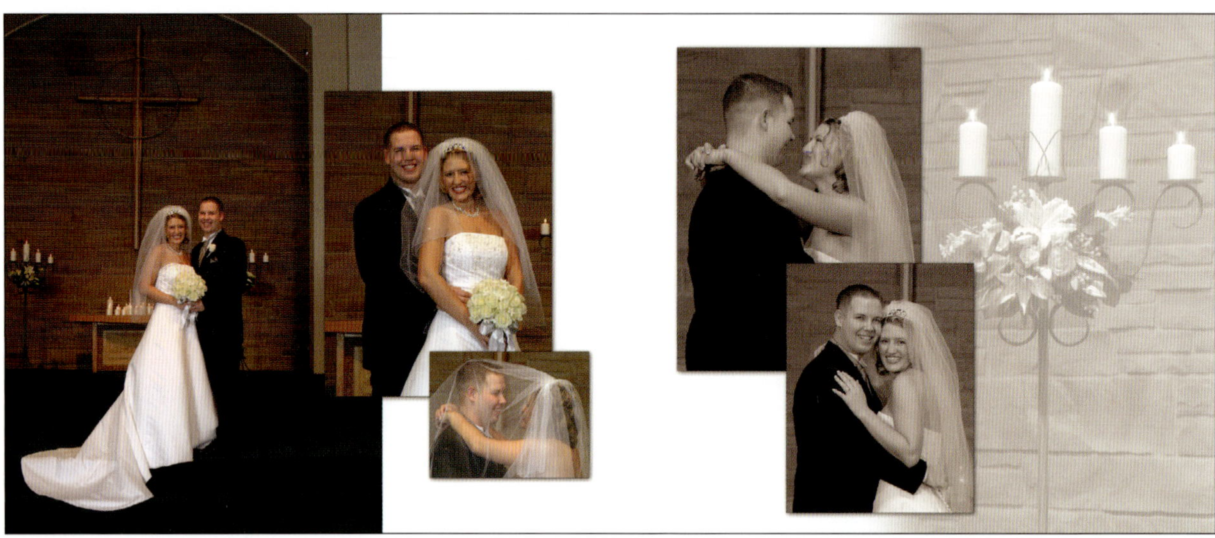

Design notes

The candle image was taken using a four-point star filter. All three images on the right page were changed to the same shade of sepia, and then the candle image was made partially transparent and given a soft edge. You'll learn how to do the soft edge with a layer mask in Design 19.

Photoshop CS includes an action in the Actions palette called Sepia Toning, but I prefer a softer sepia tone with lower contrast.

To create more than one sepia image, create an action. Whereas most of the Designs begin in the page spread window, this one begins in the individual image windows.

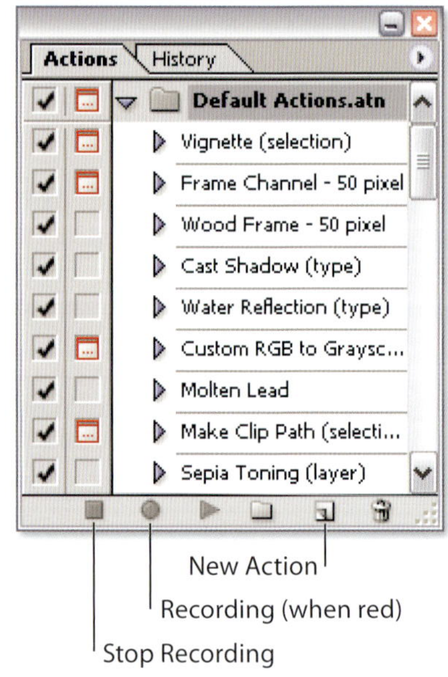

Creating an action for sepia tone

We'll record the action while we change the first image to sepia. First open all three images in their own windows in Photoshop.

1. If the Channels palette is not visible on-screen, choose it on the Window menu.
2. With the first image window selected, click the New Action icon in the Actions palette.
3. Type a name for the action, such as "Custom Sepia," then click Record.

4. From the Image menu, choose Mode and then choose Lab Color.

   If the window contains more than one layer, you'll see a warning about flattening. Click Flatten.

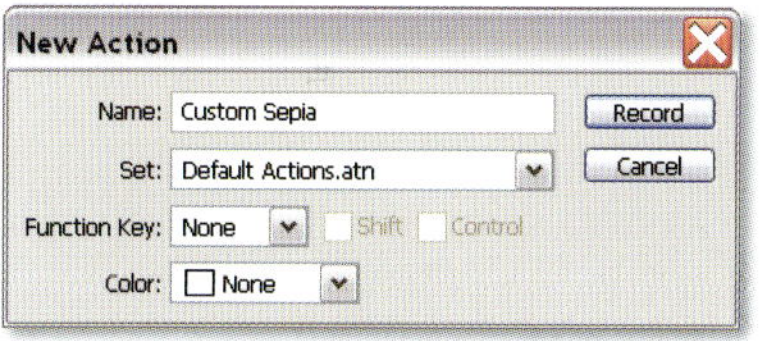

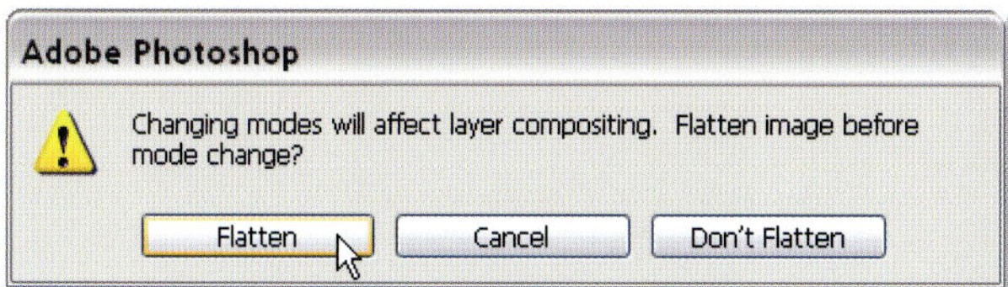

5. In the Channels palette, select the Lightness channel.
6. From the Image menu, choose Mode and then choose Grayscale. Click OK to discard the other channels.

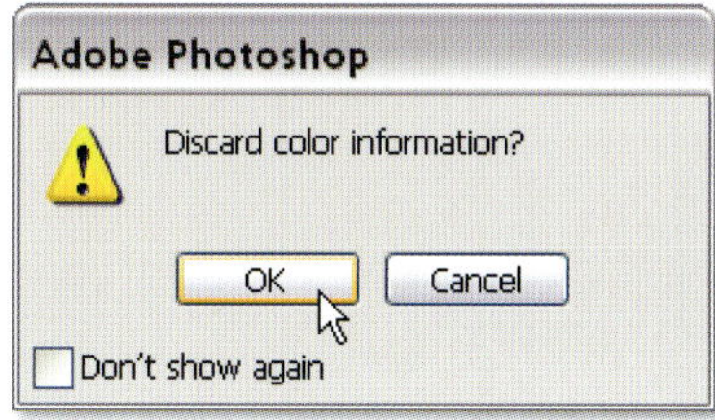

7. From the Image menu, choose Mode and then choose RGB Color.

   The appearance of the image does not change, but switching back to RGB mode is what allows you to apply a sepia tone to the black and white image.

8. Press Ctrl+L (⌘-L) for Levels.
9. Choose the Red channel and drag the midtones slider to 1.20.
10. Choose the Blue channel and drag the midtones slider to .85.

    Apply further adjustments to the Red and Blue channels if necessary, until you have the sepia tone you like. Click OK.

11. In the Actions palette, click the Stop Recording icon.

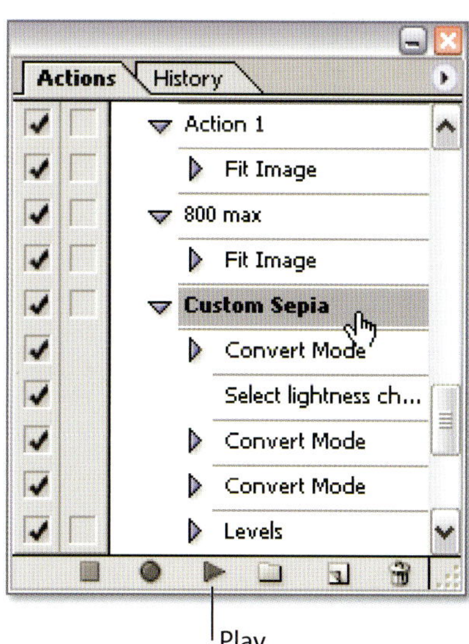

Applying this sepia tone to the other images

1. Select the window containing the second image.
2. In the Actions palette, select the new action.
3. In the Actions palette, click the Play icon.
4. Select any other windows you want to change to sepia and play the action again.

Design 19: Creating a soft edge with a layer mask

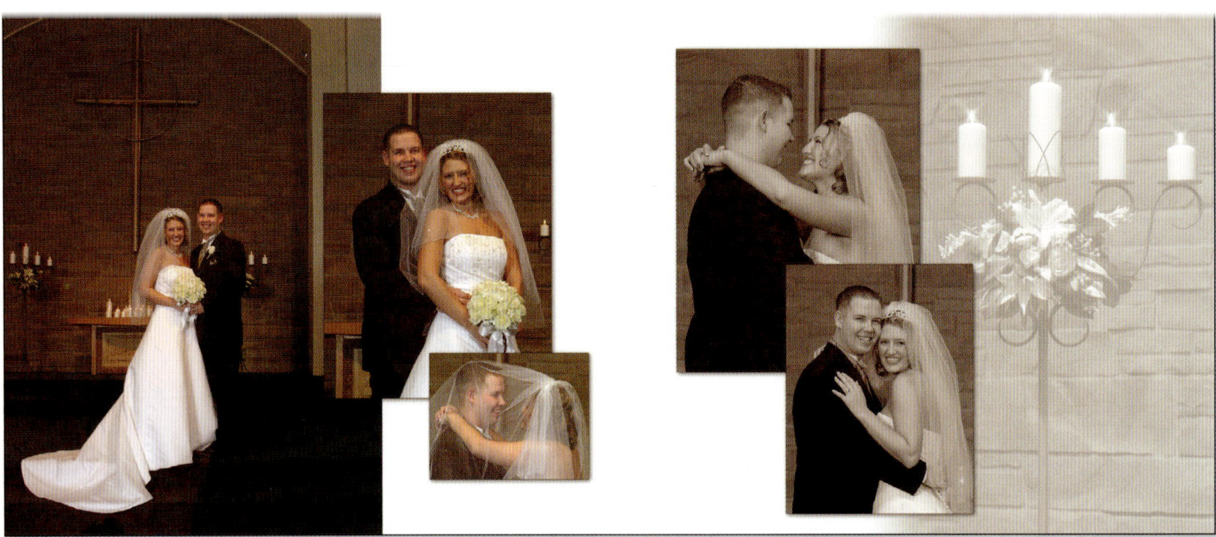

Design notes

The nice thing about using a layer mask for this procedure is that you're not actually deleting part of the image—only hiding it. After you create the soft edge, you can then move the feathered area to adjust its appearance.

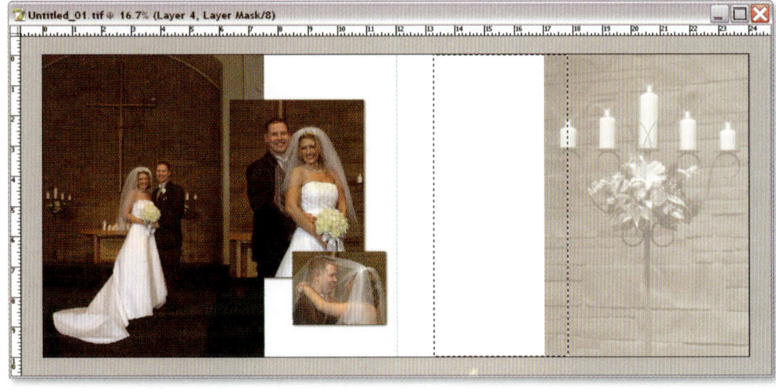

When you fade the edge of an image, be careful to avoid leaving any trace of the straight image edge. Leaving the image edge looks less than professional.

When you create a selection and then add a large amount of feathering, be aware that the feathering extends out in both directions from the selection. For instance, a feather of 80 pixels extends 40 pixels on each side of the selection. Knowing this can help you decide where to place the selection and how much of a feather to apply.

1. Scale the image to fill the page from top to bottom.
2. Lower the opacity of the image until you like its appearance.
3. With that image layer selected in the Layers palette, click the Add Layer Mask icon at the bottom of the Layers palette.

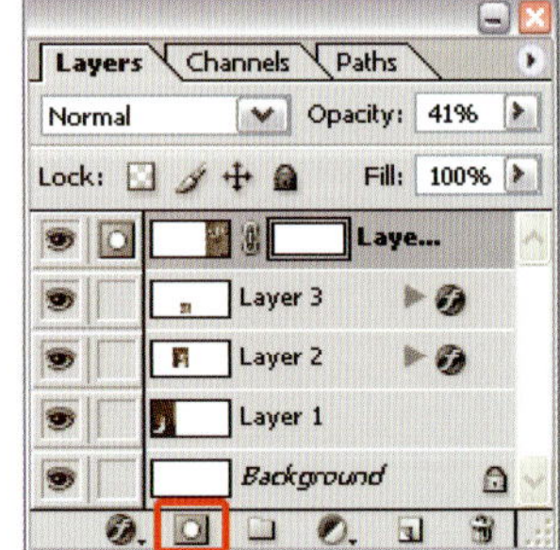

Add Layer Mask icon

4. With the Marquee tool, drag out a selection that overlaps the edge of the image.
5. Press Ctrl+Alt+D (⌘-Option-D) for Feather, and enter a number around 80. Click OK.
6. Press D to set the default colors to white and black.
7. Press Ctrl+Backspace (⌘-Delete) to "fill the selection with black" (which makes the selected part of the image transparent because of the layer mask).

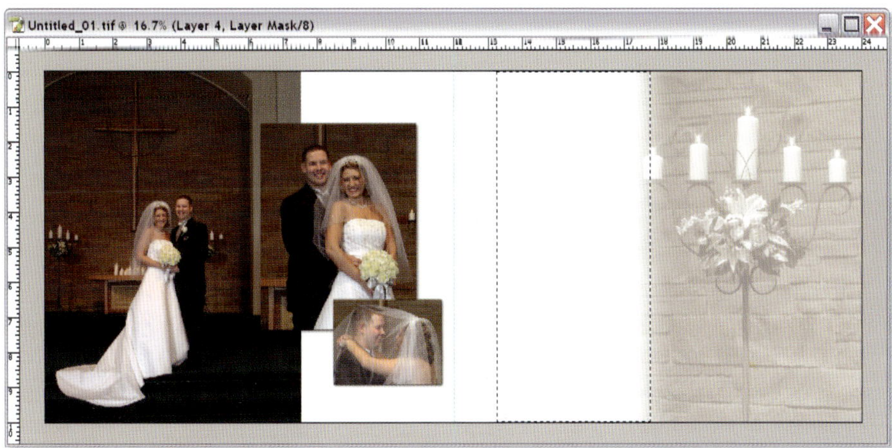

8. To adjust the location of the feathered edge, press V for the Move tool.
9. Press Ctrl+D (⌘-D) to deselect, and then click the Link icon between the layer and its mask in the Layers palette to separate the mask from the image.
10. Use the arrow keys to move the selection.

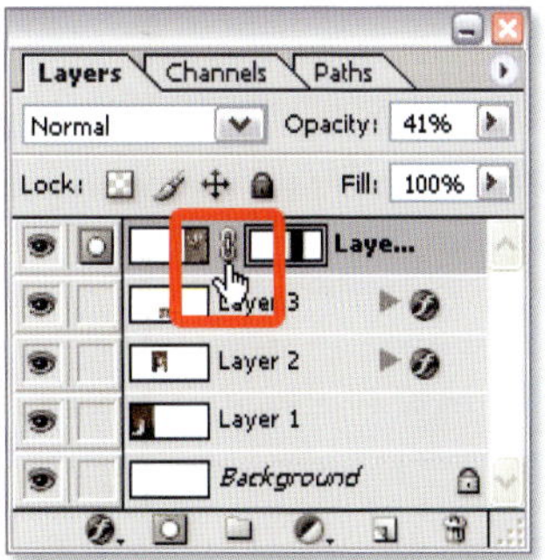

Click here to unlink the layer and the mask.

If you come back to this image later and want to move the location of the feathered edge, make sure the layer mask is selected in the Layers palette.

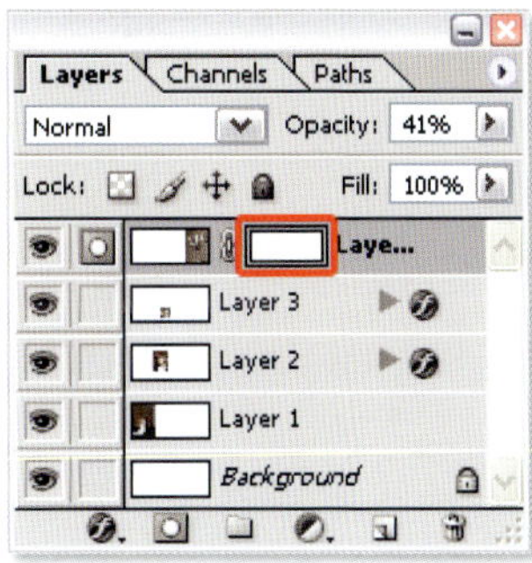

Click here to select the mask.

Design 20: Adding coordinating frames

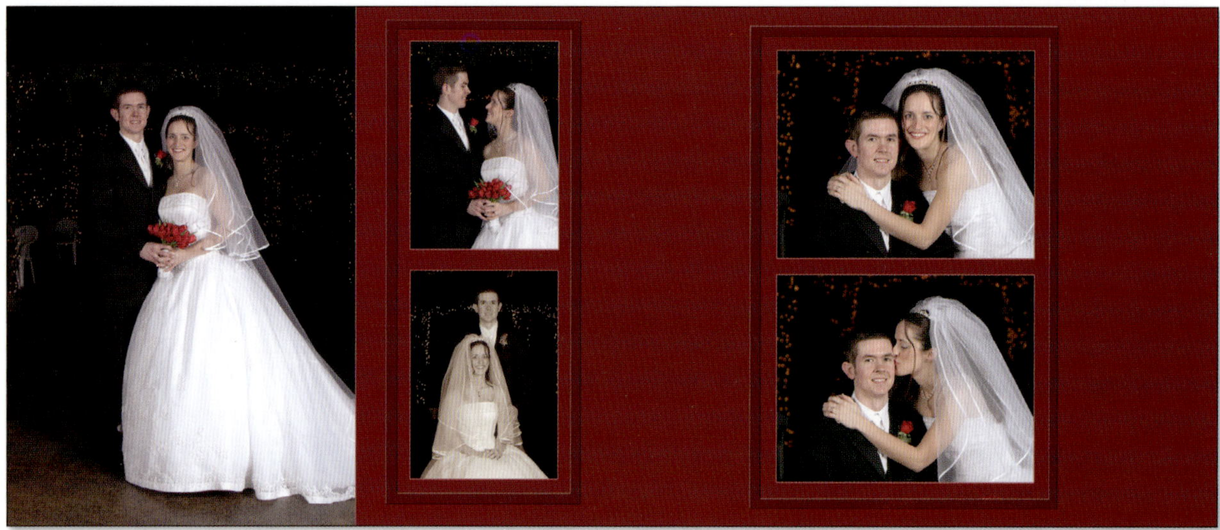

Design notes

This effect creates a frame in a color that coordinates with the background color. First, you'll fill the Background layer with color. You'll create a frame and change its color by changing only the brightness. Next you'll add a layer style to the frame. And as a final touch, you can add a layer style to each image.

Filling the background with color

1. In the toolbox, click the Set Foreground Color swatch and click in the Color Picker to define a color. Click OK.

   You can also click in one of the images on the page to sample a coordinating color. It's not important to specify the exact color at this point because it's easy to change it later.

2. In the Layers palette, click the Background layer and press Alt+Backspace (Option-Delete) to fill it with color.
3. If you want to adjust the color, press Ctrl+L (⌘-L) for Levels.
4. In the Levels dialog, choose the color channels (Red, Green, and Blue) one at a time and drag the Input Levels sliders to adjust the color.
5. With the RGB channel selected, drag the Output Levels sliders to adjust the brightness.

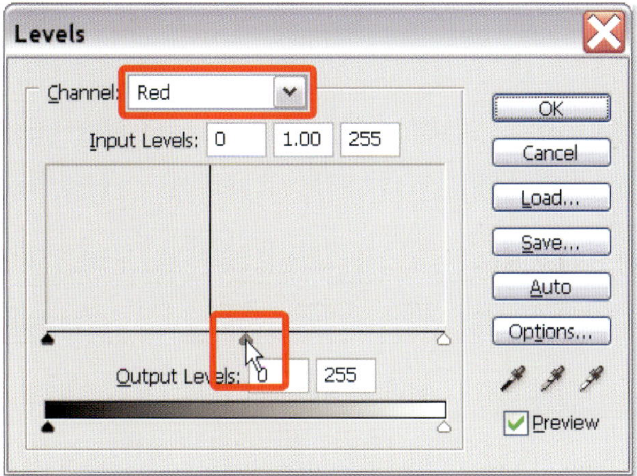

With the Red channel selected, drag the Input Levels sliders to adjust the Color.

Creating the frame and adjusting the luminosity

1. Press Ctrl+' (⌘-') to show the grid, if it's not already displayed.
2. Make sure the colored Background layer is selected in the Layers palette.
3. With the Marquee tool, drag out a selection around one image (or however many you'd like to frame together). Hold the spacebar and watch the grid to create a selection with even spacing all the way around the image or images.

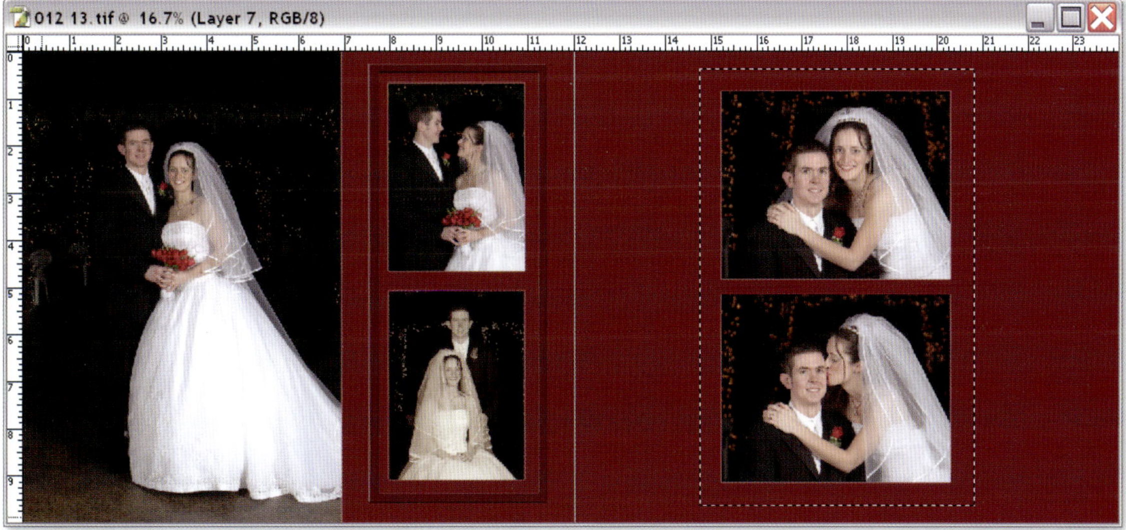

4. Press Ctrl+J (⌘-J) to copy the selection and paste it onto its own layer.

5. Hold Ctrl (⌘) and click the image icon for the new layer to select the color block.
6. From the Select menu, choose Modify and then choose Contract. Enter a number such as 40. Click OK.
7. Press Delete.
8. Press Ctrl+L (⌘-L) for Levels.
9. Drag the Shadows or Midtones input sliders to the right to darken the frame as much as you'd like.

For any other frames on this page spread, use the Eyedropper (I) to select the color you created for the first frame. Create a new frame with the Marquee tool as described above, and then press Alt+Backspace (Option-Delete) to fill the frame with sampled color.

Adding a Bevel and Emboss style to the frame

1. From the Layer menu, choose Layer Style, and then choose Bevel and Emboss.
2. Set these parameters:

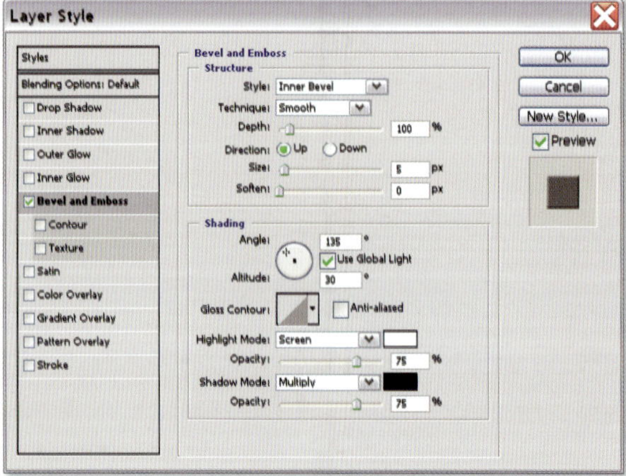

Adding Outer Glow to the images

1. In the Layers palette, double-click the image icon for one of the framed images.
2. Choose Outer Glow.
3. Set the parameters you'd like for the Outer Glow. Click OK.
4. Copy this layer style to the other images by dragging the style name in the Layers palette, just below the names of each of the other layers.

Design 21: Creating a beveled black frame

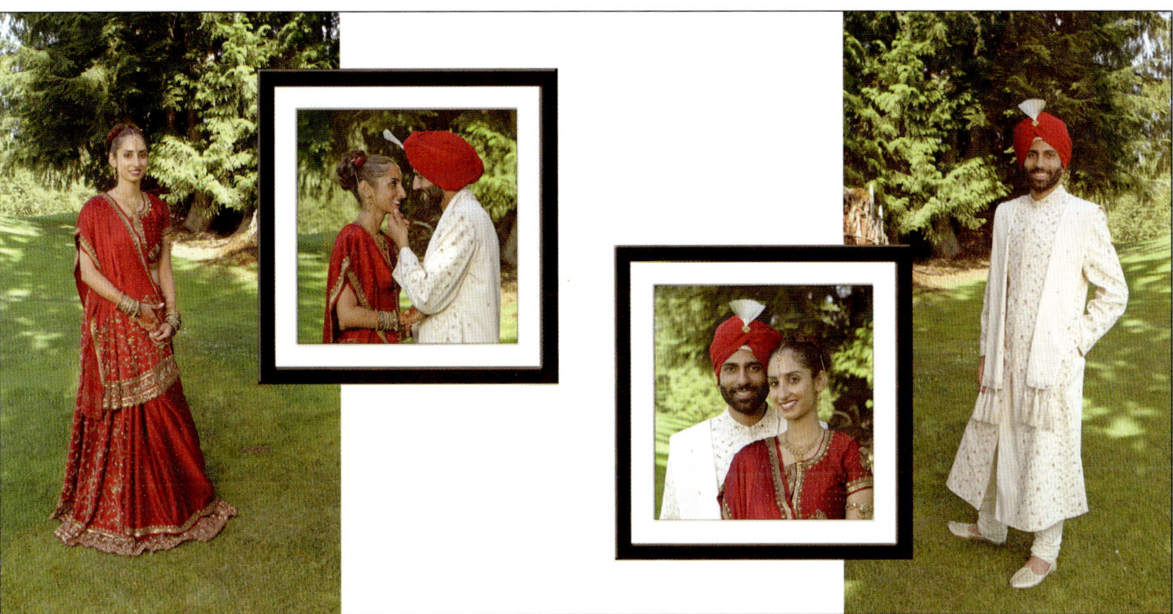

Design notes

A black frame works nicely around an image with no mat or with a white mat. This technique includes how to create a virtual mat with a dimensional effect.

Before you begin, make sure you have cropped the image exactly the way you'd like it to appear in the page spread. Perform the following procedure in the individual image window before pasting it into the page spread window.

If you want a black frame with no mat, skip the procedure for adding the white mat.

Adding the white mat

1. In the individual image window, press D to set the default foreground and background colors to black and white.
2. Press Ctrl+A (⌘-A) and Ctrl+Shift+J (⌘-Shift-J) to select the image, cut it, and paste it onto its own layer.
3. From the Image menu, choose Canvas Size.

4. Check the Relative option.
5. Look at the canvas width and height displayed and enter the size you want for the white mat for both Width and Height.

   If you're using inches for your units of measure, typing 1 for each dimension will give you a half-inch mat all the way around the image. Try a number and click OK to see what it looks like. If you'd like the mat larger or smaller, choose Undo from the Edit menu, open the Canvas Size dialog again and type a new number.

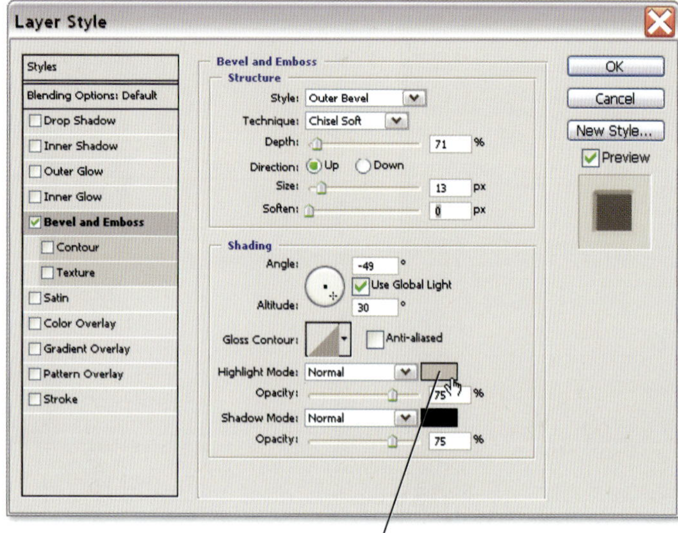

Click here and choose a light gray.

6. Double-click the image icon for the image layer in the Layers palette and click Bevel and Emboss.

   Set the options shown here. You'll need to click the color swatch for Highlight Mode and choose a light gray. This gives you the best look for the virtual mat effect.
7. Click OK. This adds the white mat and the virtual mat effect around the image.

Adding the black frame

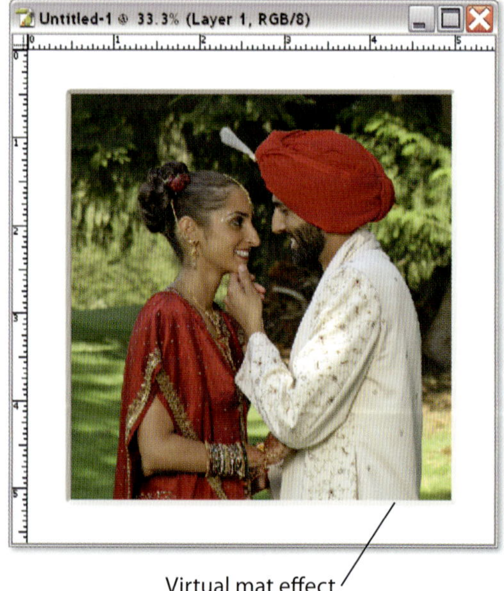

Virtual mat effect

1. After you've added the white mat (above), press X to switch the foreground and background colors (making black the background color).
2. Press Ctrl+E (⌘-E) to merge the two layers.
3. Press Ctrl+A (⌘-A) and Ctrl+Shift+J (⌘-Shift-J) to select, cut, and paste the image and mat onto a new layer.
4. From the Image menu, choose Canvas Size.
5. Make sure the Relative option is checked and type the size you want for the black frame for both Width and Height. Try choosing a size that's one-half to one-quarter the size of your mat. Click OK.

   You'll see your image with a white mat and a black frame. Now you need to put the black frame on its own layer so you can give it a beveled edge.

6. Click the Visibility icon in the Layers palette for the layer with the image and white mat.

   This temporarily hides that layer.

7. Press W for the Magic Wand tool and set the Tolerance to 1 in the options bar.

8. In the Layers palette, select the Background layer and then click the black frame to select it.

9. Press Ctrl+Shift+J (⌘-Shift-J) to cut the selection and paste it onto its own layer.

Try creating a frame that's half the width of the mat.

Giving the frame a beveled edge

1. Double-click the image icon for the frame layer, and then choose Bevel and Emboss.

2. For Style, choose Inner Bevel.

3. For Direction, choose Down.

4. For Depth and Size, move the sliders until you like the appearance of the bevel.

   Make a note somewhere about the settings you used for this bevel if you'll be creating a matching frame for the same page spread. You'll be flattening this image so you can move the image and frame together onto the page. After flattening, you'll no longer be able to see the Bevel and Emboss settings in the Layer Style dialog.

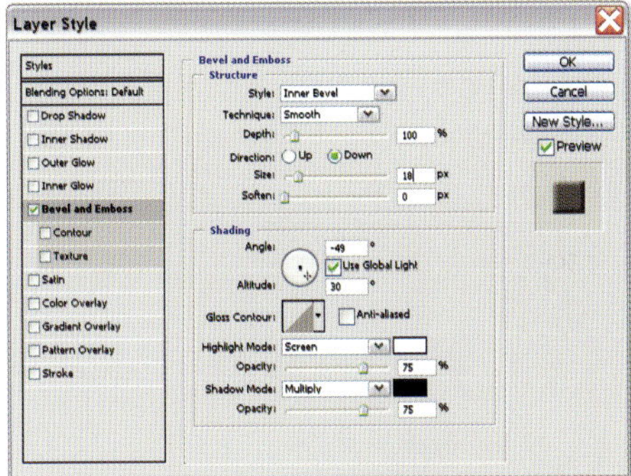

5. Set the Shading Angle to 135 degrees. Click OK.

6. From the Layer menu, choose Flatten Image.

Now you can copy the flattened framed image into the page spread by dragging the layer from the Layers palette into the page spread window.

Design 22: Scaling images to the same size

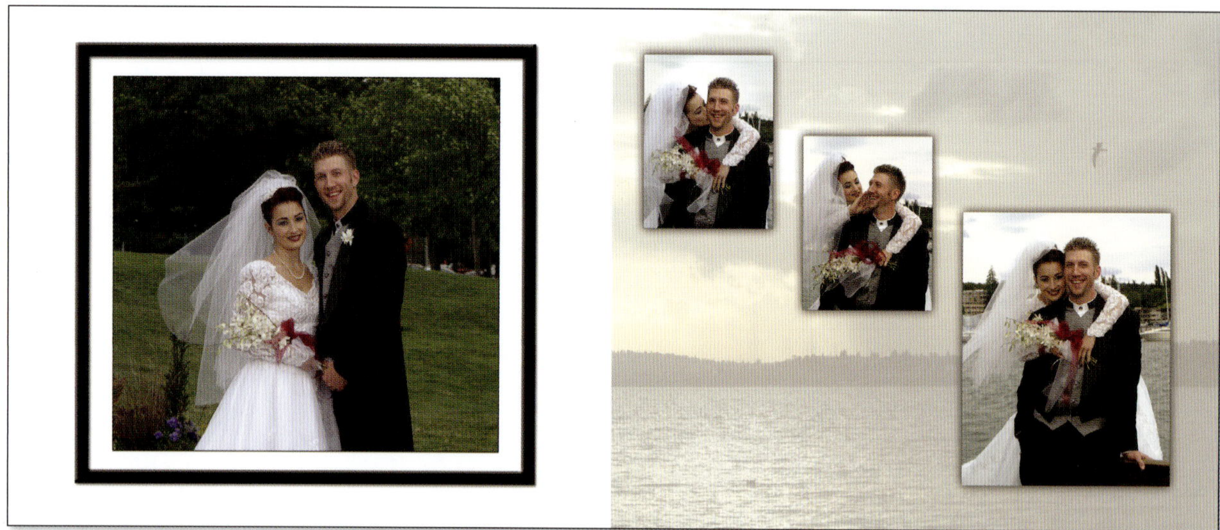

Design notes

In many cases you'll want to scale images to the same size to provide repetition in the design. There are a number of ways to do this. For example, you can place guides around the first image, place the second image directly over the first image, and then scale it down until it's almost exactly the same size, trimming part of the image if necessary. If you want to be very precise, use the method below.

Scaling the first image

1. Place the first image in the page spread window.
2. Make sure the Info palette is visible on-screen.

   If you don't see it, choose Info from the Window menu.
3. In the Layers palette, select the layer containing the first image.
4. Press Ctrl+T (⌘-T) for Free Transform.
5. Holding Shift, drag a corner of the image to scale it down to the size you'd like.
6. Watch the numbers in the Info palette as you drag. When the image is the size you'd like, make a note of the exact width and height.

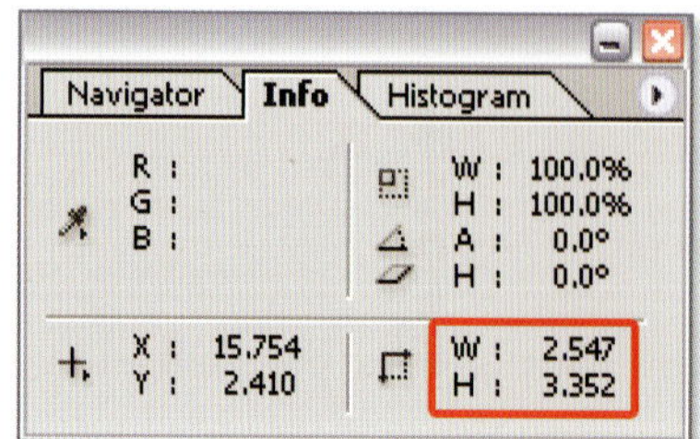

If you need to see the size of an image later, you can hold Ctrl (⌘) and click the image icon in the Layers palette. The image is selected, and its dimensions appear in the Info palette.

7. Press Enter to accept the transformation.

Cropping the second image

1. In the window for the second image, press C for the Crop tool.
2. In the options bar, enter the width and height that you wrote down after resizing the first image.

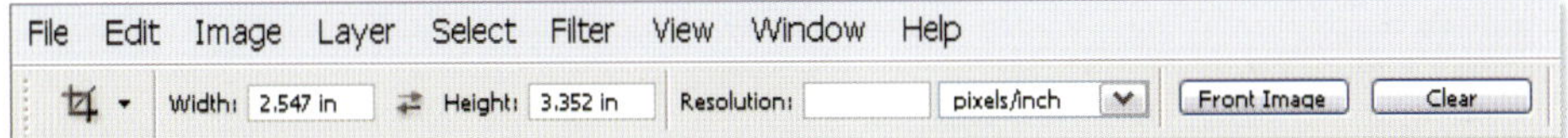

3. Drag out a crop boundary in the image and position it appropriately.
4. Press Enter.

   This gives you the correct aspect ratio for the second image. However, when you paste it into the page spread, you'll still need to scale it down.

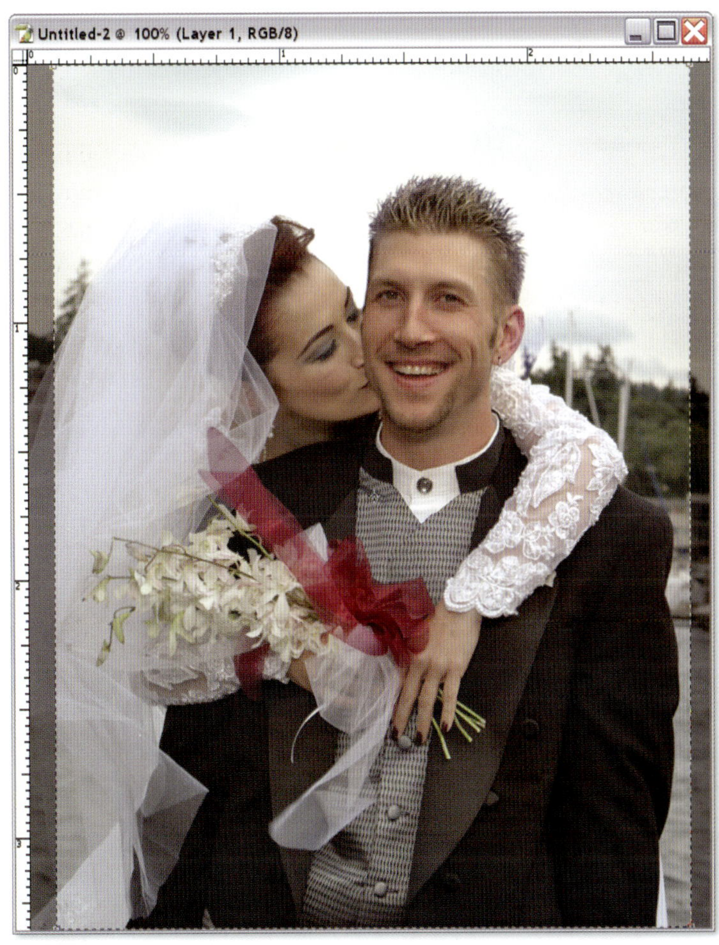

Pasting and scaling the second image

1. Drag the second image into the page spread window.
2. Press Ctrl+T (⌘-T) for Free Transform.
3. Holding Shift, drag to scale the image, watching the numbers in the Info palette as you drag. Scale it to exactly the same size as the first image.
4. Press Enter to accept the transformation.

To learn about creating a beveled frame like the one on the left page, see Design 21.

Design 23: Creating gradient fills

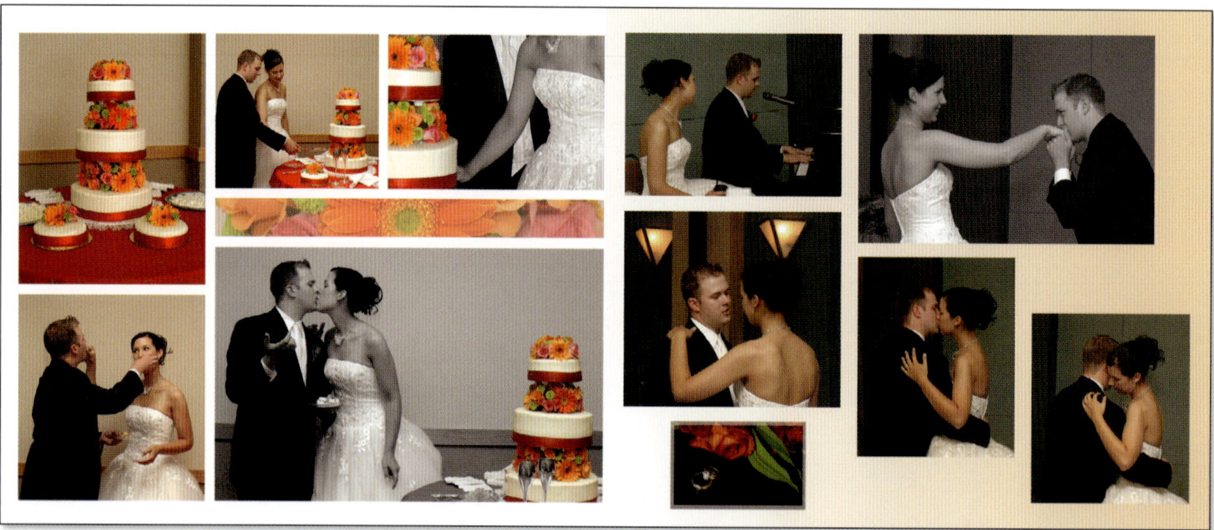

Design notes

You might decide to do one or two pages like this in an album, but more than a few of them would make the album too busy. Because there was so much going on here, I decided not to apply any layer styles at all.

The close-up of flowers used on the cake page was cropped from an image of the cake, and then the opacity was lowered. At full opacity, this image was too bold and stole attention from images that were more important.

Leaving the images on the right page on a white background looked too plain in comparison to all that's happening on the left page, so I created a gradient fill for just that side of the page spread.

To learn how to create an image that's partly in color and partly in black and white, see Design 33.

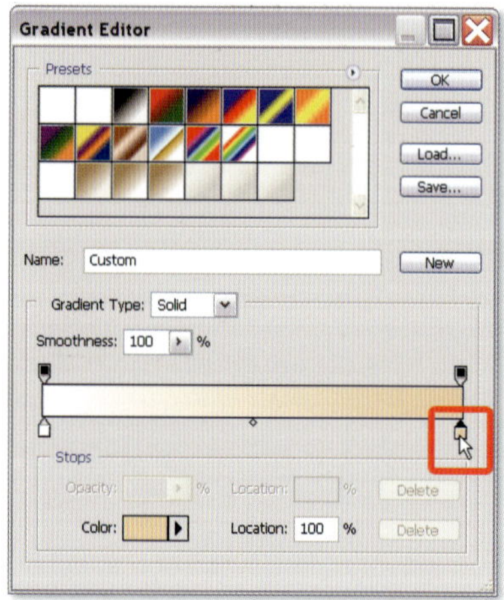

Double-click the color stops to set the beginning and ending colors of the gradient.

Creating a gradient fill

If you create the gradient fill on its own layer, you'll be able to adjust the opacity later to make the effect more subtle. You can also change the color easily later using Levels.

1. Drag the window out so you have space around the canvas.

2. With the Marquee tool, drag out a selection that covers half the page.

   It's easy to do this precisely if you have a guide at the halfway point and Snap checked on the View menu.

3. Press G for the Gradient tool, and click the Gradient color swatch in the options bar.

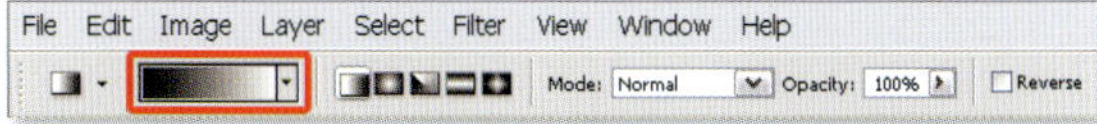

4. In the Gradient Editor dialog, double-click the left color stop and set it to white. Click OK.

5. Double-click the right color stop and set it to a color you choose, or sample a color from an image on your page. Click OK to close both dialogs.

6. Using the Gradient tool, click just outside one side of the selection and drag to just outside the other side of the selection.

The gradient colors extend between the location where you first click and the location where you later release the mouse button, wherever those locations happen to be outside the selection or area. If you start and end the gradient some distance outside the area, you'll only see the middle of the gradient. To see the entire range of color, click and release just outside the borders of the selection.

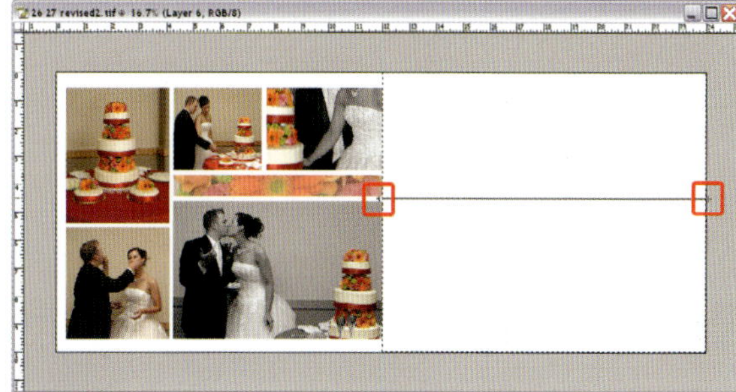

With the Gradient tool, drag just outside the borders of the selection on each side.

Variation

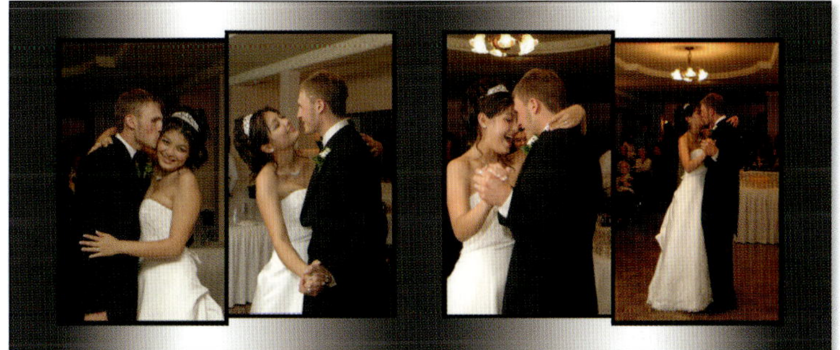

You can create more than one gradient effect in an area, as shown in the illustration above. Simply click to add more color stops, and double-click each one to set the color. Then drag the diamond sliders to adjust the location of each gradient.

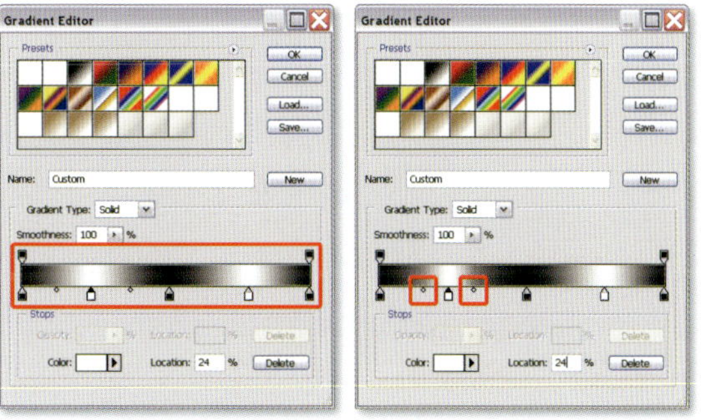

Click to add additional color stops.

Drag the diamond sliders for each selected color stop to adjust the location of each gradient.

Design 24: Adding text

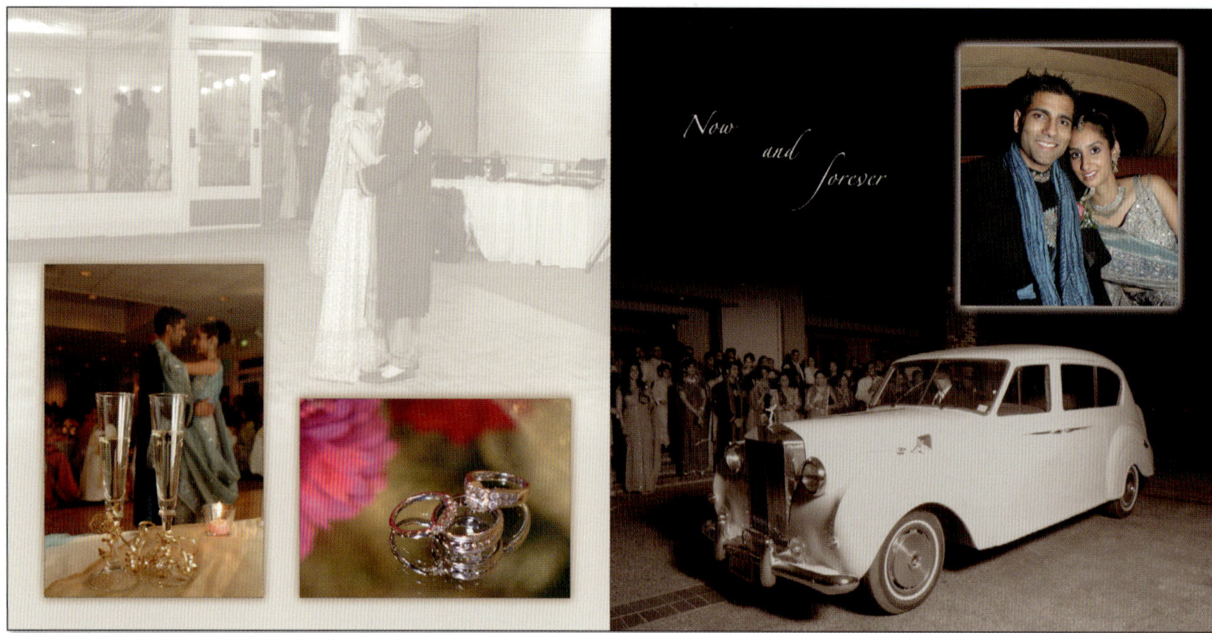

Design notes

After the design is complete, it's time to decide about text. I've tried asking brides to provide me with text, but it doesn't work well. They might suggest playful quotes that seem like a good idea at this moment in their lives but that will not match the quality of timeless elegance portrayed by the images. If you do manage to get a copy of the vows, a line or two works nicely on the ceremony page. Among the fonts I use are Monotype Corsiva and Zapfino. I recommend keeping text to a minimum. Think about clients reading the text every time they open this album for the rest of their lives.

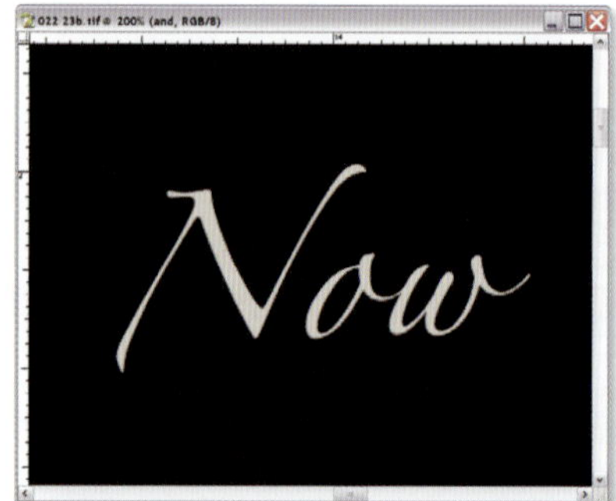

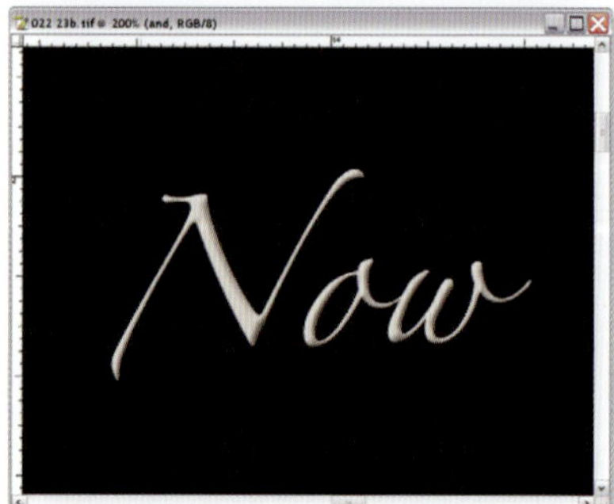

Text with a bevel and emboss style applied.

The Zapfino font was used in this example and each word was entered on its own layer. This way I was able to move each word exactly where I wanted it. Adding a bevel and emboss style to text is a nice way to give it a finished look.

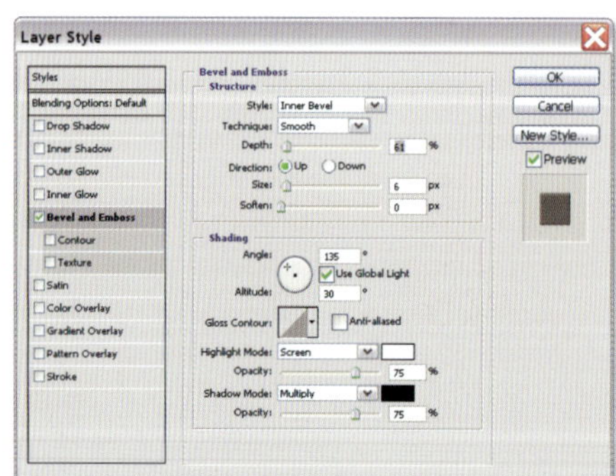

Design 25: Fading an image to black

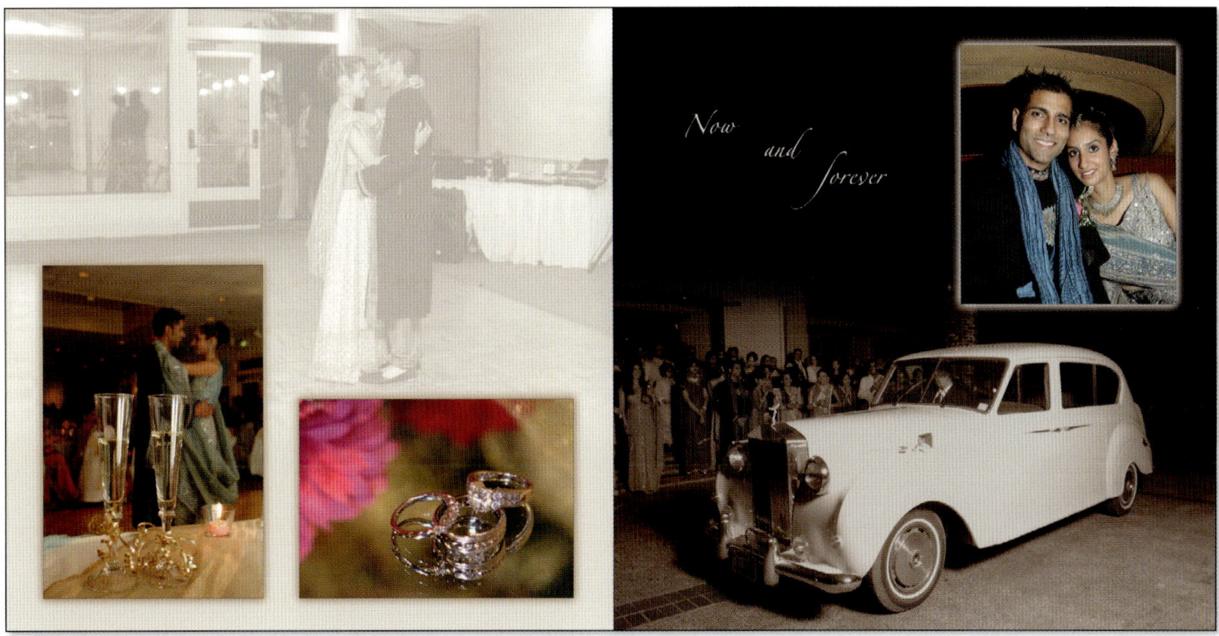

Design notes

This is a good option when you want to use a background image that doesn't fill the page. In addition to filling the page with a coordinating look, it provides room to place pictures of the subjects without hiding part of the background image. In this example, fading to black worked well because the image became naturally darker near the top. Changing the image to sepia also helped to make the transition look natural.

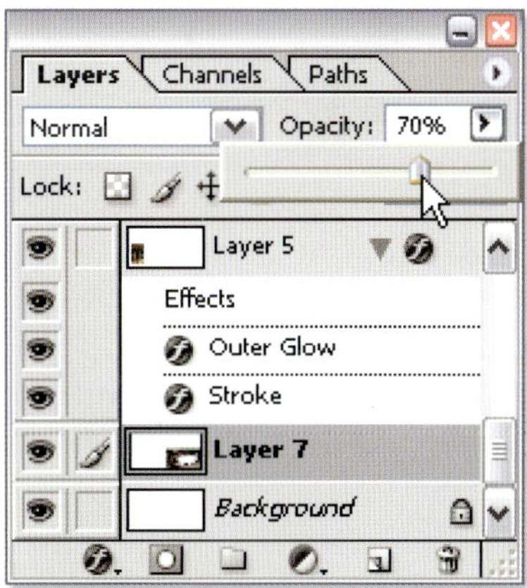

1. In the Layers palette, drag the image layer to just above the Background layer. Lower the opacity to about 70%.
2. With the Marquee tool, drag out a selection that overlaps the top of the image.
3. Press Alt+Ctrl+D (Option-⌘-D) for Feather and enter something like 100.
4. Press Delete.
5. Click the Background layer.
6. Press D for default colors, and press Alt+Backspace (Option-Delete) to fill the Background layer with black.

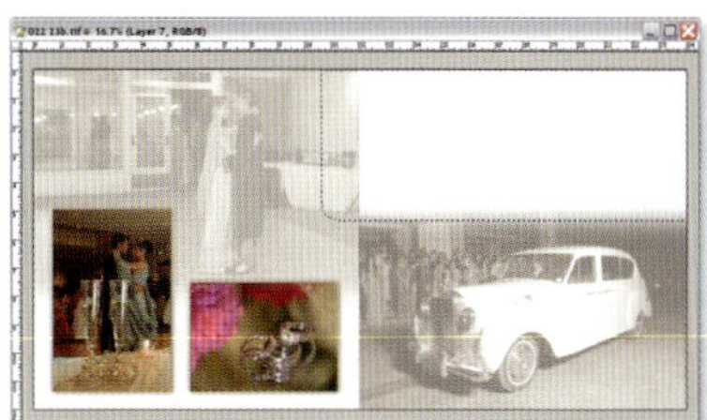

Because the car layer is semitransparent, the black in the Background layer shows through it, helping to blend it in at the feathered edge.

Design 26: Straightening skewed and crooked images

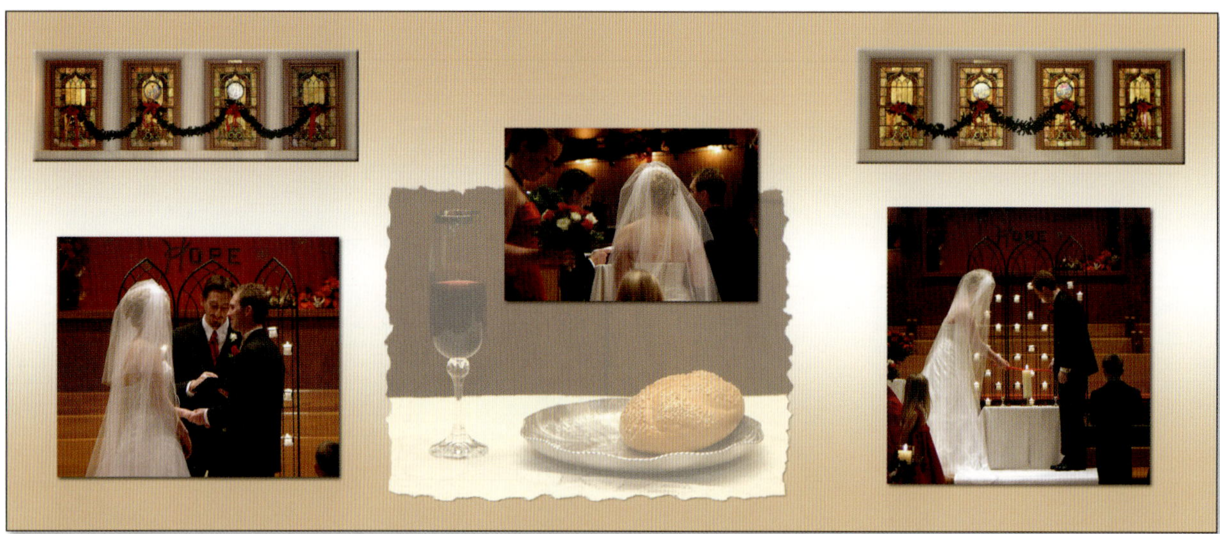

Design notes

The stained glass windows in the image above were high up on the walls of the church. Because they were shot from below, they originally appeared skewed, as you can see in the illustration at the right.

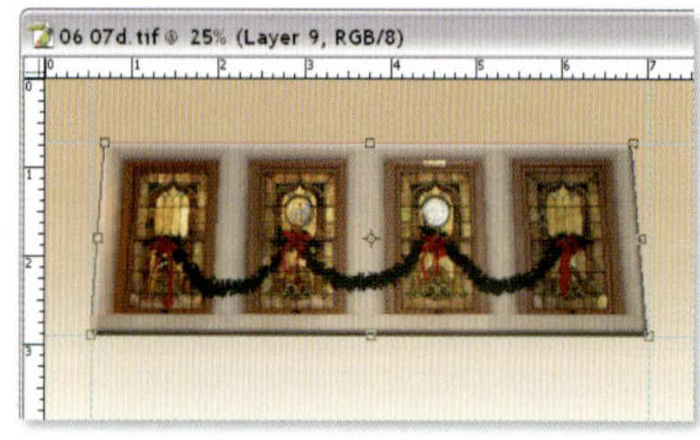

Place guides at the corners of the image.

Skewed images can be straightened using this method:

1. Zoom in on the image by pressing Z for the Zoom tool and clicking the image.
2. Drag out guides, placing them at the widest corners of the image.
3. With the image layer selected in the Layers palette, choose Transform from the Edit menu and then choose Skew.
4. One at a time, drag the top corners of the image until the sides are vertically aligned with the guides. Make sure the top edge of the image is still aligned with the horizontal guide.
5. Press Enter to accept the transformation.

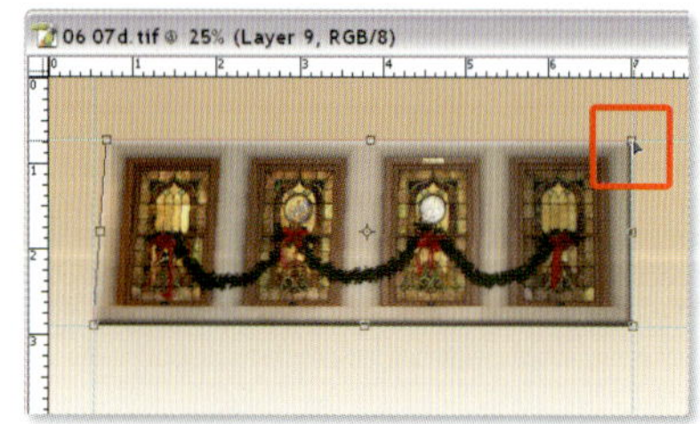

Use the Skew command to straighten the image.

Here's a handy way to straighten an image if the camera wasn't quite straight when the image was shot.

1. Click and hold on the Eyedropper tool and choose the Measure tool at the bottom of the pop-up menu.
2. Click and hold at one end of an edge that should be horizontal.

If the image contains an element that can easily be set to vertical, drag out a measuring line on the vertical element instead.

3. Drag along the chosen edge and release the mouse when you have a line that precisely follows the edge.
4. From the Image menu, choose Rotate Canvas and then choose Arbitrary.

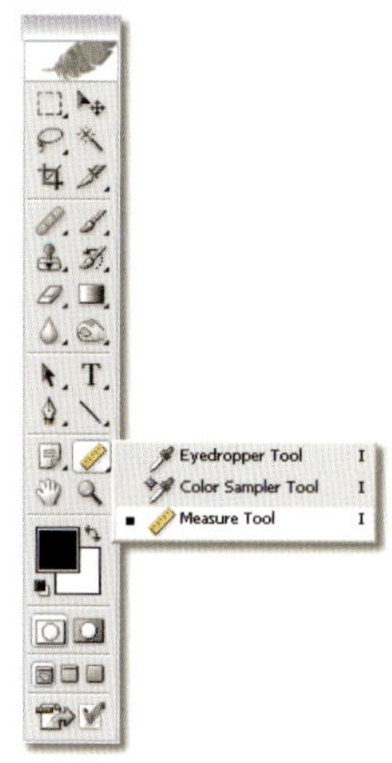

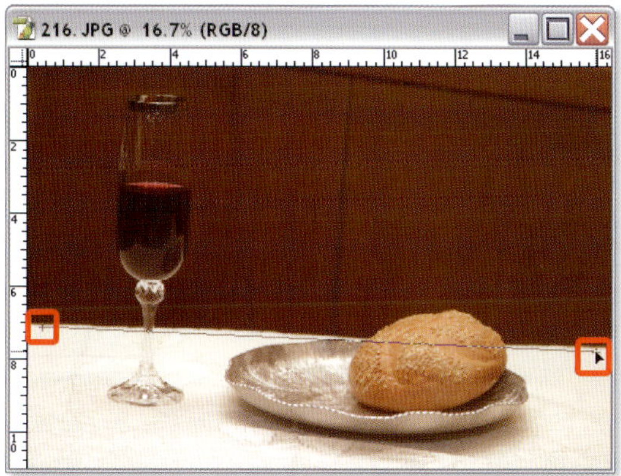

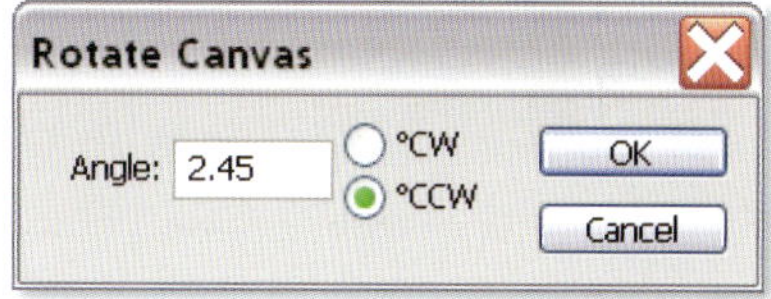

You'll see the angle of rotation necessary to straighten the image. Click OK.

After straightening in this way, you'll need to crop the image to remove the areas of background color added at the corners.

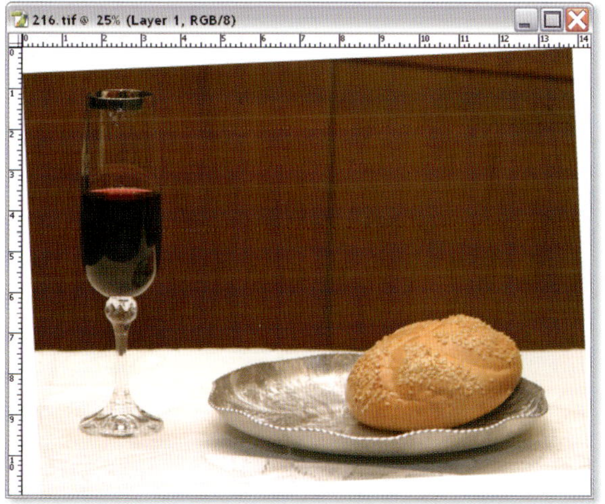

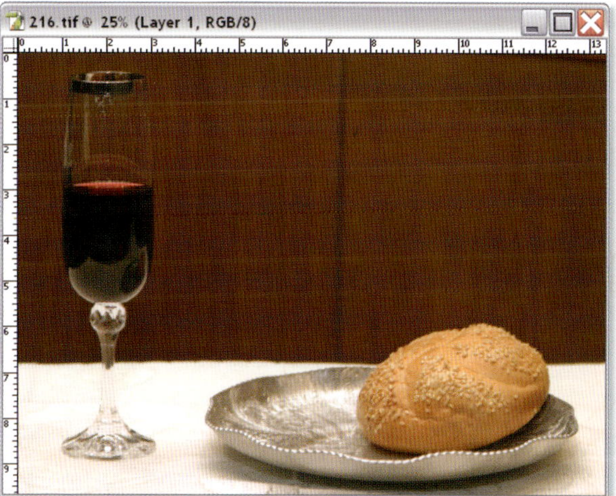

Design 27: Creating the look of torn paper

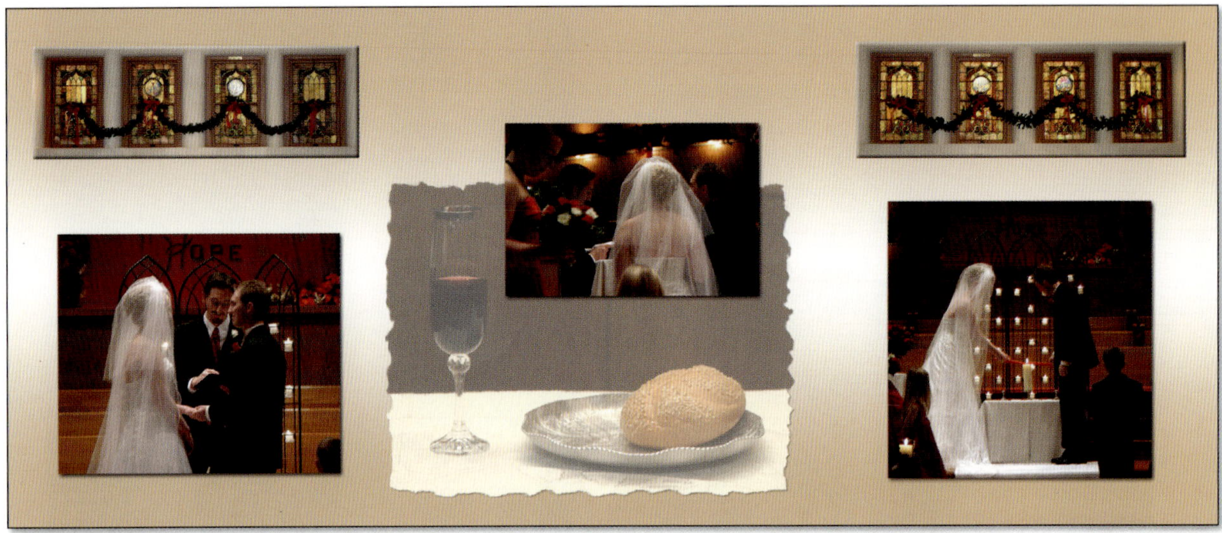

Design notes

Be careful about using casual edges like "torn paper" next to formal images with straight edges. Depending upon what's shown in the images, it may look incongruous to contrast edges in this way.

In this example, the torn paper effect was softened by making the image semitransparent, thus setting it off in more than one way from the other images. Moreover, it's a detail image, whereas the images with straight edges are of the subjects. Using the same edge effects for similar images lends a sense of repetition and harmony.

Torn paper effects seem to look more realistic with pointed corners rather than with rounded ones.

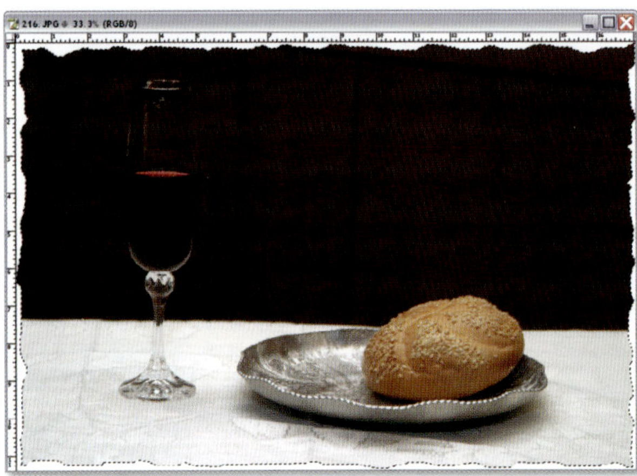

1. Using the Lasso tool, drag erratically to create an uneven edge all the way around inside the edges of the image.
2. Press Shift+Ctrl+I (Shift-⌘-I) for Inverse.
3. Press Delete to remove the straight edges of the image.
4. Press Shift+Ctrl+I (Shift-⌘-I) for Inverse again, to select the "torn" image.
5. Press Ctrl+Alt+J (⌘-Option-J) cut the image and paste it onto its own layer, if its not already on its own layer.
6. Click the Smudge tool.
7. Choose a 9-pixel brush from the options bar, and set the Hardness to 100%.

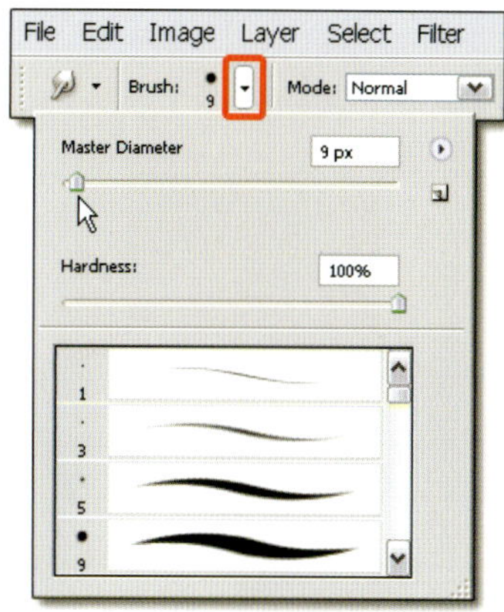

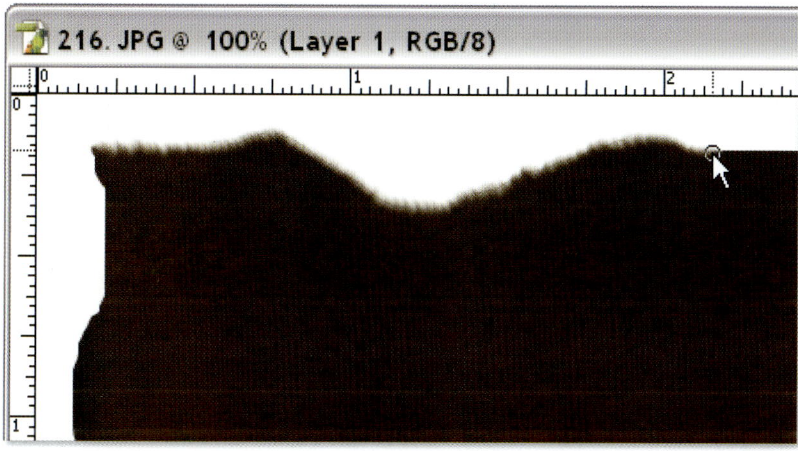

8. Zoom in on the edge of the image, and scrub with tiny perpendicular motions all along the edge to soften it.

Adding a shadow

To give the torn edge a more realistic look, add a small drop shadow.

1. Double-click the image icon for the layer in the Layers palette.
2. Click Drop Shadow.
   - For Blend mode, choose Normal.
   - For Opacity, choose 75%.
   - For Angle, choose 135.
   - Move the Distance and Size sliders until you like the appearance of the shadow.

Design 28: Creating vertical bars

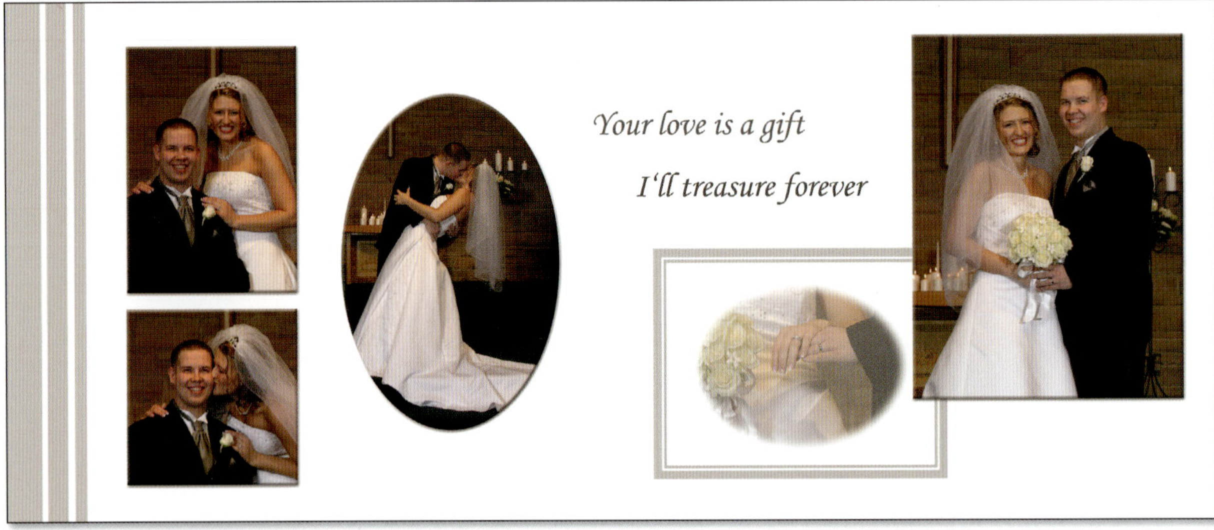

Design notes

In this design and the next, you'll learn how to create three different elements used in these pages: the vertical bars, the frame, and the soft cameo.

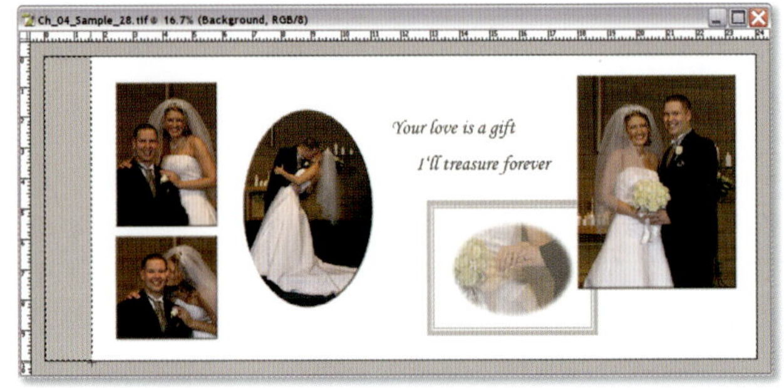

1. In the page spread window, click the Background layer in the Layers palette, and press Ctrl+Alt+Shift+N (⌘-Shift-Option-N) to create a new layer.
2. With the Marquee tool, drag out a selection on this new layer for one wide bar (which you will divide into three).
3. Click the Set Foreground Color swatch in the toolbox and click a medium gray.

   The exact color isn't important since it's easy to change later.
4. Press Alt+Backspace (Option-Delete) to fill the selection with the color you chose.
5. Drag out a narrow selection inside the bar to create the first gap, then press Delete.
6. Using the arrow keys, move the selection to a new location (if you want both gaps to be equal), and press Delete again.

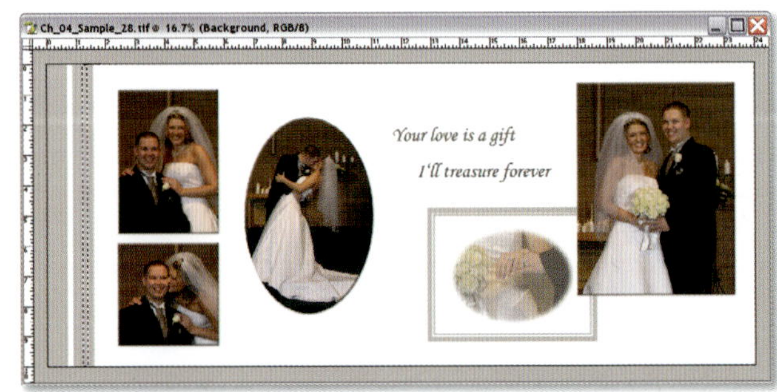

Design 29: Creating a vignetted cameo

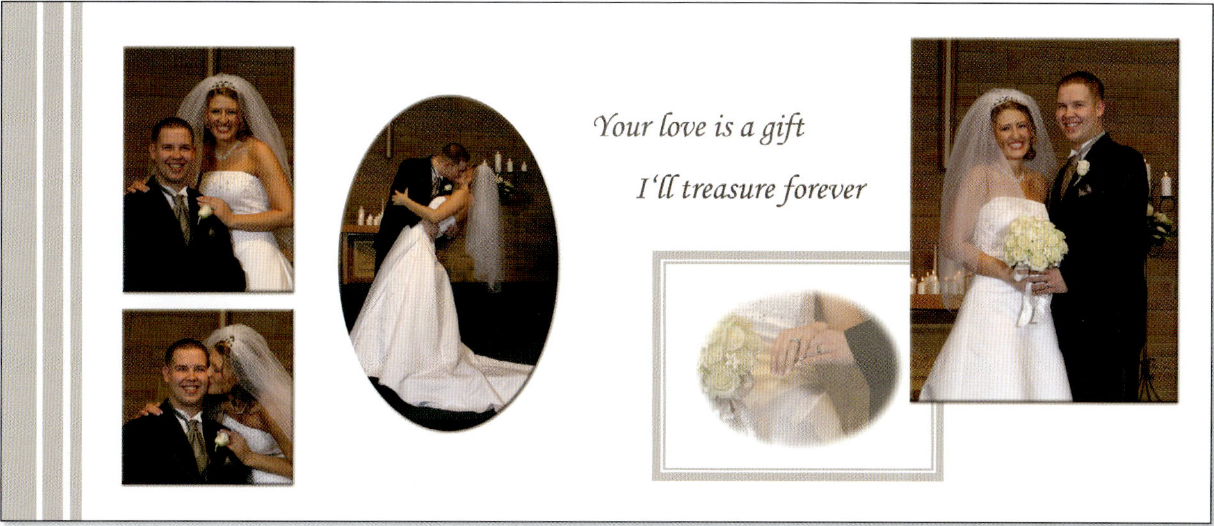

Design notes

This cameo image would have looked strange with a dark frame. It's a soft, faded design element, and the appearance of the frame should complement that look. You'll lower the opacity of the cameo image and the frame the same amount.

1. With the image layer selected in the Layers palette, use the Elliptical Marquee tool to drag out a selection.
2. Press Alt+Ctrl+D (Option-⌘-D) for Feather, enter something like 30, and press Enter.
3. Press Shift+Ctrl+I (Shift-⌘-I) for Inverse.
4. Press Delete.

   If you try this feather and find that you want a different amount, click the Elliptical Marquee step in the History palette to undo the feathering and then apply a different feathering amount. Make sure you don't leave any trace of the formerly straight edges of the image.

Creating the frame

1. With the cameo layer selected in the Layers palette, press Ctrl+Alt+Shift+N (⌘-Option-Shift-N) to create a new layer above it.

2. With the Marquee tool, drag out a rectangle for the frame around the vignette.

3. Press I for the Eyedropper, click the vertical bars to sample their color (if you want these to match), and then press Alt+Backspace (Option-Delete) to fill the frame with color.

   This temporarily hides the cameo image.

4. From the Select menu, choose Modify and then choose Contract. Enter a number such as 50.

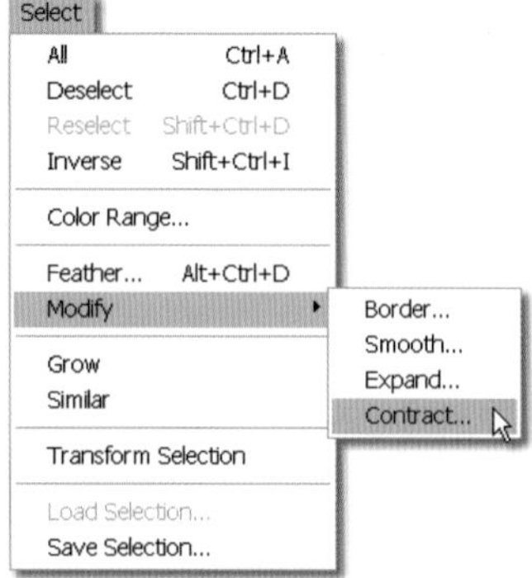

5. Press Delete.

6. From the Select menu, choose Modify and then choose Contract. Enter a number such as 20.

7. Press Alt+Backspace (Option-Delete) to fill the selection with the frame color, once again hiding the cameo.

8. From the Select menu, choose Modify and then choose Contract. Enter a number such as 15.

9. Press Delete.

Lowering the opacity of the bars and frame

1. With the frame layer selected in the Layers palette, choose Merge Down from the Layer menu.

2. Drag the Opacity slider to lower the opacity until you like the appearance.

   Note of the percentage of opacity that you chose.

3. In the Layers palette, select the layer containing the vertical bars.

4. Drag the Opacity slider to the same number as in Step 2.

Design 30: Leaving part of the background image opaque

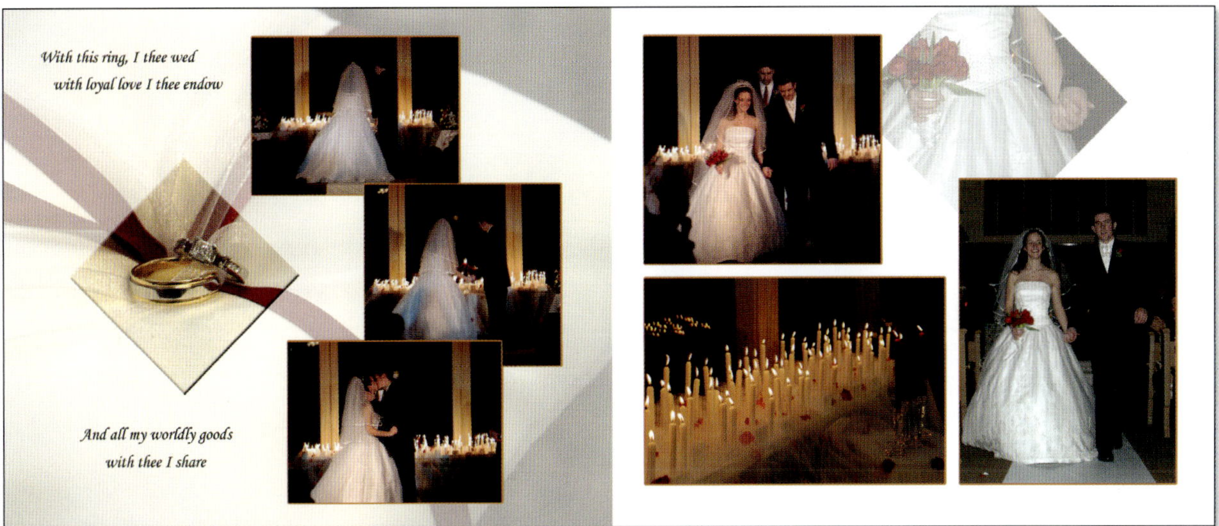

Design notes

The first step in this process involves scaling the background image and placing it exactly where you'd like it. Then you'll select a portion of the image, copy it, paste it on a new layer, and lower the opacity of only the large version of the image.

Copying part of the image

1. Scale the background image (see Design 1).
2. Place the background image exactly where you'd like it.
3. Press M for the Marquee tool and drag out a selection around an interesting part of the image.

   For a square selection, hold Shift while dragging. To move the entire selection while dragging, hold the spacebar.
4. If you want to rotate the selection, choose Transform Selection from the Select menu. (If you don't want to rotate the selection, go to step 7.)
5. Drag outside the selection to rotate it the way you'd like.

   If you want the image at a specific angle, such as at 45 degrees (as in the illustration), watch the numbers on the options bar as you rotate. Holding Shift constrains the rotation to various useful increments.
6. Press Enter to accept the transformation (or Esc to cancel it).

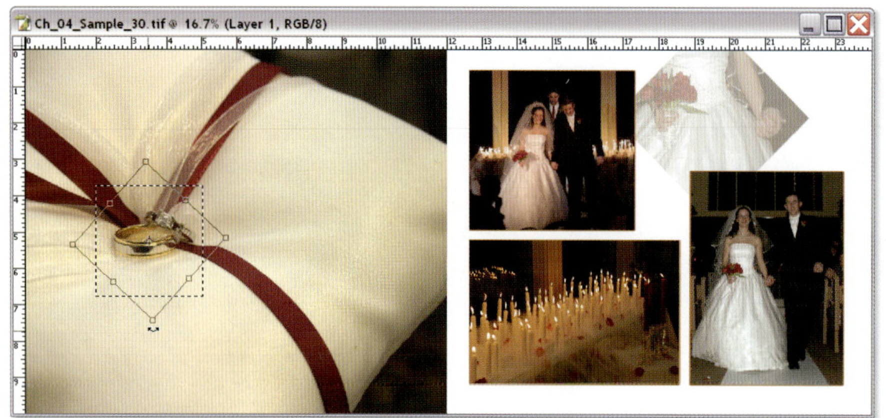

Hold Shift while rotating to constrain the angle of rotation.

7. Press Ctrl+J (⌘-J) to copy the selection and paste it in the same location on its own layer.

Lowering the opacity of the background image

1. Select the background image layer in the Layers palette.
2. Drag the opacity slider until the image appears as faded as you'd like. The background image in the illustration was set to 31% opacity.

Adding a layer effect to the opaque image

Now that you have the background faded, you're better able to see what a layer effect will look like when you apply it to the part that remains opaque.

1. In the Layers palette, double-click the image icon for the layer with the opaque image.
2. Choose Bevel and Emboss.
3. Here are the Bevel and Emboss settings used in the example:

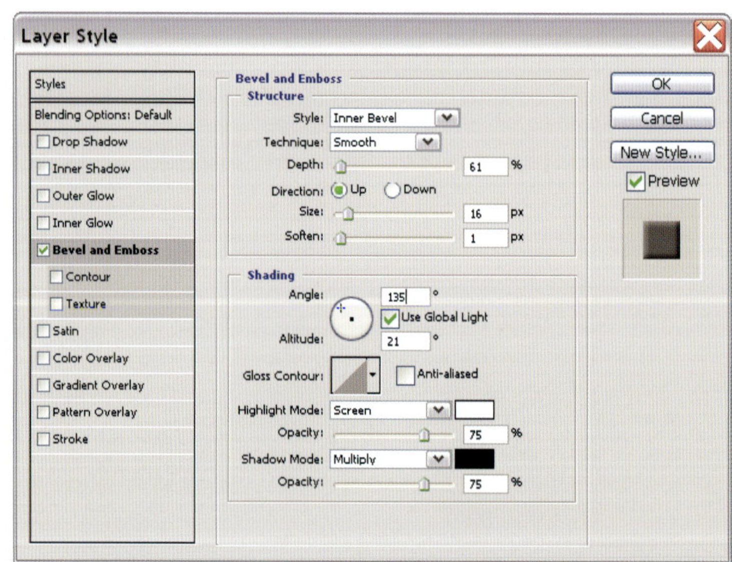

Design 31: Cutting out design elements from the background

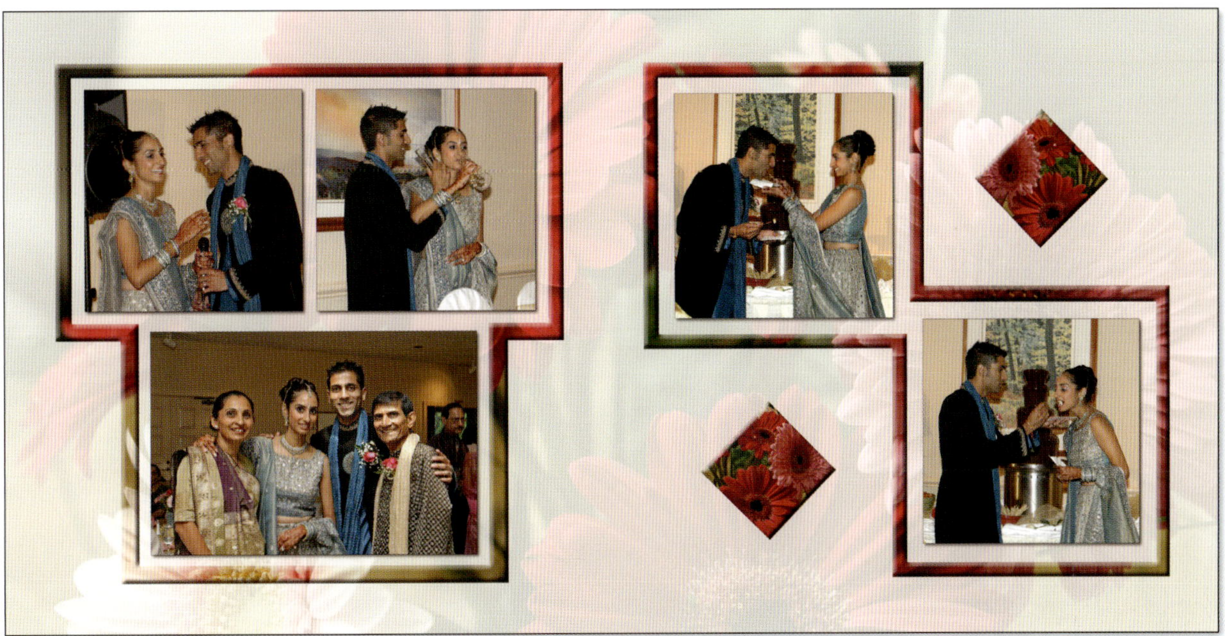

Design notes

Here's another variation of how to cut out parts of a screened-back image so that portions of the full-opacity version show through.

Creating two versions of the image

1. Fill the page spread with a background image and drag that layer to just above the blank Background layer in the Layers palette.
2. With the image layer selected in the Layers palette, press Ctrl+J (⌘-J) to duplicate it.
3. Click the Visibility icon for the new layer to temporarily hide it.
4. Click the original background image layer and lower the opacity to something like 25%.
5. Press Ctrl+E (⌘-E) to merge this layer with the Background layer and make it opaque.
6. Press Ctrl+A (⌘-A) for Select All, and then press Ctrl+Shift+J (⌘-Shift-J) to cut the image and paste it onto its own layer.

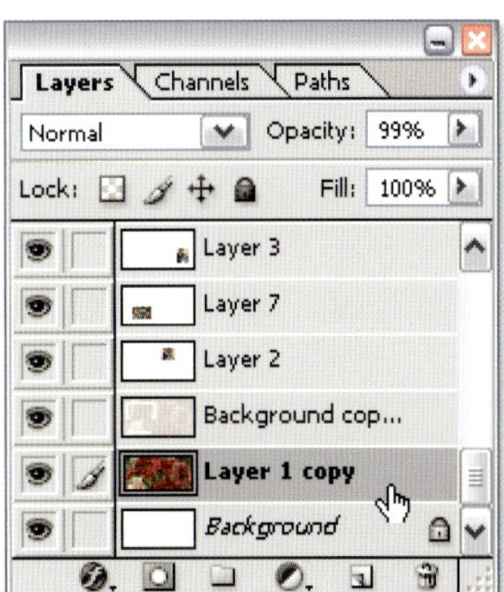

7. Click the Visibility icon again so you can see the full-opacity layer, and then drag it just under the screened-back version in the Layers palette.
8. Place the rest of the images on the page in exactly the arrangement that you'd like.

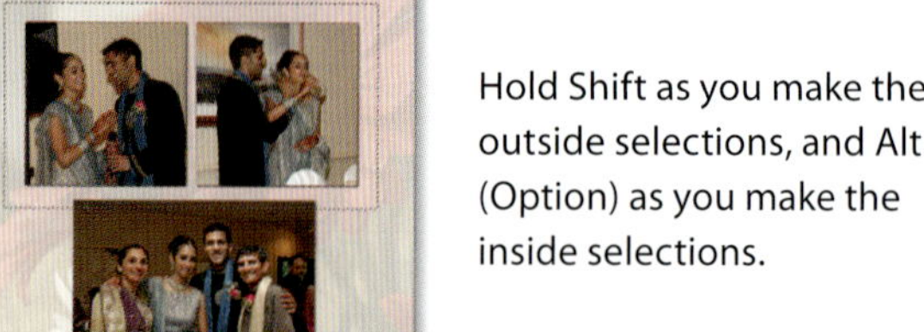

Hold Shift as you make the outside selections, and Alt (Option) as you make the inside selections.

Creating the cutout on the left page

1. With the Marquee tool, drag out a selection for the upper rectangle.

   Remember that when dragging out any of these selections, you can hold the spacebar to move the entire selection as you drag.
2. Holding Shift, drag out a selection for the lower rectangle.
3. Holding Alt (Option), drag out a selection inside the upper rectangle to create the top portion of the frame.
4. Holding Alt (Option), drag out another selection inside the lower rectangle to create the lower portion of the frame.
5. With the *full-opacity layer* selected in the Layers palette, press Ctrl+J (⌘-J) to copy and paste the selection onto its own layer.
6. In the Layers palette, drag the new frame layer above the screened-back layer.

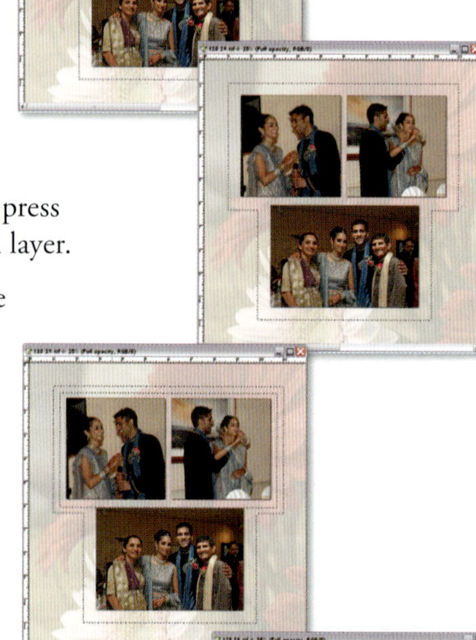

Creating the cutout on the right page

Use the same technique for the cutout frame on the right page.

1. Drag out a marquee for the outside of the upper frame, and then, while holding Shift, drag out a marquee for the outside of the lower frame.
2. Hold Alt (Option) and drag inside each of these selections to join the frames into one selection.
3. With the full-opacity layer selected in the Layers palette, press Ctrl+J (⌘-J) to copy and paste the selection onto its own layer.

Now you can give each of the frame layers a final touch by applying the Bevel and Emboss style, as in Design 2.

Design 32: Creating more design elements from cutouts

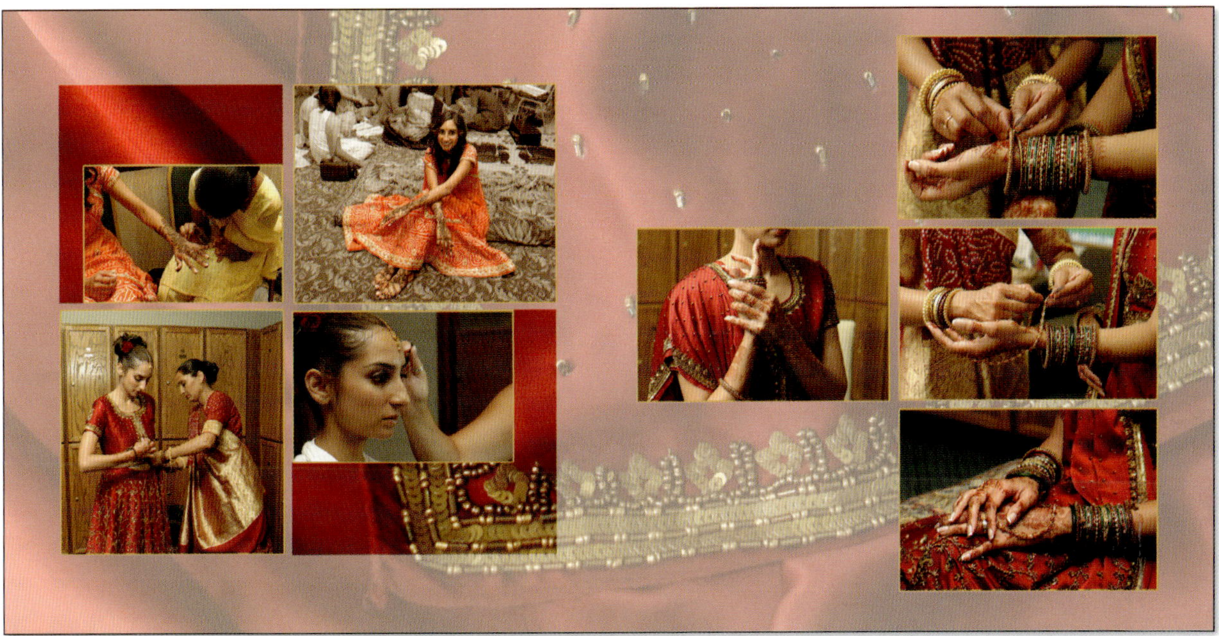

Design notes

This technique is a third design idea for cutouts. In this variation, the cutouts were used to visually create a nice, square block from four images with different sizes and shapes. These images were given a gold stroke using a color sampled from the fabric in the background image.

First create an opaque, screened-back image of the background over a full-opacity version as described in Design 31. Then you're ready to create the cutouts.

1. Drag guides out of the rulers and position them around the larger images in the block.
2. Make sure Snap is checked on the View menu.
3. Using the Marquee tool, start at the inside corner of the top left image, and drag out a selection that aligns exactly with the edges of the two adjacent images.
4. Make sure the screened-back image layer is selected in the Layers palette, and press Delete.

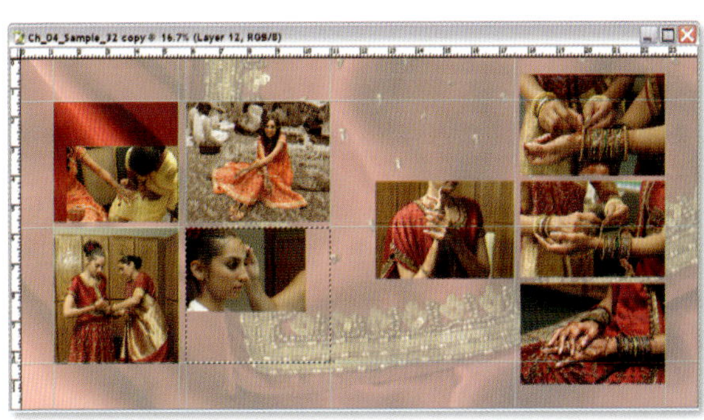

Design 33: Creating a spot color image

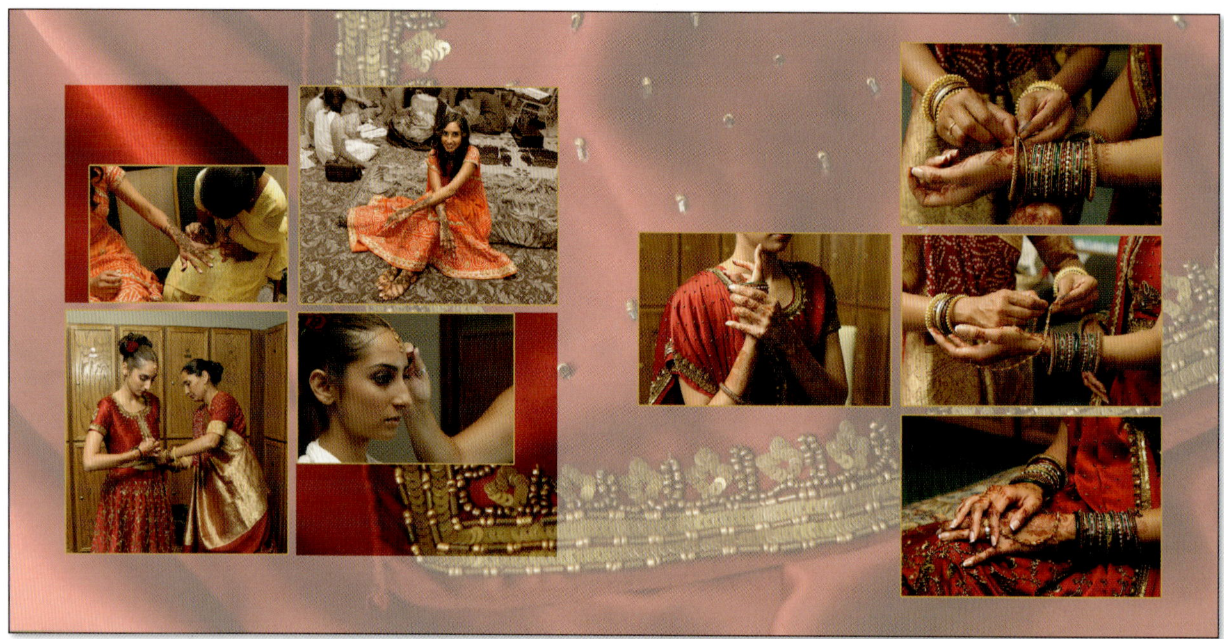

Design notes

Sometimes you'll want to create an image that's mostly black and white or sepia, with parts of the image in color. When you create an image like this, consider slightly lowering the saturation of the color layer. You might find that this gives the image a softer, more realistically "hand-painted" appearance.

First create two versions of the same file

1. Open the file and crop it the way you'd like to use it on the page.
2. In the History palette, right-click (Ctrl-click) the Crop step, and choose New Document.

Turn one of the versions into a sepia image

1. In the new document window, find your custom Sepia action (created in Design 18) or the default Sepia Toning action in the Actions palette.
2. Click the Play icon.

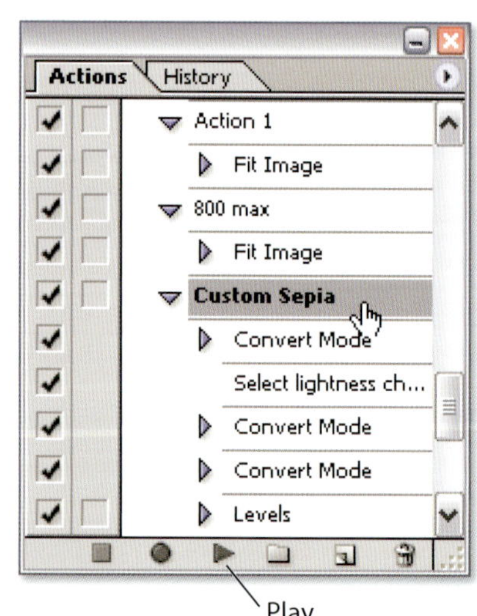

Then paste part of the color version into the sepia image

1. In the window for the color version, press Z and drag around a portion of the image to zoom in.
2. With the Lasso tool, carefully select around the area you want to see in color.

   Hold Shift and drag to add to the selection. Hold Alt (Option) and drag to remove part of the selection.
3. From the Select menu, choose Feather and give the selection a 2-pixel feather.
4. Holding Shift, drag the selection from the color window to the sepia window.

   Holding Shift allows you to paste a selection into exactly the same location in the target window as in the source window, if the two documents were cropped exactly the same way.

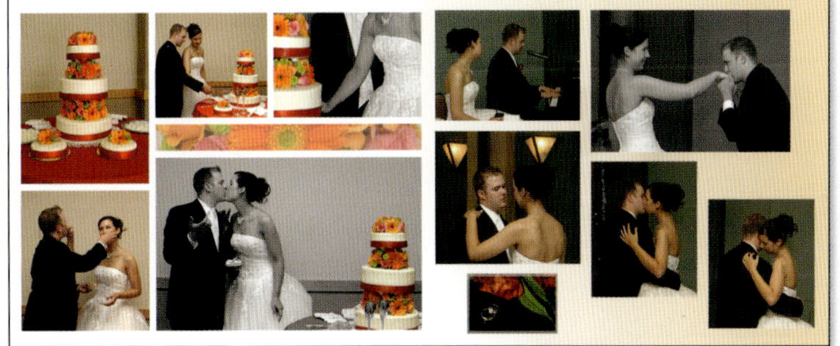

Here's another example of a spot color image.

Aligning the images

If for some reason the two images didn't line up, here's a way to align them.

1. In the Layers palette, select the upper image layer.
2. Drag the opacity slider to lower this layer's opacity to 60%.
3. Press Z and click to zoom in.
4. Press V for the Move tool and use the arrow keys to align the image as well as you can with the image below it.
5. Drag the opacity slider back up to 100%.
6. To check for perfect alignment, click the layer for the top image, and then click that layer's Visibility icon while carefully watching the image. If nothing appears to shift when you turn the visibility off and on, you know it's perfectly aligned.
7. If the image seems to shift, then click the visibility icon again to make the layer visible and use the arrow keys to adjust the image placement. Check alignment again by clicking the Visibility icon and watching for the image to shift.

Design 34: Designing the last page

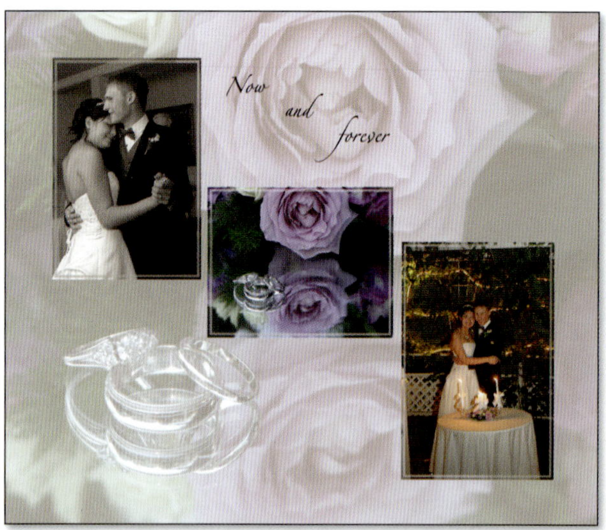

Design notes

The repetition of the flower image shown both large and small makes this composition intriguing. Notice that the other images were carefully placed so they didn't hide the most interesting elements of the background. The way the three opaque images were cropped and the pattern in which they were laid out provide the eye with a natural curve to follow from upper left to lower right.

Creating inner borders

1. In the Layers palette, select a layer for one of the images and press Ctrl+J (⌘-J) to create a duplicate layer.
2. In the Layers palette, click the lower layer to select it and then drag the Opacity slider to approximately 50%.

   You won't see a change in the appearance of the image at this point, since the semitransparent image is hidden behind the opaque version over it.
3. In the Layers palette, click the upper layer to select it and then click the Add Layer Mask icon at the bottom of the Layers palette.
4. Hold Ctrl (⌘) and click the image icon in the Layers palette for the upper layer to select the image.

5. From the Select menu, choose Modify and then choose Contract. Enter a number such as 30. Click OK.
6. Press D to set the default foreground and background colors.
7. Press Ctrl+Backspace (⌘-Delete) to "fill with black," allowing the transparent layer to show through the layer mask.
8. From the Select menu, choose Modify and then choose Contract. Enter a number such as 15. Click OK.
9. Press Alt+Backspace (Option-Delete) to "fill with white," bringing the opaque version of the image back into view.

Repeat this procedure for any other images on the page where you want to apply the inner border.

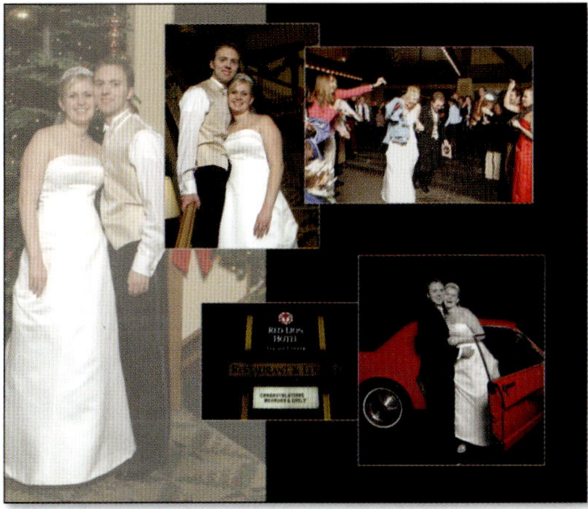

The image with the car in this page was done using the method explained in Design 33. The file was duplicated and one version was changed to black and white. In that case, the subjects were carefully selected with the Lasso tool and then the black and white subjects were Shift-dragged into the color image. The black-and-white/color image was then flattened and dragged into the page spread window.

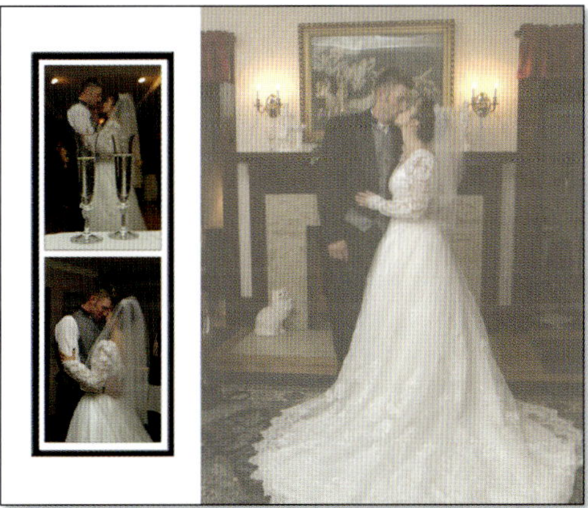

Design 35: Creating a dimensional screened-back frame

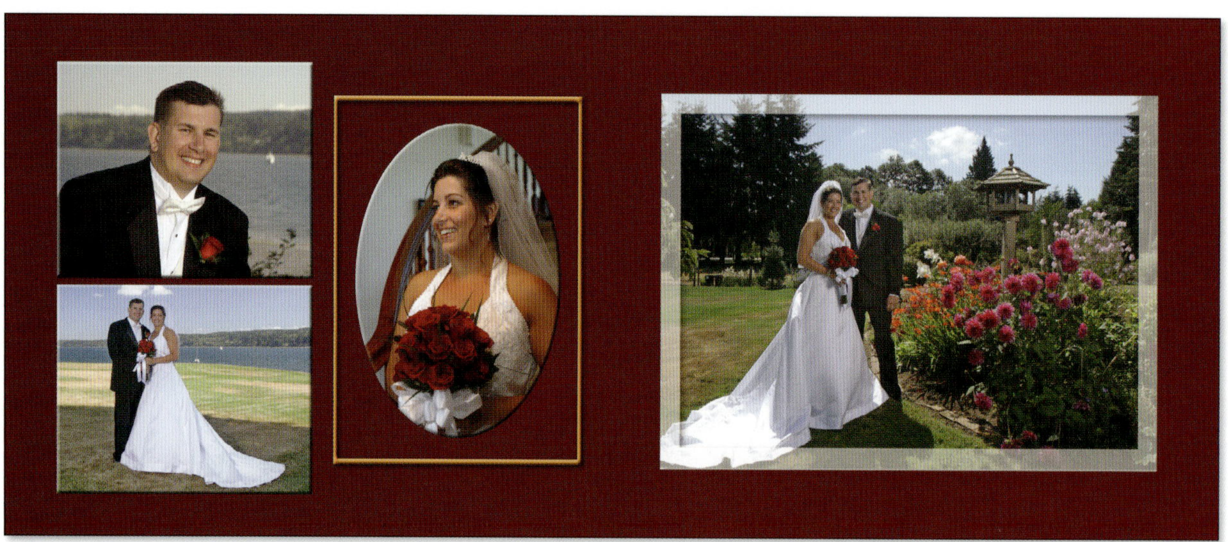

Design notes

You can create different variations of the kind of frame you see on the right page, and we'll look here at how to do three of them. You'll be making part of the image semitransparent, and because you won't want a background color showing through, you'll also learn how to make the screened-back frame opaque.

Creating the frame

1. Hold Ctrl (⌘) and click the image icon for the image in the Layers palette.
2. Because you'll need to load this selection again later, choose Save Selection from the Select menu. Type a name for the selection such as "Frame" and click OK.
3. From the Select menu, choose Modify and then choose Contract. Enter a number such as 100.
4. Press Ctrl+Shift+J (⌘-Shift-J) to cut and paste the selection onto its own layer.
5. In the Layers palette, drag the new layer down in the list so it appears under what is now the frame.

   You won't see any apparent change after altering the layer order.
6. Click the frame layer, and drag the opacity slider until you like the transparency of the frame.

7. Double-click the image icon for the frame in the Layers palette and choose Drop Shadow. Adjust the settings until you like the appearance of the Drop Shadow.

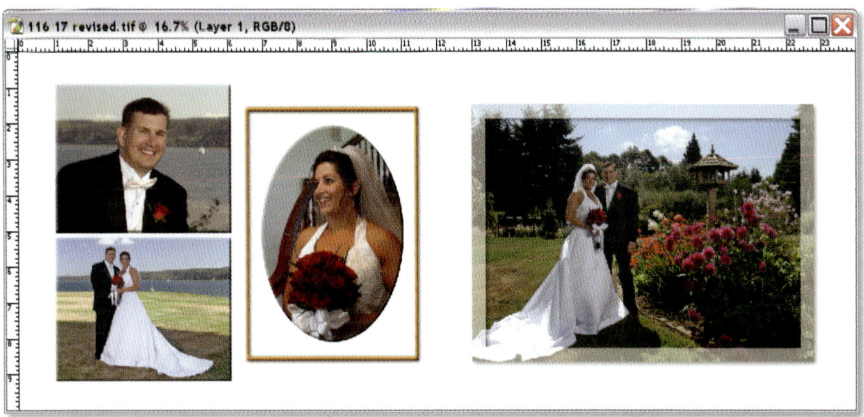

Variation 1: Adding a dimensional look to the frame

Try adding the Bevel and Emboss layer style to see if you like a dimensional look.

1. In the Layers palette, double-click the image icon for the frame layer.
2. Choose Bevel and Emboss and try these settings:
    - Style: Inner Bevel
    - Depth: 50%
    - Direction: Up
    - Size: 35 pixels

Variation 2: Removing the shadow on the outside of the frame

If you'd rather keep the flat look of the frame, you may want to remove the shadow on the outside of it so you can apply a different style there.

1. In the Layers palette, click the frame layer.
2. Make sure you like the style or styles you've applied to the frame. (After merging down, you will no longer be able to change the styles.)
3. Press E for Merge Down.

   This merges the frame with the image below it.

4. From the Select menu, choose Load Selection. Choose your Frame selection, and click OK.

5. From the Select menu, choose Inverse.

6. Press Delete.

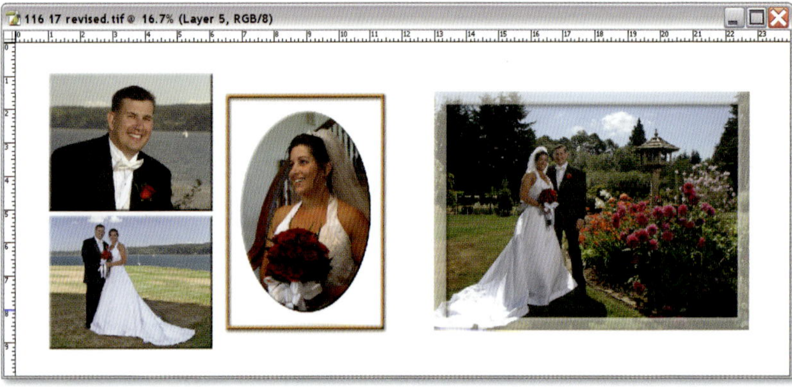

Using the framed image over a background image or color

If you add a background color behind your framed image, you'll probably find that you don't like the effect of that color showing through your semitransparent frame. Here's how to make the frame opaque.

1. If the frame and image are not just above the blank (white) Background layer in the Layers palette, drag them so that they are. Make sure the frame is still on top of the image layer (if you haven't already flattened them).

2. If you haven't merged the frame with the image layer, click the frame layer, and choose Merge Down to merge it with the image.

3. From the Select menu, choose Load Selection. Choose the Frame selection, and click OK.

4. Choose Merge Down again to merge the image and the frame into the Background layer.

5. Press Ctrl+Shift+J (⌘-Shift-J) to cut and paste the image onto its own layer.

Now the frame is opaque, and you can add a background color that won't show through it.

Design 36: Designing the cake page

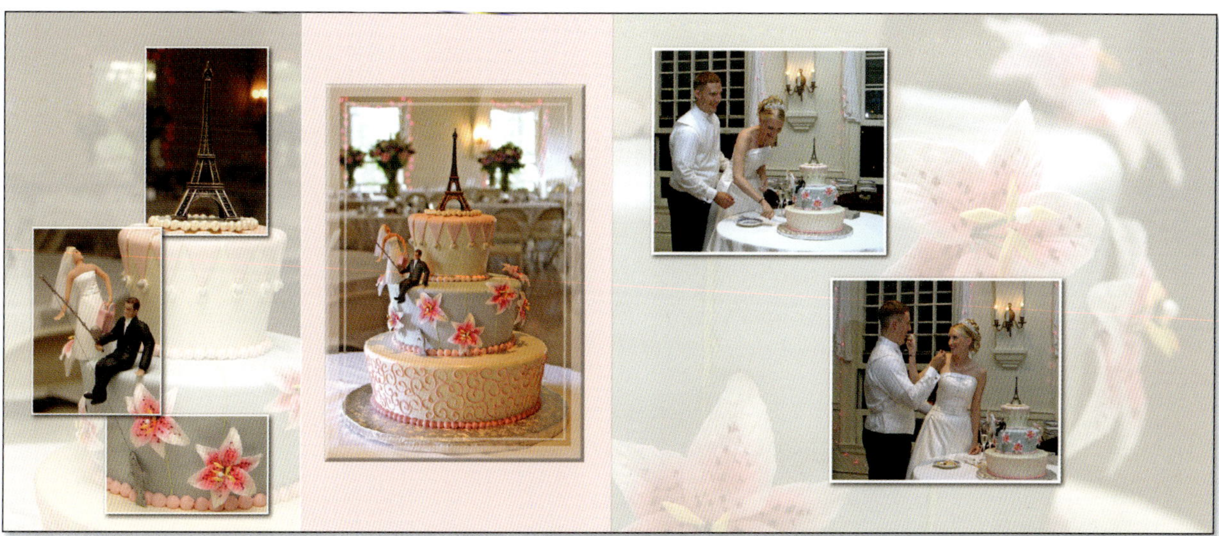

Design notes

This was a beautiful, whimsical cake, and the clients wanted to remember it in detail. On the left page, sections were copied and pasted in place before the background was screened back.

The kind of stroke we've used so far has been an outside stroke. Outside strokes are applied outside the borders of the image, and they're rounded at the corners. If you'd like to apply a stroke with square corners instead, you can use an inside stroke. Be aware that inside strokes obscure part of the image. For inside strokes, you might want to leave a little extra room when you crop so the stroke doesn't come too close to important elements in the image. Each image with a stroke on this page also has a small drop shadow applied.

Applying an inside stroke

1. With the Marquee tool, select a section of the image that you want to remain opaque.
2. Press Ctrl+J (⌘-J) to copy and paste that section onto its own layer. Repeat for the other sections of the image that you'd like to remain opaque, copying each section from the background image.
3. Double-click the image icon for one of these layers in the Layers palette.
4. Choose Stroke and set these parameters:

- Size: 9 pixels (15 for the larger images on the right)
- Position: Inside
- Opacity: 100%
- Color: White

5. Choose Drop Shadow and create a small drop shadow.
6. Copy the layer styles and paste them into the other layers (See Design 6).
7. Click the background image layer in the Layers palette and lower the opacity to something like 35%.

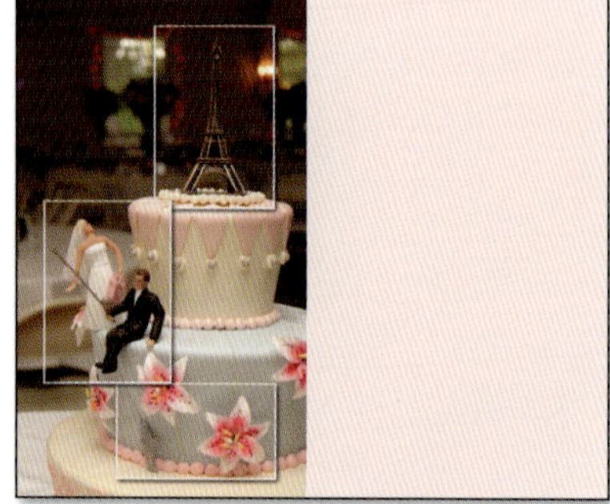

Add an inside stroke and a drop shadow to each copied section.

Creating a beveled plaque

1. In the Layers palette, select the layer for the plaque image and press Ctrl+J (⌘-J) to create a duplicate layer.
2. Ctrl+click (⌘-click) the image icon for the new layer to select the image.
3. From the Select menu, choose Modify, and then choose Contract. Enter a number such as 75 pixels. Click OK.
4. From the Select menu, choose Inverse, and then press Delete.
5. Click the lower layer and drag the Opacity slider to something like 30%.
6. Click the upper layer and drag out a selection inside the remaining opaque image.
7. Holding Alt (Option), drag out another selection inside the first to create a thin double selection.
8. Press Delete.

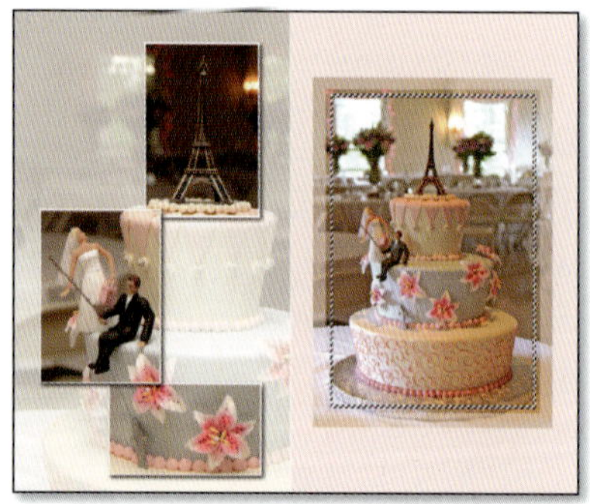

Lower the opacity of the background image....

Now give the lower layer a bevel.

1. Double-click the image icon for the lower layer in the Layers palette (the layer that was screened back) and click Bevel and Emboss.
2. Set these parameters:
   - Style: Inner Bevel
   - Depth: 171%
   - Direction: Up
   - Size: 21 pixels

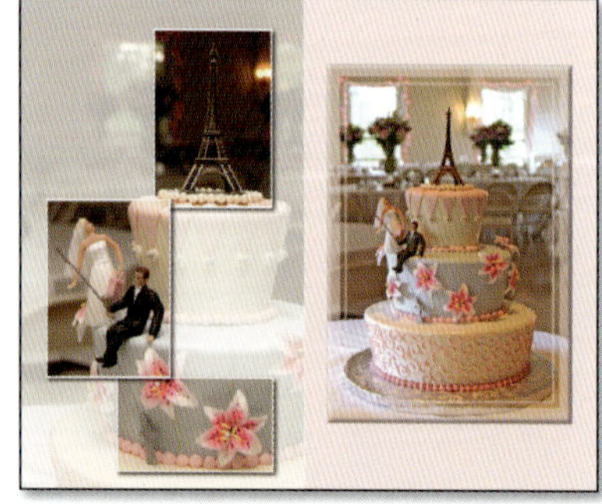

...and then create a beveled plaque.

Design 37: Adding a border to several images together

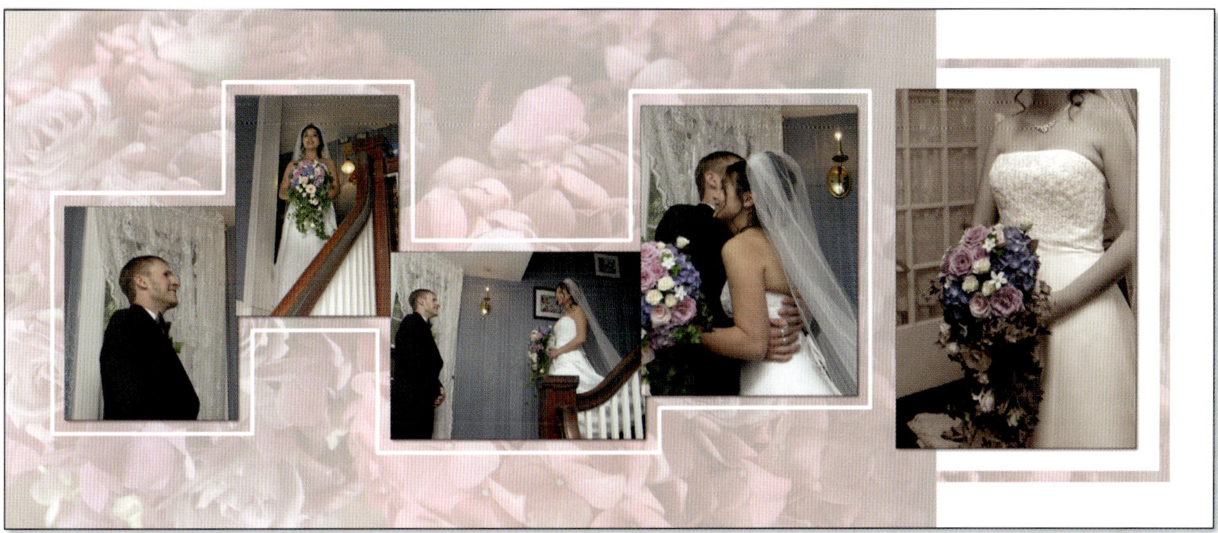

Design notes

You'll create this border using a layer mask. You'll have a layer filled with white on top of a semitransparent image. When you add a layer mask to the white layer, the white will be completely hidden at first. Then you'll "paint with white" where you want the white borders showing through the mask.

You could achieve this same effect by simply erasing through a screened-back layer so the white Background layer shows through underneath. But if you erase, you can't easily correct mistakes. By painting away portions of the image using a layer mask, however, you can always restore parts of the image later by "painting with black."

It's important to finish the procedures in all four of these sections before starting another task or closing the document. Having the correct layer selected and the correct foreground and background color settings is the only way to make this technique work.

Creating a layer mask

1. Scale up your background image to the appropriate size and place it where you want it in the page spread. Scale all the other images and place them in their final locations.

   If you move them later, you'll have to redo the white border.

2. Lower the opacity of the background image to something like 35%.
3. Click the background image in the Layers palette and press Ctrl+Alt+Shift+N (⌘-Option-Shift-N) to add a new layer.
4. Press D for Default Colors. This gives you a foreground color of black and a background color of white.
5. Press Ctrl+Backspace (⌘-Delete) to fill the new layer with white.

   At this point, the background image will be hidden behind the layer of white.
6. Holding Alt (Option), click the Add layer mask icon at the bottom of the Layers palette to hide (or mask) the white layer.

   If you look at the layer mask on this layer in the Layers palette, you'll see that it's filled with black, making the layer of white completely transparent. You'll also notice that since you have a layer mask selected, the default colors in the toolbox have switched places, giving you white for the foreground color.

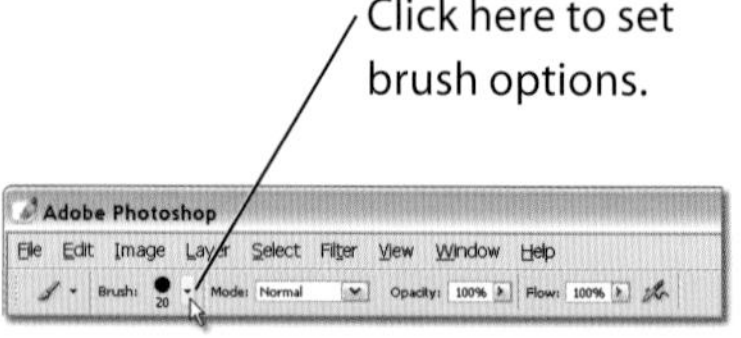

Setting the brush size

1. Press B for the Brush tool. If this selects the Pencil tool, press Shift+B to select the Brush tool.
2. Click the arrow next to the brush size indicator in the options bar.

   This opens the Brush Preset Picker.
3. For Master Diameter, drag the slider to 20 pixels.
4. For Hardness, drag the slider to 100%.

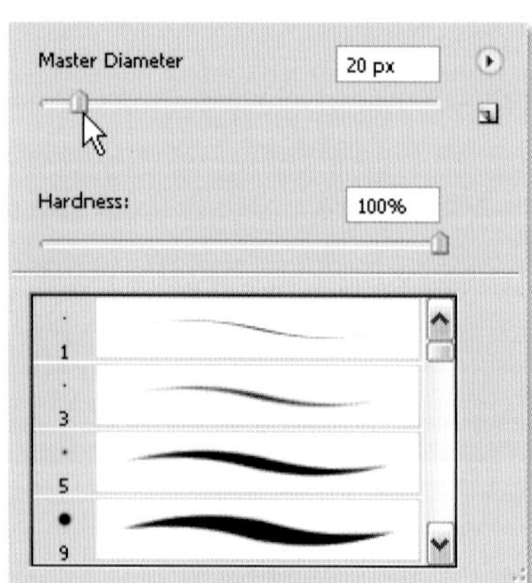

Set these options for the brush.

Adding the white border

It's important that you've followed the previous two sections carefully before proceeding. This way you'll have the layer mask selected, the correct default foreground and background color settings, and the correct brush size.

1. Drag guides out from the rulers, and place them exactly where you want to draw the border around the images.
2. On the View menu, make sure Snap is checked, and make sure that Guides is checked on the Snap To submenu.
3. Draw the border using these steps:

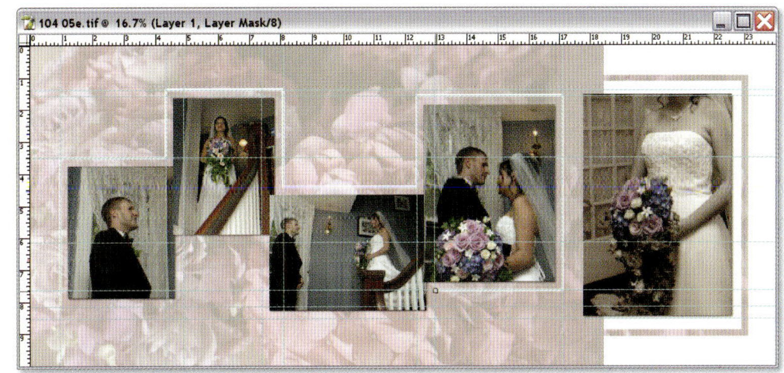

- Position the cursor at the intersection where you want the first line segment to begin.
- Click and release the mouse button.
- Press and hold Shift to constrain to a straight line.
- Still holding Shift, position the cursor at the intersection where you want the line segment to end.
- Click and release the mouse button. The straight white line is drawn for you.
- Continue holding Shift and click at the intersections all the way around to have Photoshop draw each section of the border.

This technique works as long as you go around the border in one direction, clicking at each consecutive intersection. If you skip around in the border, you'll need to release Shift to start a new path or unwanted lines will be drawn.

Repairing the border

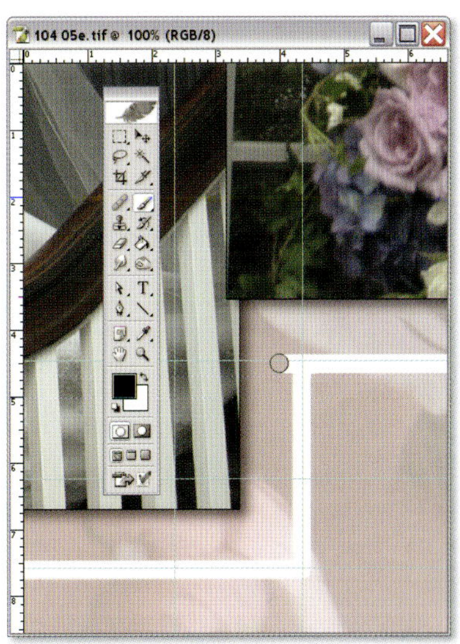

If you need to fix any of the corners after creating the whole border, you can do this by "painting with black."

1. Make sure the layer mask icon is selected in the Layers palette.
2. Press X to switch the foreground and background colors, giving you black for the foreground and white for the background.
3. Uncheck Snap on the View menu.

   If Snap is on, the repairs you try to make will remove the corners of the border.
4. Zoom in close to the image and paint back in the areas you didn't mean to remove.

When you "paint with black," you're making transparent the portions of the white border that you want to hide.

Design 38: Creating a coordinating frame

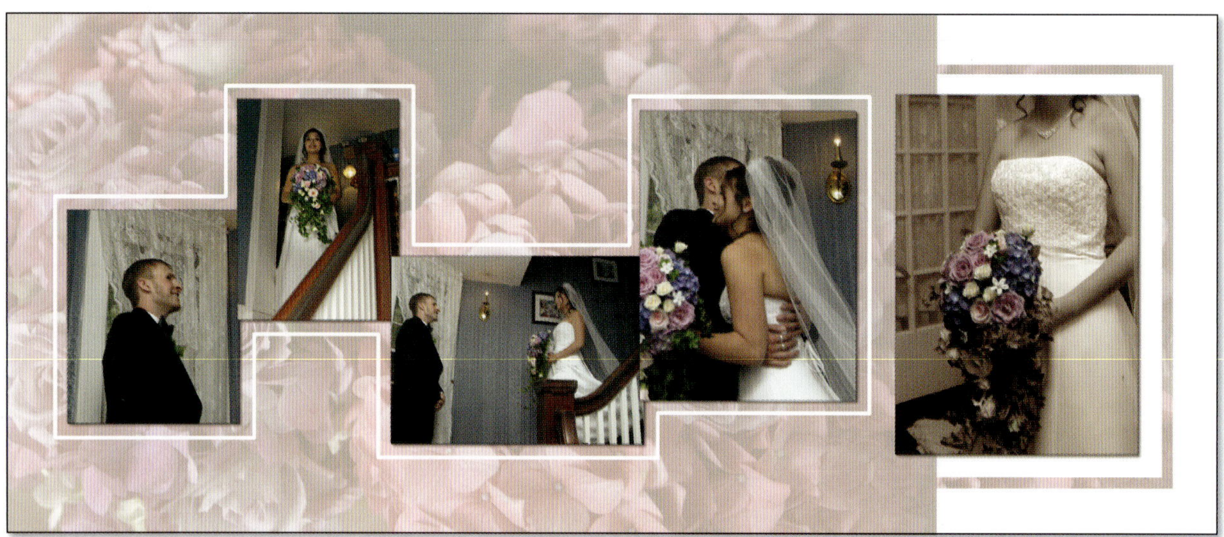

Design notes

The frame on the right page is a nice way to tie an image in with the rest of the page and to set it apart in a special way at the same time.

This technique works well with background images that are relatively uniform in appearance. If you have an image with areas that are very different, the frame may not match the background as well at the edges where they meet after you've moved the frame.

Before you begin this technique, make the background image opaque as explained in Design 14, cut it, and paste it on its own layer.

1. With the Marquee tool, drag to create a selection outside the image.

   It doesn't matter where the left edge of the frame is since this part will eventually be hidden behind the background image.

2. Holding Alt (Option), drag again to select the inside of the frame.
3. Drag the selection over the background image.
4. Make sure the background image layer is selected in the Layers palette.

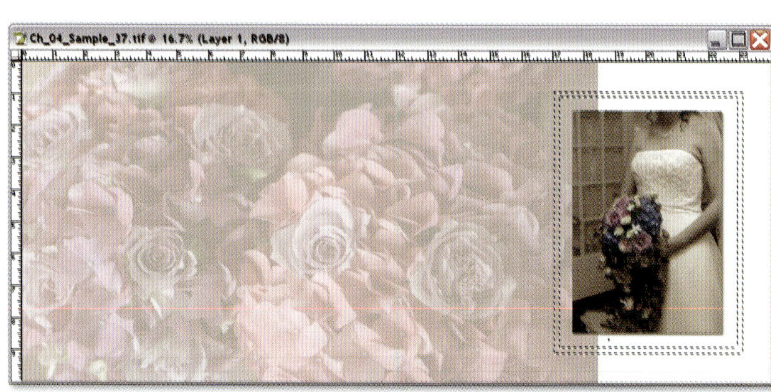

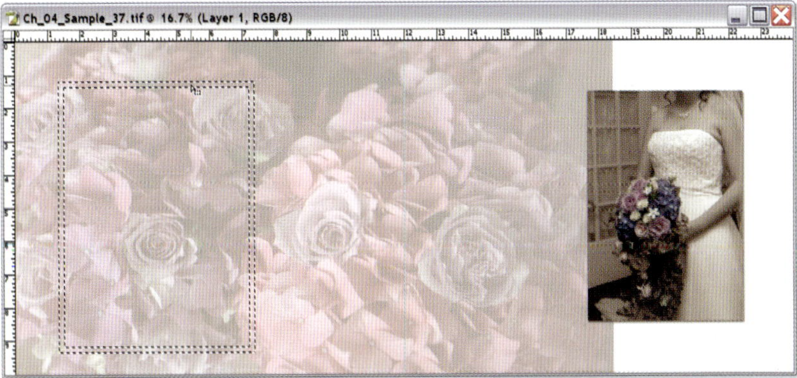

5. Press Ctrl+J (⌘-J) to copy and paste the frame of the background image onto its own layer.
6. Press V for the Move tool and drag the frame back into place so it frames the image again.

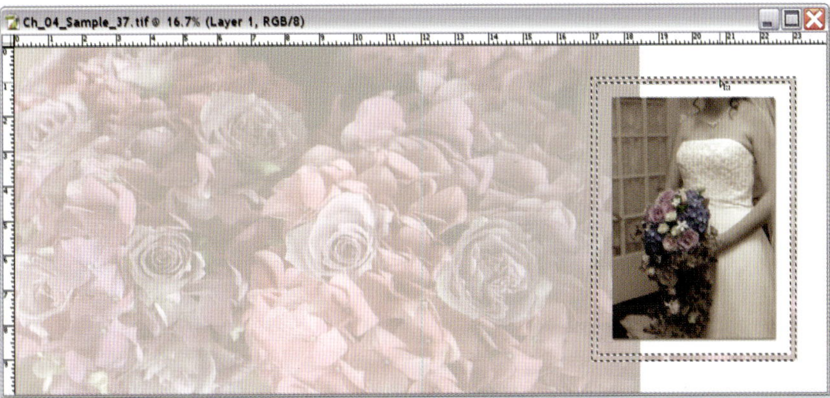

Blending the frame and the background image

You may need to do a little blending where the frame and the background image meet.

1. In the Layers palette, drag the frame layer under the layer containing the opaque background image.
2. Click the background image layer in the Layers palette and press Ctrl+E (⌘-E) for Merge Down.
3. Zoom in so you can easily see one of the points where the two elements meet.
4. With the Smudge tool and a 10-pixel brush set to 20% opacity, drag with tiny scrubbing movements over the line to blend it.

Design 39: Creating a cutout border

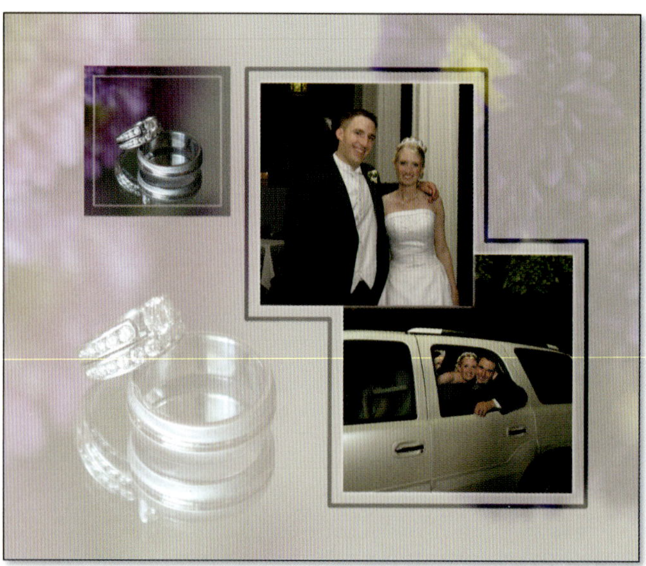

Design notes

This technique is similar to the one in Design 37. As with that technique, it's important to complete all three parts of the procedure without doing another task or closing and reopening the page spread window.

Before creating the border, scale the background images and the other images and place them exactly where you want them on the page. If you move them later, you'll have to redo the cutout border.

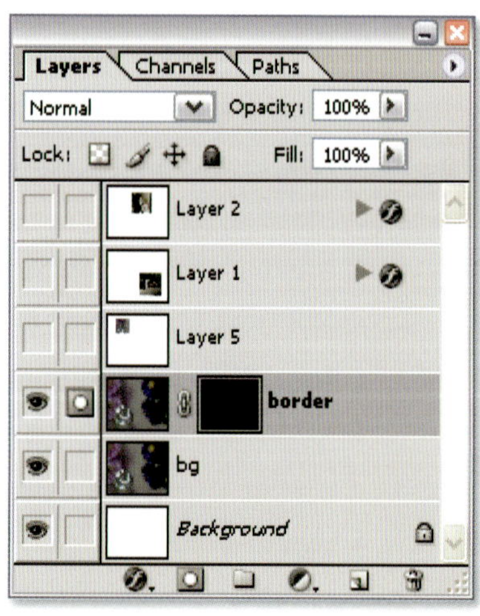

Creating a layer mask

1. In the Layers palette, select the layer with the background image and press Ctrl+J (⌘-J) to duplicate it.
2. Select the lower layer and set the opacity to about 35%.

   You won't see this change because the full-opacity version hides this layer.
3. Select the upper layer in the Layers palette.
4. Holding Alt (Option), click the Add Layer Mask icon to create a layer mask that hides or masks the full-opacity version.

Now anything you paint with white in this layer mask will cause the opaque image underneath to show through.

Creating a cutout border

1. Press D to set the default colors. This gives you a foreground color of white and a background color of black.
2. Click the Brush tool. In the options bar, set Brush Size to 20 pixels and the Hardness to 100%.

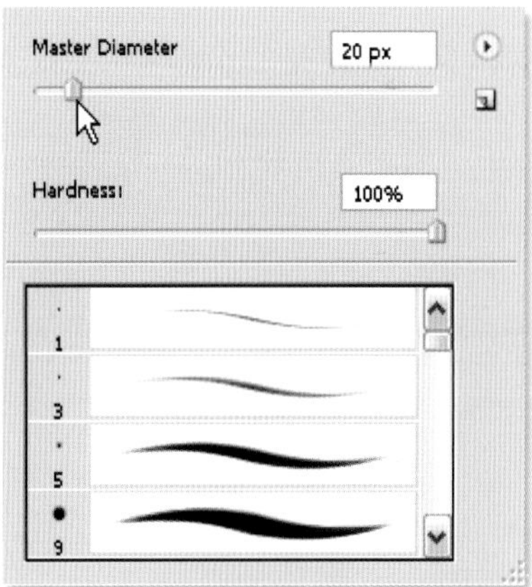

3. Drag out guides and place them around the images where you want the borders to create an intersection at each corner.
4. On the View menu, make sure Snap is checked, and make sure that Guides is checked on the Snap To submenu.
5. Draw the border using these steps:
   - Position the cursor at the intersection where you want the first line segment to begin.
   - Click and release the mouse button.
   - Press and hold Shift to constrain to a straight line.
   - Holding Shift, position the cursor at the intersection where you want the line segment to end.
   - Click and release the mouse button. The straight line is drawn for you.
   - Continue holding Shift and click at the intersections to have Photoshop draw each section of the border.

This technique works as long as you go around the border in one direction, clicking at each consecutive intersection. If you skip around in the border, you'll need to release Shift to start a new path or unwanted lines will be drawn.

Repairing the border

If you need to fix any of the corners after creating the whole border, you can do this by "painting with black."

1. Press X to switch the foreground and background colors.
2. Uncheck Snap on the View menu.

   If Snap is on, the repairs you try to make will remove the corners of your border.
3. Zoom in close to your image and paint back in the areas that you didn't mean to remove.

   When you "paint with black," you're replacing the portions of the layer mask that previously were removed.

Design 40: Desaturating part of an image

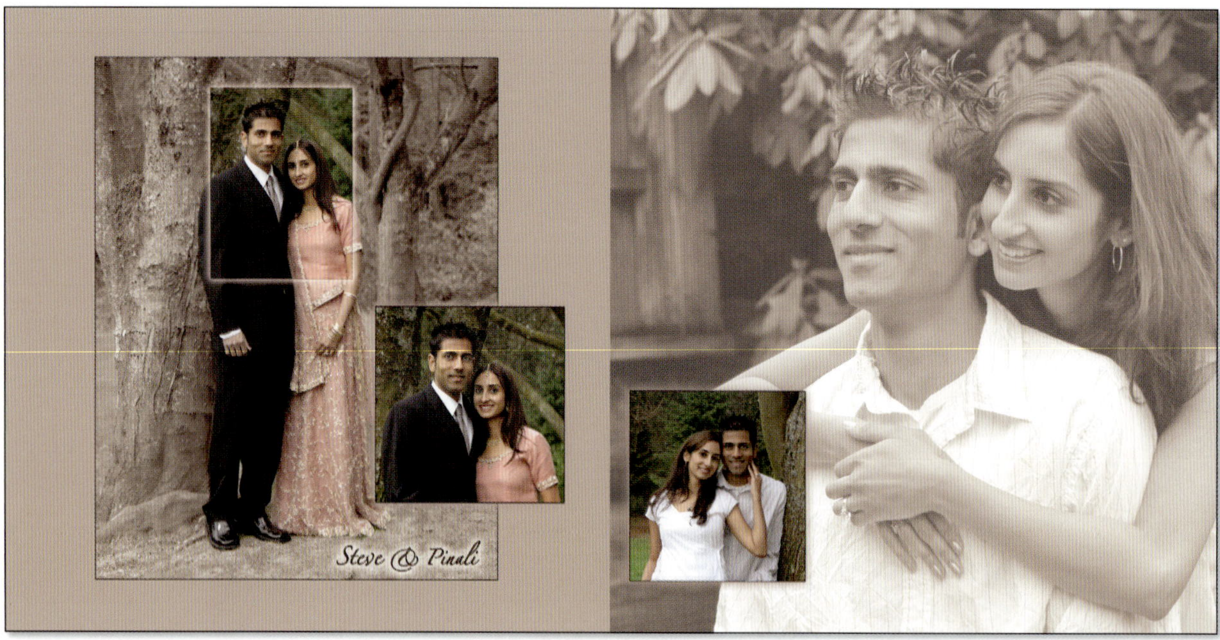

Design notes

On the left page, I wanted to create a miniature portrait inside the larger image. To do this, I first duplicated the image and created a spot color version with the full-length subjects slightly desaturated. Over this I added the fully-saturated portrait of their faces (copied from the original image), and then gave that portrait an outer glow.

The more formal poses in their formal attire were placed together on one page, and the more casual poses in their casual attire were placed on the other. Mixing these together on a page would have looked incongruous.

First create two versions of the same file

1. Open the file, and crop it the way you'd like to use it on the page.
2. In the History palette, right-click (Ctrl-click) the Crop step, and choose New Document.

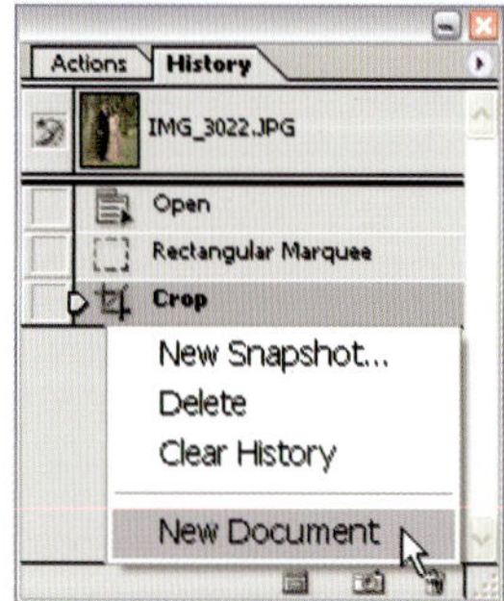

Turn one of the versions into a sepia image

In the new document window, locate the Custom Sepia action (created in Design 18) or the default Sepia Toning action in the Actions palette, and click the Play icon.

Copy and paste the subjects into the sepia image

1. In the color version, zoom in and carefully select around the subjects with the Lasso tool.

   Hold Shift and drag to add to the selection. Hold Alt (Option) and drag to remove part of the selection.

2. From the Select menu, choose Feather, and give the selection a 2-pixel feather.

3. Holding Shift, drag the selection from the color window to the sepia window.

   Holding Shift allows you to paste a selection into exactly the same location in the target window as it was in the source window.

4. From the Image menu, choose Adjustment, and then choose Hue/Saturation and drag the Saturation slider to -24.

Holding Shift, drag the selected subjects into the sepia image.

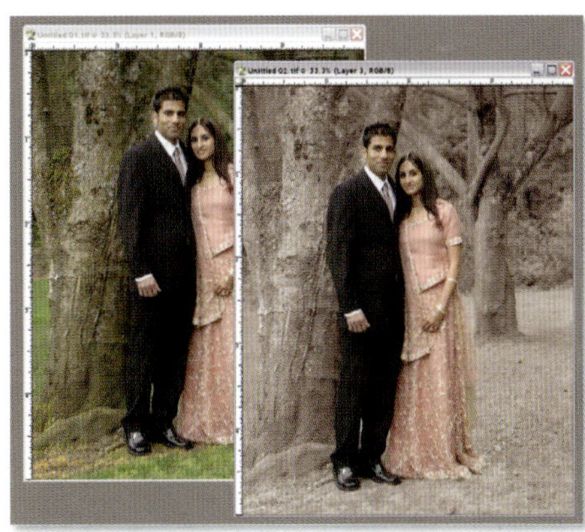

Adding the full-color portrait

1. In the window containing the full-color version of the image, use the Marquee tool to drag out a rectangular selection around the subjects.

2. With the Move tool, hold Shift and drag the selection from the current window into the sepia window.

Adding styles to the color images

1. Double-click the image icon for a layer containing one of the color images.

2. Click Outer Glow.

3. Click the yellow box and then click in a light area of the sepia image to sample a color for the outer glow. Set Blend Mode to Screen and Opacity to 75%.

4. Click to select Stroke.

5. Set the size to 3 pixels. Click the Color box, and click in a dark area of the sepia image to sample a color for the stroke.

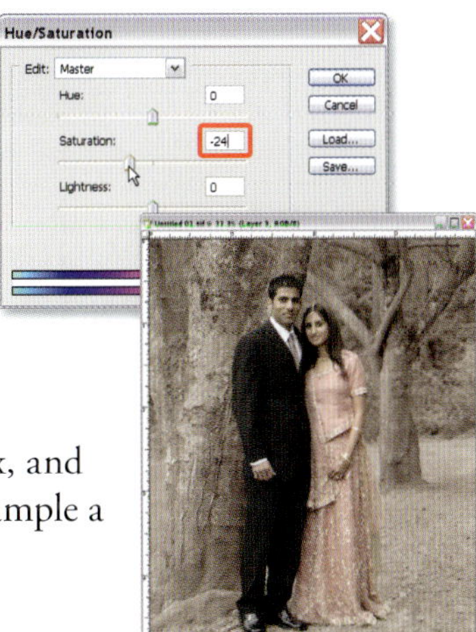

Design 41: Adding a frame with a gradient fill

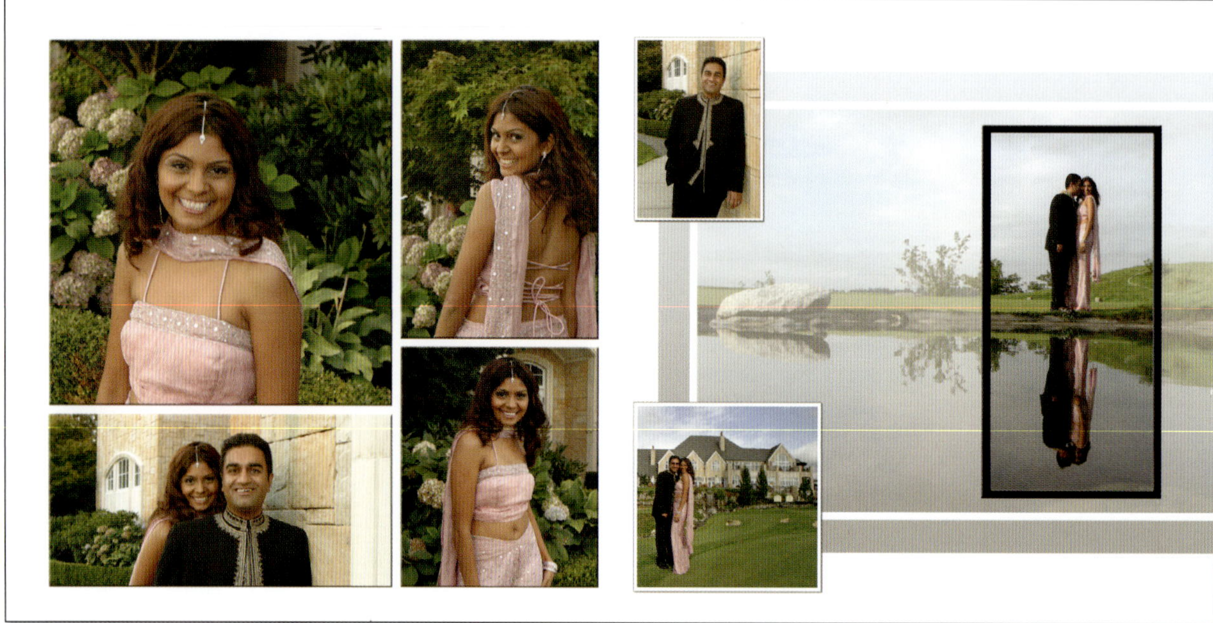

Design notes

These clients loved the rock in the image on the right, so it was impossible to make the reflection image as large as I wanted to without having the rock disappear off the page. Adding the gradient frame around the image created the illusion that the image was larger.

Here's what the page looked like before adding the gradient frame.

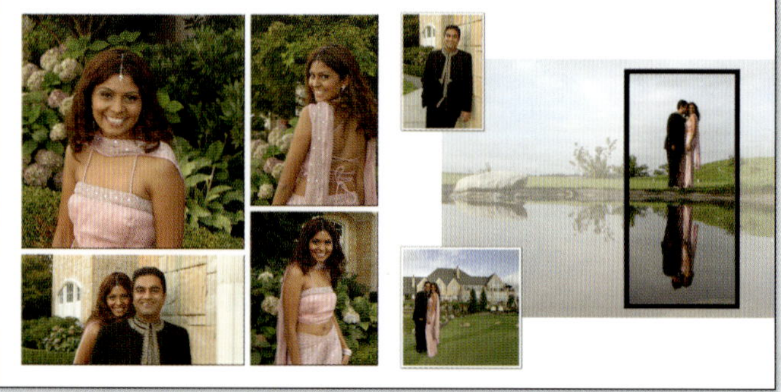

Creating the frame and the gradient fill

1. Scale the image appropriately and place it where you want it on the page.
2. Now create a frame around the image. To make precise spacing easy, drag out guides from the rulers for the outside and inside dimensions of your frame. Make sure Snap is checked on the View menu.

3. Use the Marquee tool to select the outside of the frame.
4. Holding Alt (Option), drag out another selection inside the first one, leaving precisely the same amount of blank space all the way around the image.

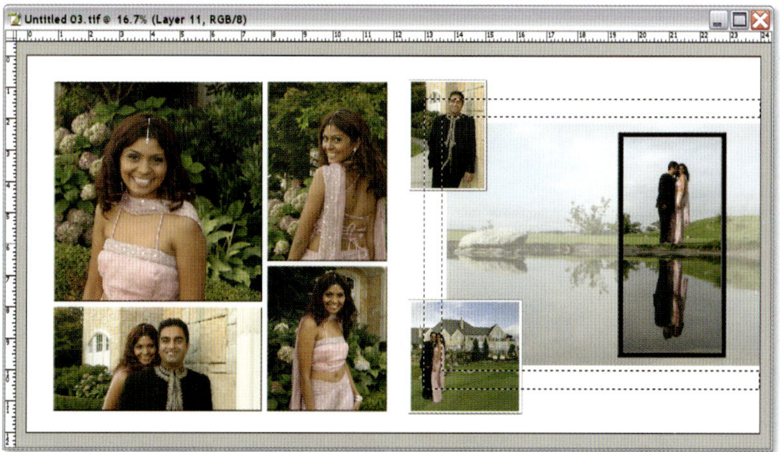

5. With the blank Background layer selected, press Ctrl+J (⌘-J) to copy and paste the white frame onto its own layer.
6. In the Layers palette, double-click the image icon for the new layer and choose Gradient Overlay.
7. Click the Gradient swatch.
8. In the Gradient Editor dialog, double-click the left color stop and set it to a color at the bottom of the image by clicking in the image with the Eyedropper.
9. Double-click the right color stop and set it to a color at the top of the image by clicking in the image again. Click OK.
10. For Style, choose Linear.

    You might also try the other Gradient Overlay styles, such as Radial and Reflected. For Reflected, change the angle and watch what happens.

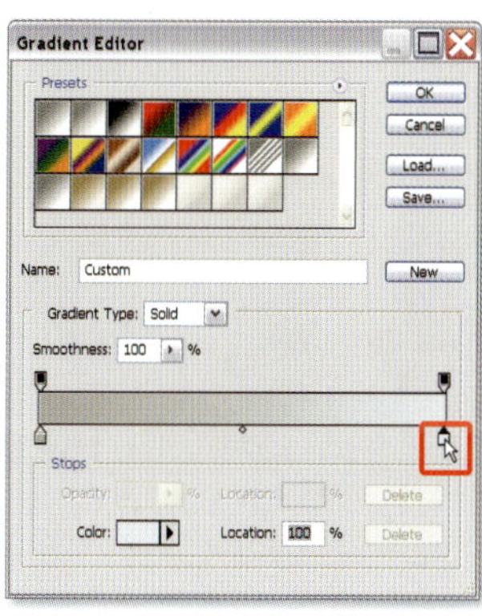

Double-click the color stops to set the gradient colors.

To learn about creating a beveled black frame like the one on the right page, see Design 21.

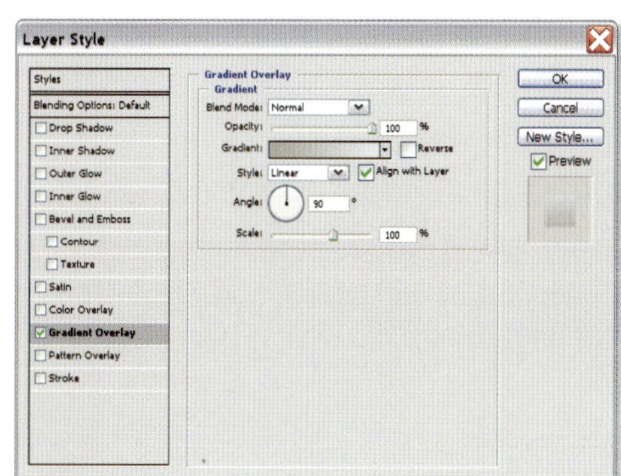

Design 42: Adding a filmstrip

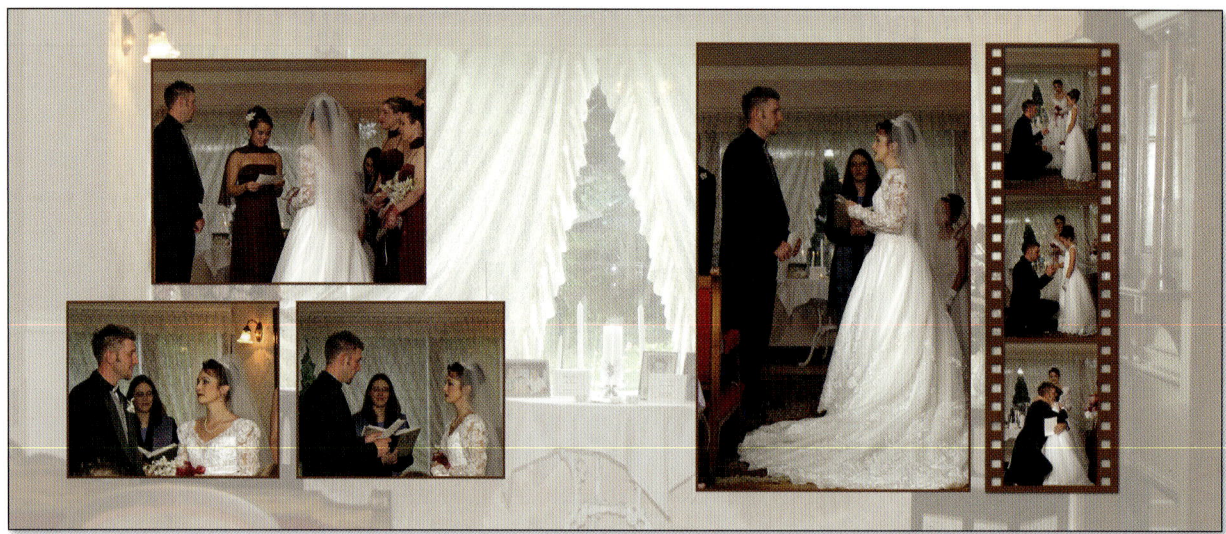

Design notes

I created this filmstrip in Photoshop, and now it's easy to drop images in behind each "negative," scaling them appropriately. Since the filmstrip is on its own layer, the color can be adjusted to match other elements on the page.

You can download the filmstrip image free at www.carilloncreek.com.

Using images with the film strip

1. Drag the filmstrip into your page spread window and scale it appropriately.
2. In the window for one of the images you want to use in the filmstrip, press C for the Crop tool. In the options bar, set Width to 1.46 and Height to 2.17.
3. Drag out a crop boundary and position it appropriately.
4. Press Enter.

This gives you the correct aspect ratio for the image. However, when you paste it into the page spread, you'll still need to scale it down. How much to scale the image will depend upon the size and resolution of your page spread window and whether you've scaled the filmstrip.

Pasting and scaling the images

1. Drag the image into the page spread window.
2. Select the filmstrip layer in the Layers palette, temporarily lower the opacity to 70%, and drag this layer just above the image layer.
3. Select the image layer and press Ctrl+T (⌘-T) for Free Transform.
4. Holding Shift, drag to scale the image.

   When the image is close to the correct size, let go of Shift for a moment and drag within the image to move it to the correct location behind the filmstrip. Hold Shift again and drag a selection handle to scale the image appropriately, so that all four edges are hidden behind the inside of the "negative" frame.
5. Press Enter to accept the transformation.
6. Crop the other two images, drag them into the page spread window, and scale them in the same way.
7. Bring the opacity of the filmstrip layer back up to 100%.

After you've placed all three images in the film strip, link their layers with the filmstrip layer so you can move all four elements together on the page. To do this, select one of the layers in the Layers palette and then click the Link icon for the other three layers.

In CS2, hold Shift and click each layer you want to link. Then click the Link icon at the bottom of the palette to link all selected layers.

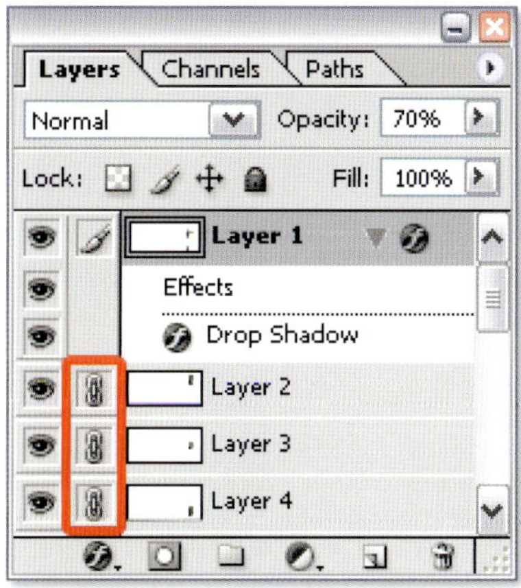

Summary of the process

5

If you've read this entire book, you have the information you need to produce digital magazine-style wedding albums. Let's look at a brief summary of the steps needed to complete your first album.

Preparing to create a sample album

- Choose a set of beautiful images to use (or wait until after an upcoming wedding). (See p. 9.)
- Research album companies and request cover material swatches and order forms. (See p. 12.)
- Buy a Colorvision Spyder or other calibration device and calibrate your monitor. (See p. 34.)
- Read at least one good book about color-correcting. (See p. 34.)
- Check with your lab about the resolution they recommend for digital album pages.
- Create a test page and send it to your lab. (See p. 68.)

Preparing to offer digital albums to clients

- Decide about pricing issues. (See p. 13.)
- Decide what to say during consultations. (See p. 16.)
- Decide how you plan to show proofs to clients (on a website or only in the studio). (See p. 28.)
- Decide how you'll select album images with clients, and which proof presentation software to use. (See p. 28.)
- Create a commission agreement form. (See p. 33.)

Creating the sample album

- Use the Photoshop File Browser for sorting, rotating, renaming, and selecting proofs. (See p. 20.)
- Create a Photoshop droplet for batch resizing, if necessary. (See p. 26.)
- Review Chapter 3, Designing Pages. (See p. 37.)
- Memorize the Photoshop keyboard shortcuts. (See p. 48.)
- Design the pages for your sample album, using only the best images. (See Chapter 4.)
- Flatten each page spread, split the pages if necessary, and save each page under a new name. (See p. 70.)
- Send the page files to the lab. (See p. 72.)
- When you receive the page prints, trim them if necessary. (See p. 73.)
- Send the page prints to the album company for mounting and binding.

One final note

If you've never thought of yourself as a graphic artist, now is the time to assume you are a graphic artist. If you're starting out with good images, and you're looking at beautiful designs and creating similar pages, your work will be beautiful!

Index

C

D

E

F

G

H

I

J

K

L

M

N

O

P

R

S

About the author

Kathy Woodford began her career as a contract technical writer in Seattle, working at Aldus (before it became Adobe). She wrote manuals and online help for such products as Aldus FreeHand and Pagemaker, and then worked for years as a technical writer at Microsoft.

Kathy took several years off to stay at home with her two daughters while they were young. When they were both in school, she started Calypsis, now a successful wedding photography business. She has used Adobe Photoshop for more than eight years. Her husband, Dale, is her business partner and technical guru, and a senior software developer at a well-known software company.